CONTENT RULES

How to Create Killer Blogs, Podcasts, Videos, Ebooks, Webinars (and More) That Engage Customers and Ignite Your Business

ANN HANDLEY & C.C. CHAPMAN

WILEY

John Wiley & Sons, Inc.

Library of Congress Cataloging-in-Publication Data:

ISBN: 978-0-470-64828-5 (cloth); ISBN: 978-0-470-94869-9 (ebk);
ISBN: 978-0-470-94871-2 (ebk); ISBN: 978-0-470-94872-9 (ebk)

Printed in the United States of America.

10 9 8 7 6 5 4 3 2 1

For Colin.
Miss you every day.
—A.H.

Goofy Monkey, Buddy, and Sticky Noodle—
I do everything to keep you smiling.
Now and always.
—C.C.

Contents

PART FOUR

Foreword

"Marketing is about publishing great content."

How many times have you heard a statement more or less like this? Tons, right? By now every marketing professional and entrepreneur on the planet understands this fundamental truth. We don't need convincing.

But what the many content-marketing experts have failed to do is tell us how to create that content.

What, exactly, should I do?

In my experience, the art and science of creating content had never been adequately explained to marketers. Perhaps you would build a web site and spend a bunch of cash on the design. But the best that the designers could do with the content was put in some filler text. Okay, then what? You stared at "Lorem ipsum" for days not knowing what to write, and then defaulted to some gobbledygook-laden drivel about your products and services. Ugh.

There is a better way, and this book will show it to you.

The answer: Tell stories.

Think about it. All good films and all good fiction are really about the story, right? Without a compelling, conflict-driven story, all the other elements don't mean much.

Here is a classic story line from countless books and movies:

Boy meets girl.

They fall in love.

Boy loses girl.

Boy (and sometimes girl) is miserable for most of the action.

They finally get back together.

They get married.

How and why they break up and then what they do to get back together are what make the story interesting.

How interesting would that same book or movie be were it to have this plot:

Boy meets girl.

They fall in love.

They get married.

At best, such a plot would be an insufferable bore. At worst, it becomes propaganda.

In fact, it's just the sort of propaganda most marketers and business writers construct every day: "Here's our product. It is great. Here are customers who say it is great. Now buy some of our product." Sadly, this classic propaganda-driven marketing is everywhere. It's not just text-based content, either. Video and other information is also mainly propaganda.

As you read the book, you'll be reflecting on how you can introduce storytelling into your work. How can you make your content interesting, like a great movie or novel? How can your web site, blog posts, videos, and other materials be made more interesting?

Ann and C.C. show you how!

Throughout *Content Rules*, you'll learn how to construct interesting and valuable information using many of the same skills that journalists and storytellers use. You'll learn how to identify an audience, how to develop a distinct point of view and voice, and how to construct a narrative that is exciting and engaging.

Content Rules includes many success stories from consumer brands, B2B outfits, government agencies, and other organizations—together with "ideas you can steal" from each.

When I created the New Rules Social Media Book Series with John Wiley & Sons, I said that it was essential to have a book about how to create killer content. And I knew just the people to do it. Ann and C.C. are storytellers, journalists, and marketers. In my opinion, that's the perfect combination of skills and expertise to identify and deliver rules that we can all use to create killer blogs, podcasts, videos, ebooks, webinars, and more.

I've followed the work of both Ann and C.C. with keen interest for nearly five years, learning from them as they pave the way forward to new forms of marketing. They must have more than a thousand blog posts, hundreds of videos, and dozens of articles between them. Now, in one place, you have access to their greatest hits.

—David Meerman Scott
Author of *The New Rules of Marketing & PR* and
the new book *Real-Time Marketing & PR*
www.WebInkNow.com
twitter.com/dmscott

Acknowledgments

You know how people say they wouldn't be standing here if it weren't for the support and friendship of certain people? So we, too, are surrounded by countless treasured friends and colleagues who helped to make this book possible. Many of them are quoted here. But in addition, we give special thanks to:

J.C. Hutchins, Clarence Smith Jr., Steve Coulson, Mitch Joel, Julien Smith, Amber Naslund, Ron Ploof, Christopher Penn, Whitney Hoffman, Tamsen McMahon, Michelle Wolverton, Lauren Vargas, Mark Yoshimoto Nemcoff, Kristina Halvorson, Matthew T. Grant, Stephanie Tilton, Steve Garfield, Jay Baer, Joe Pulizzi, Amy Black, David Armano, Lee Odden, Ted Page, Mack Collier, C.K. Kerley, D.J. Waldow, Leigh Durst, Shelley Ryan, the amazing Shannon Vargo, the executive team at MarketingProfs—Allen Weiss, Roy Young, Sharon Hudson, Valerie Witt, Aaron Lorentz, and Anne Yastremski—and (saving the best for almost last) to Vahe Habeshian: a thank you doesn't quite express the depth of gratitude. Finally, a very special thank you to David Meerman Scott, who knew what this book was before we did.

Last, but certainly not least, we thank our loving families. Writing is lonely. But it's only tolerable when—at last!—you open the office door, and there they are.

Big Fat Overview
(Sometimes Called an Introduction)

Blogs, YouTube, Facebook, Twitter, and other online platforms are giving organizations like yours an enormous opportunity to engage directly with your customers or would-be customers. That's a lucky thing, because instead of creating awareness about your company or your brand solely the old-school way (by annoying people with advertising, bugging them with direct mail, or interrupting them with a phone call during dinner), you now have an unprecedented and enormous opportunity.

Now, thanks to the advent of the Internet and, more specifically, the rise of web-based tools and technologies, you can create online content—blog posts, videos, webinars, and web sites—that will attract customers to you, so you won't have to chase after them. What's more, you can entice your customers to share that content with each other, all across the Web.

Produce great stuff, and your customers will come to you. Produce really great stuff, and your customers will share and disseminate your message for you. More than ever before, content is king! Content rules!

Of course, like most things in life, such luck—the opportunity to have your customers tell your story for you—comes with a hitch. Content may rule, but your online content must be the right sort of content: Customer-focused. Authentic. Compelling. Entertaining. Surprising. Valuable. Interesting. In other words, you must *earn* the attention of people.

That sounds like work, doesn't it? It is. It's work to create and publish compelling stuff that will:

- Appeal to your would-be constituents.

- Give them something they find value in.

- Keep them coming back for more.

Today, however, every company has become a de facto publisher, creating content that's valued by those they want to reach. We're hesitating as we write that word *publisher*, by the way, because to many of you it implies the production of books, magazines, and the like. Most businesses don't have a lot of experience with publishing, nor do they see themselves as publishers. Rather, they are in the business of whatever they are in the business of (making things, or selling services, or what have you).

But when we say that businesses are becoming publishers, we're referring not to the process of putting ink to paper or printing and binding books but to the notion that creating and delivering relevant, valuable information to people will drive new business to you. Figuring out what your prospective customers are interested in, creating stuff that meets those needs, and delivering it to them is what you need to do. And that, by the way, is exactly what publishers do.

But organizations or individuals like you looking to build their business online have to take it further: You need to create stuff that will help your clients, you need to become a trusted resource your customers can then look to, and you need to get buyers to take action when they are ready. Your company can now publish the kind of content that will cultivate a base of fans, arouse passion for your products or services, and, ultimately, ignite your business.

The problem, of course, is that doing so successfully is a challenge. What does it mean to create content that's remarkable? And how can you do it consistently? How can you be heard above the noise? Why doesn't your blog have any comments? It's *hard* work, right?

Yes, it is. A survey of more than 1,000 businesses this past spring found that "producing engaging content" is the top challenge in content marketing programs. (See Figure I.1.)

That's where this book comes in. It demystifies the publishing process and shares the secrets of creating remarkable blogs, podcasts, webinars, ebooks, and other web content that will attract would-be customers to you. It walks you through the fundamentals of how to create bold stories, videos, and blog posts. And then, once you've created the content, it tells you how to share it

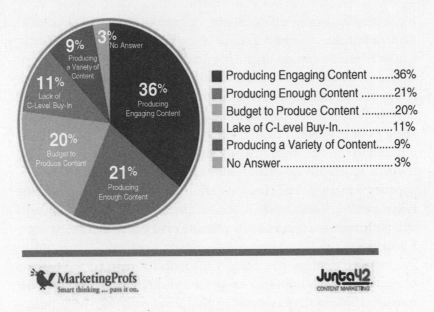

Producing Engaging Content 36%
Producing Enough Content 21%
Budget to Produce Content 20%
Lake of C-Level Buy-In.................11%
Producing a Variety of Content......9%
No Answer..................................3%

Figure I.1 Biggest Content Marketing Challenge

widely online to cultivate fans, arouse passion for your products or services, and ignite your business.

In other words, this book equips you for success. It will serve as a one-stop source on the art and science of developing content that people care about, content that will drive your business. Some companies have already figured it out; they are already publishing great content to establish credibility and build a loyal customer base. To inspire and inform your own efforts, here we'll share how they are doing it.

How This Book Works (and Three Promises to You)

This book is part of the New Rules of Social Media Series, produced by John Wiley & Sons with David Meerman Scott. With his *The New Rules of Marketing & PR* (John Wiley & Sons, 2007, completely revised in 2010), David pioneered the idea of creating remarkable content to connect online with buyers. David's book (and others in this series, including *Inbound Marketing* by Brian Halligan and Dharmesh Shah, and Steve Garfield's *Get Seen*) examines the importance of creating remarkable content but does not delve into the nitty-gritty of how you might go about doing so. And that is where this book comes in. It complements the others in the series by laying out the how-to.

Think of it as a little like the notion of having a baby: It's easy enough (and loads of fun!) to imagine and conceive a child. But tending to the demands of a wriggling, persistent creature—*and consistently! Forever and ever! Like for the rest of your life!*—is another thing entirely. That's where the hard work comes in. But like parenting itself, content done right delivers in amazing ways and is ultimately a rich and rewarding experience. In other words, it's worth it.

Did that analogy just scare you? Does it feel like a sentence of sorts, or too daunting a task? Are you thinking you'd rather remain childless than commit to that level of work? Well, here's where the analogy starts to crumble a bit: Not everyone *has* to become a parent, obviously. But if your company has a web site, you have essentially already given birth. And producing content isn't nearly as forbidding as it sounds, because this book is the field guide you need for identifying your audience, creating great content, and getting that content to your targeted community.

This brings us to the point of this section's heading: *how this book works.* Aside from a quick bit in Chapter 1, we're not going to spend a lot of time here on setup, convincing you that the rules have changed, that product-centric communications and marketing-speak are selling your brand short, and so on. (In other words, we're guessing you are already convinced of the need for killer content.) But if you need a more detailed rationale, we'd suggest David Meerman Scott's *The New Rules of Marketing & PR* as a primer.

Rather, we're going to pick up where *The New Rules of Marketing & PR* leaves off. We're going to talk about *how* to create and share remarkable content: the elements, necessary inspiration, and some handy tools. In other words, we're not going to focus on *why* content rules, but about *how* to create the stuff that truly does.

As we do, we'll promise you:

- *Not to be boring.* Some business books really plod along, don't they? We've written this book in a digestible, how-to format. Skim it. Jump around. Put it down and come back and pick it up later. It's designed for that.

- *To give some context.* You'll notice that we borrowed liberally from the literary and journalism worlds in this book so we could better explain points and concepts. In part, it's because our backgrounds are in both, so they are worlds we know and are continually inspired by. But it's also because marketing can learn a lot from the art and style of storytelling (literature) and the fundamentals and science of good reporting (journalism). Those endeavors have been matching content with audiences longer than anybody, and it's hard to find a better inspiration for clear, accessible communication. (If you can, let us know.)

- *To draw plenty of road maps.* The first part of this book (appropriately called Part One) introduces and elucidates the rules for creating great content. Part Two offers specific how-to steps to creating an array of content you might want to develop, by type. Part Three offers 10 case studies of content that converts. And last, Part Four is a handy content checklist against which you can measure your own content development efforts.

And finally, a clarification: When we use the word *business* in this book, we're describing any kind of business, either one that sells to other businesses (business-to-business, or B2B) or one that sells to consumers (business-to-consumers, or B2C). What's more, when we use *business* (or *brand*, *company*, or *organization*) in this book, we're really talking about any kind of entity or individual, including corporations, entrepreneurs, nonprofits, sole practitioners or consultants, artists, government agencies, churches, schools, hospitals, political candidates, sports teams, community groups, and rock bands, along with butchers, bakers, and candlestick makers. Similarly, when we use the term *buyer*, we also mean subscribers, voters, donors, applicants, attendees, worshippers, or new members.

In other words, these content rules apply to anyone looking to do business, get subscribers or clients, win votes, or find donors or constituents of any kind. We also realized that if we consistently included all of the people we are actually referring to when we say *businesses* or *organizations* or *buyers*, you would find it annoying. And so would we.

Why We Need Some Rules, but Not Others

Most of us learned how to write in school. As impressionable children we learned how to compose essays or term papers according to a specific formula: Each new thought is awarded its own paragraph, and each paragraph consists of a topic sentence, several body sentences, and a concluding sentence.

The topic sentence is the powerful ringleader of a paragraph and states the main point. Supporting body sentences are the flunkies, backing up whatever the topic sentence asserts and doing the necessary dirty work of explaining and completing the main assertion. The concluding sentence is the hefty thug at the end, and he throws his weight around a little to be sure you get the point.

That's a perfectly fine way to write an essay or a blog post or a white paper or just about any kind of written content. But the problem is that such a rigid composition formula suggests that there is only one way to write: a sort of secret code to writing that you must crack to do it well. Then there are all those convoluted and complicated rules of grammar and punctuation and usage, which only compound the anxiety. (We're talking about *who* versus *whom*, split infinitives, and *affect* versus *effect*.)

It's no wonder, then, that many of us are paralyzed when confronted with a blank page. We often think there's a right way and a wrong way to write, and we often do just about anything to avoid writing altogether.

As content creators, we understand the anxiety surrounding publishing your writing for others to read. We're in the clarity business, simplifying people's convoluted ideas and wrestling their wild, out-of-control text into something more civilized and comprehensible. If everyone knew how to write and did it well, people like us would be out of work.

We're imagining that as you read this you're perhaps thinking, "Wait a sec: *Writing?* Isn't this a book about creating content that rocks?"

Well, there's a link between the two that is sometimes obvious (as when you are writing a blog post or an ebook) and sometimes less so (as when you might be creating a webinar or a video script). But what's more fundamental is that anxiety about writing often spills over into anxiety about creating content generally, resulting in content that's stilted and uncomfortable sounding, or not at all like something a human being might have written to engage other human beings. That anxiety is also what makes some people a little shy or fearful about creating content that's different—and possibly extraordinary.

The truth is that creating content does not have to be complex. There is no rigid formula you must learn in order to do it well. By applying a few general rules, anyone can begin producing great stuff. What's more, it's a tremendous opportunity. It's awesome to have the ability to connect to customers and would-be customers directly, in a language they understand. It's surprisingly satisfying to spark a direct dialogue with them. It allows you to look at things from your customers' points of view and inspires you to create content that will resonate with them.

And while we are on the subject of simplifying: We've intentionally used a direct, pragmatic, nonbusiness vocabulary wherever possible. In part that's because we wanted to keep the advice equally accessible for the church minister who is trying to get more of the devoted to attend more regularly, for the small business owner trying to sell more widgets, and for the marketer or agency for a larger organization trying to provide the best possible service to the client. In business, people love to complicate concepts with their own lexicons. So we wind up with text that tends to obfuscate rather than illuminate, or with copy that feels off-putting instead of friendly.

Like you with your customers, our goal here, too, is to engage rather than repel. We don't want readers to feel like they need to know the formidable (and often silly) language of business. In other words, we've used ordinary language here, so as not to paralyze any of you.

The inherent tension in marketing is that companies always want to talk about themselves and what their products or services can do. Everyone else, meanwhile, only wants to know what those products or services can do *for them.* Creating content as a cornerstone of your marketing allows you to truly place yourself in your customers' shoes, to adopt their vantage points, and to consider their thoughts, feelings, and needs. In short, it allows you to get to know the people who buy from you better than any customer survey or poll ever could.

We want each of you to create amazing content that is compelling to you and your community. That is the goal of this book: to be a beacon to the hapless and anxious, lighting the path toward content that will help you connect deeply with your customers and ignite your business.

In collecting and vetting these Content Rules, we have relied on the keys of good storytelling and journalism, and on the fundamentals of marketing. We've created these rules for writers and nonwriters alike, making the rules accessible and, we hope, memorable.

We're a little nervous about using the word *rules* in the title of this book; however subtly, the title seems to be undermining the very point we're making about flouting rigid conventions. But what follows are not so much strict rules as guidelines, really. Unlike laws, which suggest fixed codes of behavior with dire consequences if they are broken, guidelines are a handy and broad set of suggestions meant to simplify your life and ease the anxiety you might have about creating content. Think of these rules as you might bumpers on a bowling lane: They not only greatly improve the chances that you will bowl a strike but also, at the very least, keep you well out of the gutter.

PART ONE

The Content Rules

CHAPTER 1
The Case for Content

About a year or so ago, Ann was thinking of buying a digital camera to take on a trip to Armenia. She's not an expert photographer, so she didn't need anything with bells and whistles. She merely wanted something as slim and light as an ATM card to slip in her pocket (and cheap, too, in case it fell out). She wanted it to do nothing more than quickly and easily record the memories she would make there.

The problem, of course, wasn't that she couldn't find something to fit the bill. Rather, she couldn't decide from among the array of choices. Each of the major camera makers (like Canon, Kodak, Sony, Nikon, Pentax, and so on) had a product that was suitable. So which was the right camera for her?

A few years ago, she might have flipped through a back issue of *Consumer Reports* for some advice, or consulted a buying guide. But this time, she started her search online, consulting the camera makers' own web sites to compare features and read reviews.

She also sought advice from friends and followers on social networks like Twitter. Somewhere along the way, her search caught the attention of Kodak's then–chief marketing officer (CMO), Jeffrey Hayzlett, whose team monitors Twitter for queries such as Ann's. Jeffrey subsequently reached out to Ann directly on Twitter to suggest his company's own point-and-shoot pipsqueak, the EasyShare. Oh, and if she had any unanswered queries about point-and-shoot products, Jeffrey added, ask away!

It's cool that the CMO of a $7.6 billion company reached out to a single consumer. But what's really going on isn't just cool;

it's a major shift in how companies are marketing themselves online. Kodak might be on Twitter, but it and other companies are also creating blogs, publishing podcasts and webinars, launching Facebook pages, and more. Kodak knows that it doesn't have to wait for *Consumer Reports* to review its latest point-and-shoot; it can publish the specs itself and help customers come to Kodak.

Sears knows this, too, which is why in early 2010 it launched the Sears Yard Guru (www.searsyardguru.com) to help would-be buyers of lawn mowers narrow their search according to their own yard's size and terrain. So does industrial equipment auctioneer Ritchie Bros. Auctioneers, which publishes and maintains RitchieWiki (www.ritchiewiki.com) to share information about heavy equipment. Or MC^2, an exhibit and event marketing company that churns out blogs, ebooks, and white papers (www.mc-2.com). Or Landon Pollack, who launched his nonprofit StubbyDog (www.stubbydog.org) as an online magazine with a mission: to rebrand the much-maligned American pit bull terrier.

What's up with that? Why are companies like Kodak and Sears and Ritchie Bros, or any of those profiled in this book, bothering to invest so much in online content? Because it's both efficient and increasingly imperative that companies create online content as a cornerstone of their marketing—for three reasons:

1. *The notion of marketing to your customers by interrupting them repeatedly with advertising or other marketing messages is simply not enough any more.* Creating brand awareness through buying mass media or begging some attention from the newspapers, magazines, or other media that cover your market is selling your brand short.

   In other words: The rules have changed. David Meerman Scott explained this first and best in his seminal book *The New Rules of Marketing & PR:* "Prior to the Web, organizations had only two significant choices to attract attention: buy expensive advertising or get third-party ink from the media. But the Web has changed the rules."

2. *Customer behavior and expectations are shifting.* Ann's approach to buying a point-and-shoot digital camera was neither unusual nor unique; you've probably done similar research for your own buying decisions. Likewise, your potential customers are going online to search for information about the stuff you sell: everything from lawn mowers to cameras to consulting services to circuit-board solder paste to what band to go see on a Friday night.

Your customers read blogs, they google their purchases, and they query followers on Twitter or friends on Facebook. They are always educating themselves by researching purchases online before they make them.

Overwhelmingly, consumers depend on search engines to help them shop online, writes Debra Miller on the Compete.com blog about a February 2010 study of how shoppers buy: "Three out of five shoppers said that they always or often use search engines when shopping online," reports Miller. "More consumers use search engines than they do coupon sites, retailer e-mails, consumer reviews, or shopping comparison sites." (See Figure 1.1.)

This means, of course, that your key to igniting sales is to create online content and optimize it so that it appears on the first page of search results when your customers search for you or the products or services you sell.

3. *Everyone is the media. Everyone is a publisher.* Technology has enabled connections. There is no longer a high barrier to publishing online. The ease and low cost of publishing via blogs, videos, podcasts, forums, and social networks like Twitter and Facebook mean that businesses can reach their customers directly with relatively little cost. The idea of publishing material to attract a certain audience isn't reserved for an elite few who can afford the printing and distribution costs. "As brands, we become

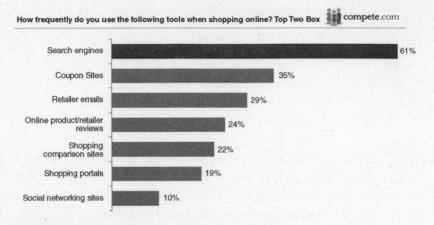

Figure 1.1   Research Tools for Online Shoppers

Source: http://blog.compete.com/2010/02/22/online-shopper-intelligence-study-released

media," says Brian Solis, author of *Engage* (John Wiley & Sons, 2010). In other words: *You* are a publisher; *you* are the media.

What that really means is that you can reach your potential buyers directly. And, of course, they can speak directly to you as well. You now have the ability to engage in direct conversation.

What Is Content, and What Can It Do for You?

So what is content, exactly?

Content is a broad term that refers to anything created and uploaded to a web site: the words, images, tools, or other things that reside there. All of the pages of your web site, then, are content: the home page, the About Us page, the Frequently Asked Questions (FAQ) page, the product information pages, and so on. All of the things you create as part of those pages or as part of your marketing—your videos, blogs, photographs, webinars, white papers, ebooks, podcasts, and so on—are content, too. And finally, all of the things you publish at outposts that are off of your own site—your Facebook page, your Twitter stream, your LinkedIn group page, for example—are forms of content.[1]

Obviously, you don't have to publish through all of those channels to have a noticeable online presence. As you'll see with the companies we profile, your online content can take countless forms, depending on various factors: the needs and preferences of your audience, your goals, your company's expertise and brand, as well as available time, talent, and budget.

You can use the concepts in this book to infuse all of your web content with energy, life, purpose, and value. But this book maintains a specific focus on how to create content for marketing: creating and sharing relevant, valuable information that attracts people to you and creates trust, credibility, and authority (among other things) for your business and that ultimately converts visitors and browsers into buyers.

That's precisely the point of creating killer content—to convert browsers into buyers and customers into regulars or (better yet) rabid fans, ambassadors, and advocates. You do that by deepening your relationship with them, over time, by repeatedly and consistently creating content they care about and want to share freely with their friends or colleagues, and by encouraging them to engage with you and to sign up for things you publish (like an e-mail newsletter or a webinar) or to download a white paper or an ebook.

"The one who has the more engaging content wins, because frequent and regular contact builds a relationship" that offers lots of opportunities for conversion, says Joe Pulizzi, author (with Newt Barrett) of *Get Content, Get Customers* (McGraw-Hill, 2009). "Advertising is a luxury," Joe says, "but content is survival."

---

[1] This is probably a good time to make a distinction between content and copywriting. The two are often confused, but web content isn't the same thing as copywriting. Copywriting is about using words to promote through advertising, sales collateral, brochures, or other marketing messages that interrupt—like radio or television advertising or direct mail. (Confusing things further, "copy" was used in the newsrooms Ann worked in to refer to news articles and other content prior to editing and printing—but that's a whole other story.)

Done right, the content you create will position your company not as just a seller of stuff, but as a reliable source of information. And its benefits compound, adds social media strategy consultant Jay Baer, who calls content an *information annuity*. (Don't you love that phrase?) Likewise, Marcus Sheridan of River Pools calls content "the ultimate gift that keeps on giving." (More on Marcus and River Pools in a minute.)

Unlike other kinds of marketing, content marketing "doesn't have an expiration date," Jay Baer says. What you create online will be searchable indefinitely. "It generates Web traffic (via search and social media linkages) and helps remove purchase impediments every day of every month. Your potential customers have questions about your company, your products, your services, your competitors. Creating and propagating smart, optimized content that succinctly answers those questions is the most direct line to sales and loyalty."[2]

Specifically, creating content as a cornerstone of your marketing can:

- Attract customers.
- Educate your buyers about a purchase they are considering.
- Overcome resistance or address objections.
- Establish your credibility, trust, and authority in your industry.
- Tell your story.
- Build buzz via social networks.
- Build a base of fans and inspire customers to love you.
- Inspire impulse buys.

Does it seem weird to talk about your marketing as *inspiring* or *credible* or *trustworthy*, or *telling a good story*? Does it seem

---

[2] www.convinceandconvert.com/convinceconvert-news/why-content-marketing-matters-to-me-and shouldto-you

radical? Does it make you a bit skeptical and nervous all at once? If so, why?

Perhaps such descriptors are more often applied in other realms—to a favorite magazine or newspaper, or maybe even to a friend—rather than marketing. But why not steer your marketing to another level? Why not create value? Why not provide your customers with a steady flow of high-value content that, as marketer Len Stein describes, is "packed with utility, seeded with inspiration, and that is honestly empathetic"? "Anything less will not suffice in a world where consumers can simply click away or spin around and mount a Web-wide counterattack on brands that refuse to walk their talk," says Len, founder of New York's Visibility Public Relations.[3]

In other words, create awesome stuff! And then use what you create as the foundation of meaningful conversations to engage with your customers. Regard your content as something *more:* as something other than just words and images on a page—as an extension of your brand. Just as a person is more than flesh and bones and hair and teeth, good content, too, is more than text and graphics and video. It's an embodiment of your brand. It's designed to inspire people to read more, or view more, or get to know and love your company a little more. Good content can quickly become the soul of your brand to the online world.

Web content allows your visitors to get involved—to comment and share and engage and *click here.* As Arianna Huffington said during her keynote speech at a MarketingProfs event in Arizona in late 2008, "If you are consuming old media, you are consuming it on your couch. If you are consuming new media, you are consuming it on your horse."

What Arianna meant was that online content both invites and demands that its participants be engaged, involved, and active—always moving forward. Old media, like TV and other forms of broadcast, just ask that we passively sit and watch.

---

[3] "Give The Brand A Personality," *MediaPost* www.mediapost.com/publications/?fa=Articles.showArticle&art_aid=129043.

Content drives conversations. Conversation engages your customers. Engaging with people is how your company will survive and thrive in this newly social world. In other words, online content is a powerful envoy for your business, with an ability to stir up interest, further engagement, and invite connection. And that's when things get interesting.

Good Content as a Competitive Advantage

Marcus Sheridan is one of three owners of River Pools and Spa in Warsaw, Virginia. The company installs swimming pools and hot tubs throughout Maryland and Virginia. Since joining the business in 2002, Marcus has spearheaded tremendous growth at the company. Despite years of record rainfall, a housing slump, and the slacker economy, River Pools continues to grow: In 2009, it sold more fiberglass pools than any other company in the United States, where it's among the top 5 percent of all in-ground pool companies.

A big reason for that, Marcus says, is his company's approach to business. "I used to see my company as a 'pool company.' [We] installed lots of swimming pools and therefore we were a pool company.

"In hindsight, though, this mentality was all wrong," he says. "Today, I see my business as a content marketing company. In other words, my entire goal is to give more valuable, helpful, and remarkable content to consumers than anyone else in my field, which will in turn lead to more sales."

Through a steady stream of blog posts and videos (the company publishes one to three a week) and an ebook on the subject of "how to buy a pool" (with the subtext "without getting ripped off"), Marcus set out to create the most educational and informative swimming pool web site on the Internet.

"I want our web site to be an encyclopedia of pool buying," he says, not unlike a business trade magazine publisher might seek to have similar authority in any given industry. "I want someone with a question to come to our site and get an answer by reading it or watching it."

The swimming pool industry is dominated by larger manufacturers, which makes it difficult for a small, young company like the nine-year-old River Pools to compete online for general search terms like *swimming pool* or *in-ground pool.* (When a potential customer searches for swimming pool information online using such terms, Google is more likely to return results for one of the big guys, not a small outfit like River Pools.)

So, instead, Marcus focuses on lower-volume, long-tail search terms to include in his web site content—more specific search phrases that usually consist of three or more keywords. Such phrases may generate low volumes of searches and traffic compared with short-tail, or more generic, search terms, but they take searchers to sites with specific, deep content that closely matches what the searcher is looking for. Such an approach is akin to "not hitting a home run every time, but if you hit enough doubles and triples, you can win the game," Marcus says.

See Figure 1.2 for a graphic representation of a long-tail keyword search.

"Most people searching online are sophisticated," Marcus says. Most are not searching for just *pools,* as they've probably already done some preliminary research and narrowed their choices. "I put myself in the mind of the consumer and think, 'What questions do I have unanswered?'" Marcus focuses on creating long-tail content that addresses those questions, creating

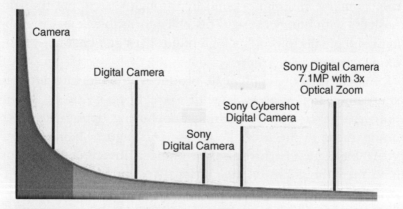

Figure 1.2   Long-Tail Keyword Search

Source: www.searchenginepartner.com/Latest-SEO-News/seo-trends-utilysing-lsi-and-the-long-tail.html

blog posts and videos about "fiberglass pool problems" and "fiberglass pool costs" and "how to choose your pool contractor." His content educates his customers about what to look for in a manufacturer and installer of pools—the hidden costs, the budgeting process, or, as Marcus says, "the good, the bad, and the ugly of in-ground pools."

"I point out the ugly, when others only talk about the good," he says.

> Marcus includes keywords and search terms in a meaningful way on his blog—not in an annoying, obvious way that gets in the way of the content itself. In the same way, you can include keywords you might be targeting, but in a natural, conversational manner. Don't make yourself look like a tool or, worse, clueless by stuffing your content full of keywords without providing context and value.

Search engines love people like Marcus; those who produce content like keyword-rich YouTube videos, blog posts, articles, and so on, consistently show up on the first page of search results for their targeted keywords. But Marcus sees the content he produces as a competitive advantage that expands and deepens his relationships with would-be customers. In other words, his customers might find him organically through search, but they do business with him because of his willingness to talk about problems and pitfalls to avoid, which builds trust and credibility and, ultimately, rabid fan loyalty.

Marcus calls the content he produces "the ultimate gift that keeps on giving" at every stage of a pool buyer's journey. When potential buyers are researching pool-buying options, content brings them to the River Pools site and piques their interest. When buyers are narrowing their choices, River Pools' content gives them the skinny on their alternatives and helps them evaluate considerations. And after the purchase, Marcus fosters rabid fan love and customer loyalty by continuing to be a resource for pool owners, with blog posts such as "Why do I have air bubbles in my pool? A troubleshooting guide."

That model—creating content that meets a buyer's needs throughout the journey toward purchase, and fostering loyalty after the fact—is, not coincidentally, the same approach as that of countless other companies (from a Pilates studio to a solder paste company to Kodak and more) that you'll read about here.

"The more valuable the information you can give to others, the more you will become viewed as an expert and therefore gain their trust," Marcus says. "The person with the abundance mentality wins."

CHAPTER 2
The Content Rules

Now is probably a good time to clarify and expand on a really important point: Creating awesome content is critical—but it's not enough. You must also develop material that meets a number of other objectives and is mindful of the conventions of good content—or (you knew this was coming!) the Content Rules.

In an age when more and more people are creating their own blog posts, filming videos, hosting webinars, and producing other content; when technology allows businesses to reach their customers directly; when customers are searching for information online and educating themselves about the products and services that interest them; when the idea of publishing material to reach a certain audience isn't reserved for an elite few who can afford the printing and distribution costs; when anyone at all can be part of the media; and when companies need to sound like what they are—organizations run by actual humans—well, we need to discredit the notion that creating content is complicated and difficult.

We promised in the introduction that we weren't going to spend a lot of time convincing you that the rules have changed—that product-centric communications sell your brand short. And we won't. Instead, here is a concise and easy-to-share list of 11 rules to help set you on the right path.

We've already been talking about the first Content Rule, "Embrace being a publisher." We'll go into more detail about the others, too. But without further fanfare, we present . . .

The Content Rules

1. *Embrace being a publisher.* You most likely already have, because you bought this book. (If you still need convincing, go back and read the introduction and Chapter 1 again.)

2. *Insight inspires originality.* Know yourself better than anyone. Get your brand story straight, and give voice to your distinctive point of view based on your mission and attributes. Know your customers, too, and what keeps them up at night. What are their concerns and objectives? What do they care about? How will your brand help them in their daily lives?

3. *Build momentum.* Why are you creating? Good content always has an objective; it's created with intent. It therefore carries triggers to action.

4. *Speak human.* Communicate your brand mission, values, and philosophy in simple terms, using the language of your customers. Speak in a conversational tone, with personality, empathy, and true emotion. Kill corporate-speak, buzzwords, and other language that makes you sound like a tool.

5. *Reimagine; don't recycle.* Recycling is an afterthought; good content is intentionally reimagined, at its inception, for various platforms and formats.

6. *Share or solve; don't shill.* Good content doesn't try to sell. Rather, it creates value by positioning you as a reliable and valuable source of vendor-agnostic information. Your content shares a resource, solves a problem, helps your customers do their jobs better, improves their lives, or makes them smarter, wittier, better-looking, taller, better networked, cooler, more enlightened, and with better backhands, tighter asses, and cuter kids. In other words, it's high value to your customers, in whatever way resonates best with them.

7. *Show; don't just tell.* Good content doesn't preach or hard-sell. Instead, it shows how your product lives in the world. It demonstrates through case studies or client narratives how your customers use your product or service, and explains in human terms how it adds value to their lives, eases their troubles, and meets their needs. Good content is not about storytelling; it's about telling a true story well.[1]

8. *Do something unexpected.* There's no business like show business, right? Occasionally adding an element of surprise to your content both drives viral sharing and enhances your company's personality. (B2B companies, we're looking at you.)

9. *Stoke the campfire.* Like a good campfire, good content sparks interaction and ignites conversation between you and your customers, and among your customers themselves, in the social sphere.

10. *Create wings and roots.* This advice is usually applied to parenting (give your children roots to keep them grounded and wings to explore new worlds). But it applies to content nicely, too: Ground your content solidly in your unique perspective and point of view but give it wings to soar freely and be shared across social platforms, all over the Web.

11. *Play to your strengths.* You don't have to create everything and publish everywhere; you don't have to do it all inclusively—create killer blogs *and* podcasts *and* white papers *and* webinars *and* ebooks *and* puppet shows *and* whatever else you can imagine. You don't have to do all of that. But you do have to do some things—and, at the very least, *one* thing—really, really well.

---

[1] Inspired by Jason Fried, co-founder of 37 Signals and co-author of *Rework* (Crown Business, 2010), writing in *Inc.* magazine.

In the coming chapters, we explain and expand on these Content Rules. Some of them are chapter headings, while others are woven into the chapters as call-outs or reinforced in the how-to section (Part Two) or success stories (Part Three).

In any case, they are all of equal import: Consider them a handy set of content commandments by which to run your own publishing efforts. We'll continue by expanding on the second rule, *Insight inspires originality.*

CHAPTER 3
Insight Inspires Originality
Who Do You Want to Attract?

When Ann was in journalism school, she learned the fundamentals of a good news story—that every article should answer the five Ws: *who*, *what*, *when*, *where*, and *why*. The idea, of course, was to tell a good story accurately and make it relevant to the reader.

Just like good journalism, good content strategy focuses on the story you have to tell and the audience you are trying to attract. These fundamental five Ws will help you focus on your customers, their needs, their preferences, and so on. Unlike journalism, though, your content strategy should begin with the *why*:

1. *Why* are you creating the content you're creating? (What are your goals?)

2. *Who* is your audience? And *who* are *you?*

3. *What* do you want the content to achieve?

4. *When and how* are you going to develop the content?

5. *Where* are you going to publish?

Question 1. Why are you creating the content you're creating?
What are your goals? What do you hope to accomplish? The cornerstone of any content strategy is to match what you want

to produce with your business objectives and strategic goals. The key here is to answer this question: How will your content strategy integrate with your other strategic efforts?

Question 2: Who is your audience? And who are you?

Who are the members of your target audience—customers or prospects? What are their preferences? Are they offline or online? What types of media or which platforms best resonate with your customers or your prospects? What are their problems? And, more important, how can you help them? "You must know your customers well enough to know what their biggest problems are," says landing-page expert Dr. Karl Blanks.

Also: Don't ignore the second part of that question: Who are you? What's unique about you? What are your point of view and your perspective?

Question 3: What do you want the content to achieve?

What effects do you want your content to have? What action do you want customers or prospects to take? And how will you measure their behavior and define the success of your efforts?

Helping your audience can take several forms: How can you help them do their jobs better, plan their vacations, buy a camera, or train for marathons? How can you anticipate and meet their needs so they start to see you as a trusted source of information they need, and not as someone who just wants to sell them stuff? You want to give their purchases a context.

Question 4: When and how are you going to develop the content?

How can you present the content in a way that best engages the intended audience? What's your budget? By what process are you going to create the stuff you need to create? What's your publishing schedule?

Question 5: Where are you going to publish?

How is your content going to be found, accessed, and shared?

Start with the Why

Here is where the second Content Rule comes into play: *Insight inspires originality*. Why? Because although you might be tempted to dive right in and start blogging or uploading videos to YouTube, you'll be far more effective if you take the time to determine *why* you are going to be creating before you actually create. Otherwise, what you do may not accomplish your goals.

Have you ever had a higher-up come into your office and demand, like a petulant child aching for a new pony, "We need a [*fill in the blank with the latest and greatest new shiny online toy that is getting lots of media coverage*]!"? It may be a Twitter account, a live-streaming video show, or a blog. If so, then your gut reaction was probably to ask the most important question: "Wait a sec. Why?"

Now, we're asking you the same.

You may have an image inside your head of the types of content you want to create. You might have grand visions of slickly designed gorgeousness that will bring customers racing to your door, money in hand. But the truth is that without a strategic plan (also known as big-picture thinking), you are doomed to fail (or, at the very least, underperform). So keep those dreams alive, but put them on a back burner for a few chapters while we lay the groundwork.

Chances are, you want to produce your online content to meet one of the following four objectives:

1. To attract new customers

2. To raise awareness about your company and create buzz about it

3. To share more information about your company online to make it easier for people to find you

4. To foster your community and give them a reason to tell others about you

(How many of you had considered that last one? We bet not many. But in the pages ahead we'll talk about why it is critical.)

A Quick and Dirty Search Lesson

Todd Defren, principal at Shift Communications, once gave a presentation that opened with the slide shown in Figure 3.1.

It sums up why posting content on your site is so important. When people search, you want them to find you.

Whole books have been written on search engine optimization (SEO) and we explain a bit more about that later. But to sum it up, the more unique pieces of content combined with the more links you have to your site from other web sites (inbound links), the higher your search ranking will be. When someone searches for "vegan dog treats" and you sell all kinds of all natural dog products, your goal should be to come up as close to the first result as possible.

But how do you secure those inbound links, you ask? By creating compelling content. Every time someone shares a link to your site in some fashion (by blogging about you or sharing a link on

Figure 3.1   Content Is to Google What Brains Are to Zombies

Twitter, for example), it boosts your search ranking. Make a video that everyone is raving about or write a blog post that people can't stop talking about, and you'll see your site start appearing much higher on the results page when people search for you or the things you sell. A higher ranking, of course, means that more people will visit your site when they search for something you sell. "It's not just about getting more traffic; it's about getting more traffic that gives a shit," says Jay Baer.[1]

Back to the Why—and Onto the Who

This exercise will help you determine why you are creating content—i.e. to reach your audience—and what content will best suit your audience's needs.

1. *Whom are you trying to reach?*

This must be the first question you answer. The more specific you can be and the more details you know, the better. If you answer "Anyone on the Web," then you are casting your net awfully wide. You're likely to catch plenty of fish, but will they be the right kind of fish? That is why knowing whom you are going after comes in handy.

Start with who your ideal customers would be. What are their ages? Where do they live? What do they do for work? Much of this may be guesswork, but forcing you and your staff to think about it is something that you should be doing already to grow your business.

---

[1] This is an actual quote uttered by Jay, as indicated by the, uh, quotation marks. We chose not to alter it or water it down as "sh*t," for example, because that seems cowardly. As a rule, we avoid cursing in business content, but sometimes it conveys a point colorfully, as in this instance. If that quote makes you reach for the smelling salts or otherwise offends, we apologize. But while we are on the subject, this is a good time to mention that you might want to develop your own policy toward cusswords. If you have a hip, edgy brand, it might suit you to drop an occasional verboten word into your content. But in general, we'd suggest avoiding a potty-mouthed free-for-all.

2. *Where do they spend their time online?*

You don't need to go through your customers' browsing history and Google search results to determine the types of sites they spend time on.

How can you find this out? There are services such as QuantCast.com that rely on demographic data to tell you where people spend their time. Yes, this is generic and anonymous, but it is a starting point.

Or you can ask them, in person or online. If you already have a customer database that you can poll by e-mail, consider a short survey asking customers which they consider their top five web sites. Get even more specific and ask them whether they use social networks like Facebook, Twitter, or LinkedIn. How sophisticated are they? Do they access online content via Real Simple Syndication (RSS)? Do they subscribe to e-mail newsletters and blogs? Such simple questions will quickly let you know where your customers are online and help you begin to conjure up what type of content will suit them.

3. *How do they access the Web?*

Are they browsing web sites on a desktop, a laptop, an iPad, or a mobile device like a smartphone? Pay attention to that last category, in particular. You might create the coolest video on the planet, but if your audience is mainly mobile, can they access it?

Also, if you are trying to reach business customers who are going to be visiting you from their work computers, you don't want to use too many fancy plug-ins or other items that might be blocked by a corporate firewall. Keep it simple and on target.

4. *What are they craving?*

Do they want to be entertained, informed, or educated? Or all three? Are they on the go and need information as quickly as possible? Do they have the time to really consume a full meal of content, or can they only snack on it?

As with any piece of content, you've got a very narrow window—often less than eight seconds, according to some reports—to engage someone before they click away. If the headline catches their attention, you've bought yourself a little more time. The only way you are going to keep your customers' attention is if you know what they want.

Again, this is a great place to ask questions: Survey your visitors to see what they'd like to see more of. Give them four or five choices, and see which rises to the top. Also, ask them what medium they'd like the content presented in. You might suddenly discover that they want more text and you've just put all your efforts into video. Create the content that your community craves.

5. *What do you want them to do?*

In the spirit of the third Content Rule (*Build momentum*), good content always has an objective; it's created with the intent to drive some action. It should therefore carry a trigger to action. What do you want your audience to take away? What do you want them to do? Buy something? Sign up for a newsletter? Visit your corporate site? Join your Facebook page? Raise their hand for a demo? Attend a webinar? Hire you as a consultant? View any content you develop as playing a role in furthering a relationship.

6. *What content do you already have?*

Take inventory of what you're already publishing and what you've already published. Leave no stone unturned: look at your online and old-school brochures, your print and online newsletters, news releases, bulletins, digital assets, VHS tapes, one-time customer communiqués, and so on. What do you already have that you might repurpose or, as we talk about in Chapter 5, reimagine?

Are you freaking out at such big questions? Don't. Asking these hard questions may not be easy or as much fun as creating stuff, but it's an important and useful exercise that will pay off.

Here's what we suggest: One day at lunchtime grab pads of sticky notes, round up your colleagues, find a place with a blank wall—and go to town having everyone write down answers to each question and sticking them up on the wall under each headline. After a set amount of time, stop; then walk through the answers. The ones no one agrees with, throw away. The ones that stay up are as good a place to start as any.

Set Your Metrics: What Does Success Look Like?

At the start of any campaign or initiative, you should ask one simple question: *How will we measure success?*

There is always one person in the room who thinks this is a simple question because it is a game of numbers. But what numbers are we talking about?

Online media are more trackable than any other media have been. But even so, you can't track everything, so how are you guaranteed to track success?

Common, yet ineffective, answers to this usually look like:

- Generating a lot of buzz and conversation online

- Having our video go viral

- A-list influencers or Web celebrities talking about us in positive ways

None of those are quantifiable and so shouldn't be true goals. Better versions of them might be:

- Generating at least 100 new mentions of our product online

- Having more than 10,000 views of our video across all sharing platforms

- Having 10 bloggers write positive posts about us

Do you see the difference? The first set of goals is vague and subjective, but the second set is clear and you can objectively determine whether you hit them. There are no gray areas in the second batch; they therefore are the type of metrics that you want to set so that you can accurately assess a project and deem it successful or not.

Here's how you might measure specific types of content.

Blogs

- *Subscribers*—The number of people who have subscribed to your blog via RSS or e-mail to get the latest content automatically.

- *Inbound links*—The number of other sites that are linking to your site. Most search engines, like Google or Bing or Yahoo!, can display this number for you.

- *Comments*—How much interaction do you have in the comments section of your blog? This is a good measure of how engaged your readers are.

- *Social validation*—How many people socially validated your content by liking it on Facebook, tweeting it on Twitter, or otherwise sharing it through social channels?

Photo and Video

- *Views*—All photo- and video-sharing services will display the number of views. If you share across multiple services, you will need to add these numbers up or use a service such as TubeMogul to do it for you. (You can also post to several video platforms via TubeMogul, by the way.)

- *Likes, thumbs-ups, and favorites*—Similar to blogs, most services have some form of so-called social validation, like the ability to like or favorite a video.

Webinars

- *Signups and attendees*—How many people took the time to fill out your registration form? How many of them actually showed up on the date and at the time to take part in the event? How many viewed it later, on demand?

Ebooks or White Papers

- *Downloads*—How many people downloaded a copy of your ebook or white paper?

In addition to having a sense of your objectives and your audience, it's equally important to have a sense of your own company's unique voice—which leads, of course, to the next chapter, "Who Are You?"

CHAPTER 4
Who Are You?

This past year, Ann was supposedly writing this book with C.C., which means that she was spending her evenings watching a lot of TV.[1] Shows she had never watched were suddenly must-see TV, especially reality shows, which handily aired more frequently than most network sitcoms or dramas. *American Idol* airs up to three times a week, for example, and she could easily burn two hours a week on *Project Runway* or its companion show, *Models of the Runway*. Together, they kept her willingly distracted almost every night of the week.

If you spend a lot of time watching competition shows like *American Idol* or *Project Runway*, you start to notice some patterns: those who emerge as finalists are the ones who, as then-*Idol* judge Kara DioGuardi was fond of telling the singing contestants, "know who they are." The designers competing for the top prize on *Project Runway* or solo artists on *American Idol* have a point of view that they express on the runway or stage. They use their

---

[1] Ann's note: Writing a book is hard work. It's daunting, huge, and terrible. What started as a kind of challenge to convince the publisher that you are an amazing person, have something to say, can sell a lot of books, and make them a lot of money, quickly disintegrates—when they believe you—into an exercise in avoidance, paralysis, distractibility, and overwhelming fear. What were you thinking? What made you think you wanted to do this? Never have mundane tasks held such allure as when I was writing this book. Never have I been so charmed by sitcoms and reality television shows, especially those programmed to run several times per week, which was a handy commitment I kept with my couch.

voices or clothing designs to express their ideas, emotions, and unique ways of viewing the world. With this point of view as a foundation, each competitor tells a story and weaves a kind of narrative. Night after night, week after week, you start to get a sense, through that narrative, of who they really are.

As much as she was trying to avoid thinking about this book, the parallel was hard to ignore (damn!): A critical step in developing great content is to develop your own distinct voice.

In literature, *voice* is the term used to describe the individual writing style of an author. It typically refers to a writer's use of a whole bunch of things—like character development, point of view, punctuation, dialogue, and so on—that contribute to the overall tone of a piece.

Voice is also the way your writing sounds when it's read. It's what the writer brings to words on the page, making it clear that they are written by a human with a certain personality and viewpoint. Voice "casts a spell," says Steven Pressfield, the author of *The Legend of Bagger Vance, Gates of Fire,* and five other books. "The right voice makes the work accessible; it gives us the tone and point of view that best illuminate the material and make it shine."

Does the idea of voice suggest something artsy-fartsy, completely outside the realm of doing business? In a word: no. In a few more words: The notion of voice actually has everything to do with your business. Voice is about how you write, certainly. But in a larger sense, it's also about how you express your brand. It's about the tone you take in all of your communications and publishing. It's about figuring out what's unique about you and your perspective.

"Before you can truly understand your customers, you have to understand yourself," says author and content-marketing evangelist Joe Pulizzi.

Your organization is struggling to differentiate in a crowded market. To succeed, you need to forge a separate and unique identity and create an enduring and memorable brand. And you need to create interesting stuff to be shared through social channels like LinkedIn, Twitter, or Facebook. In short, you have to stop sounding like everyone else.

Like the top contestants on reality TV, your content should have a tone that immediately expresses your company's specialness and your unique point of view. If someone lands on your site, or reads your newsletter, or whatever, your content shouldn't sound like your competitor's—or like anyone else's, for that matter. It should sound like you!

Most organizations readily distinguish themselves through the basics: design, graphics, logo, signage, and so on. Content is an afterthought—or sometimes barely a consideration. In graphic and web site design, for example, nonsensical Latin filler called *lorem ipsum* is commonly used as placeholder text, to show where the words will go. Since the actual words are usually added after all the other elements of a document or web site—like the typeface, typography, layout, and navigation—are squarely in place, the role of content is minimized. That's just nuts.

"I've heard the argument that 'lorem ipsum' is effective in wire-framing or design because it helps people focus on the actual layout, or color scheme, or whatever," says Kristina Halvorson, author of *Content Strategy for the Web* (New Riders, 2010). "What kills me here is that we're talking about creating a user experience that will (whether we like it or not) be *driven* by words. The entire structure of the page or app flow is *for the words*."[2]

The bottom line: Words matter. *Write differently.* The language you use and tone of your voice provide an untapped, powerful way to forge a distinctive identity, says John Simmons in his book, *We, Me, Them & It: How to Write Powerfully for Business* (Texere, 2002).

Simmons argues that companies must expand their traditional notions of corporate identity to include language, the words a company uses, and tone of voice. Branding, after all, is about differentiation. And describing a brand begins with words. Don't rely on the same tired and worn-to-the-bone words and phrases and bland corporate tone, he implores.

Typically, bland has been the tone of choice for companies, across the board. "The turn of phrase or idiosyncrasy that might signal an individual voice—emanating from family or

---

[2] www.adaptivepath.com/ideas/essays/archives/000959.php

personal history, cultural tastes, a playful sense of humor, simple, plainspoken honesty has been deleted, scrubbed clean," says B2B copywriter Richard Pelletier in an article at MarketingProfs.[3] As a result, "a growing, long-term relationship with hordes of potential customers entranced by your unique and engaging way of speaking with them slips from view." You have to show them who you are—not merely let them figure it out on their own, according to Pelletier.

A unique, human-sounding corporate voice is critical if you want to engage, stimulate, or excite your audience—especially now, when your content is increasingly an essential mechanism through which to define, enhance, and clarify who you are. Your tone of voice, in other words, is your greatest ally: It's the basis for the relationship you hope to create with your customers, along with your products, service, and culture—all the other things that go into a brand.

In the spring of 2010, Ann was a judge in a contest called the Incredibly Boring Web Content Challenge, created by the Boston ad agency Captains of Industry. Much like the Statue of Liberty attracts the poor, the tired, the huddled masses longing to be free, so Captains of Industry set out to entice the dullest, least-inspired pieces of online pabulum for a content makeover. The entries were astounding, and not in a good way. Consider Figure 4.1, from the Alberta Geological Survey: "The Buffalo Head Hills area has the highest diamond content results to date."

In other words: There's diamonds in them thar hills! And lots of 'em! Alberta, Canada, has a potential mother lode of diamonds worth billions of dollars, and the government is looking for a partner with the resources necessary to dig them up.

Or this, from Communicative Health Care Associates in Waltham, Massachusetts[4]:

Communicative Health Care Associates (CHCA) specializes in full speech-language diagnostic services, therapeutic care, and hearing screenings and through

---

[3] www.marketingprofs.com/6/pelletierrichard1.asp
[4] www.communicativehealthcare.com/services

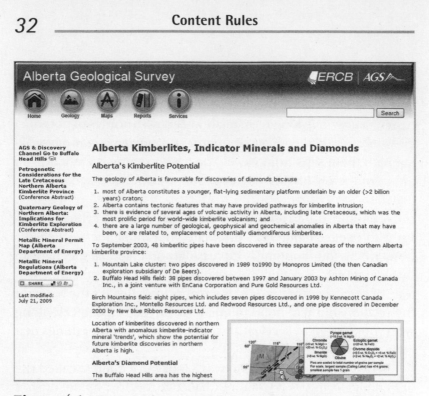

Figure 4.1   Entry in the Incredibly Boring Web Content Challenge
Source: www.ags.gov.ab.ca/minerals/diamonds/diamonds.html.

our division, Allied Rehabilitation Associates (ARA), we offer comprehensive, multidisciplinary rehabilitation services including physical and occupational therapies.

In other words: They help people speak, sign, or improve their hearing. People who have lost (or never had) the ability to hear a baby's giggle or the beating of a gull's wing as it takes flight can nevertheless communicate again, or at last.

There were plenty more examples. But notice how those two are absolutely devoid of personality, tone, and voice? Notice how they don't communicate anything of value about the identity of each organization? Or what's special about them? Or anything at all?

Contrast those two examples with the welcome message on the home page of Emma, a Nashville, Tennessee, e-mail marketing Company[5]:

---

[5] www.myemma.com

Meet Emma, the e-mail marketing and communications service that's taken a unique approach to web-based software. We think it should be easy to use (goodbye, cluttered interface). It should be made for you (farewell, generic templates). And it should even be fun (see ya around, support phone queue). It's all about e-mail marketing in style, and it's why 20,000 small and midsize businesses, non-profits and agencies have chosen Emma to power their e-mail newsletters and campaigns. And we'd love to help you.

See how you immediately get a sense of the company you will be doing business with? You get the sense that a real person, someone in tune with your needs, actually wrote the home page—and you start to get a sense of the fun, quirky, but capable company that is Emma.

Of course, there are other elements at work here: Emma's text also sounds like it is addressed to actual people—would-be customers—and it conveys what Emma can do for them ("we'd love to help you"), versus merely talking about how awesome Emma is. Notice, for example, how the page didn't say, "Emma is a full-service e-mail marketing agency based in Nashville, Tennessee. More than 20,000 organizations rely on its product and services to fulfill their e-mail marketing needs. . . ." We get into the issue of writing to your customers later in the book. For now, we're highlighting the importance of voice, because Emma has it nailed.

So does Netprospex, a Waltham, Massachusetts–based sales prospecting database and e-mail list broker. The content on the home page of Netprospex is sparse by design, straightforward, and wholly approachable. In an industry that has been associated with shady practices and marginal reputations, Netprospex wanted its voice and design to differentiate it immediately. "We considered voice and tone as much a part of the new design as we did imagery, design, and navigation," says CEO Gary Halliwell, describing the new look of his four-year-old company's site.

"We wanted the overall experience [for site visitors] to be clear and direct; we wanted them to know what to do and, just as importantly, who they were talking to when they came to our home page," Gary says. Adds Director of Marketing Katie Martell, "Our web site represents who we are as a company, and its voice says we are down-to-earth. No smoke and mirrors. Conversational. Approachable. And no ego, because the site isn't about us. It's about our customers."

The redesign had been in place for only two months when we chatted with Gary and Katie, and other features and content were still in the offing. But thus far the redesign had increased site traffic by almost 50 percent, Katie says, and upped the average time a visitor spent on the site. More anecdotally, she added, "Redesigning the site gave us the confidence to put our brand out there as a player in our space, and we know that the tone of the copy not only represented who we are as a company but also made people stick around. After all, it's easy to glaze over corporate gobbledygook!"

Speak Human: How Do You Differentiate Your Content?

Be human. "Markets consist of human beings, not demographic sectors," said Rick Levine and his colleagues, authors of *The Cluetrain Manifesto* (Basic Books, 2000), a decade ago. William Strunk and E.B. White said as much in the *Elements of Style* four decades before that, when they wrote about the importance of a straightforward communication style: *"Write in a way that comes naturally .... Be clear .... Prefer the standard to the offbeat."* (More on White in a minute.)

Are you human? Are your customers? We thought so. (And by the way: Even if you are a B2B marketer, you are ultimately speaking to other humans.) "You may be marketing to all of your customers, but remember that you are always speaking to a single person in particular," says Jellyvision founder Harry Gottlieb.

Does it sound condescending to instruct you to "speak human"? We don't mean it to be; instead, we are imploring you to create content that sounds as though a person, not a corporate department, fashioned it. How? Simply: *Write the way you talk.*

- Relax. Your voice should be natural, loose, and direct.

- Be conversational. Write a blog post, for example, as if you are writing a letter to a friend.

- Avoid marketing-speak and other jargon (see the sidebar at the end of this chapter).

- Lose the patched-together "Franken-quotes." We got this word from Matthew Stibbe of the United Kingdom's Articulate Marketing, who describes it as "that hype-loaded thing in the press release or blog post from the Senior Vice President of Marketing Bullshit."

- Use informal colloquialisms or casual expressions. "They add fizz and ginger," Matthew adds.

- Break some rules. Despite what you learned in school, you can start sentences with *and*, *but*, *so*, and *because*. So go on! And try it!

- Show, don't tell. Tell stories. Show how your products or services fit into customers' lives. Tell your audience how your stuff helps people by telling them about those people, not by talking just about your stuff.

- Worry more about creating remarkable content; worry less about being professional. The minute a client starts talking about a need to come across as professional, "I start worrying," says Matthew Stibbe, "because that's when the buzzwords, the 'end-to-end,' 'win-win' jargon comes out. No one believes you when you use language like that."

Lighten up. Any writer will tell you that to write well you have to care about what you are creating. (If you aren't interested in it, your audience won't be, either.) But we need to take it up a notch for businesses: You've got to care, certainly. But you also have to approach it with a sense of enthusiasm . . . and even fun.

Look at the examples from the Boring Web Content Challenge mentioned earlier: Why do people approach business with such grim seriousness? Perhaps people take themselves a little too seriously because they are afraid that others won't. Or perhaps some companies think they need to speak in a certain stiff way to appear credible. In business, it's tempting (and easier) to use the same boring words everyone else uses. But you'll be far more approachable (and a whole lot more engaging) if you lighten up a little. "I'd worry less about shocking customers than I would about boring them," says Jellyvision's Gottlieb.

We can think of very few industries in which a business might need to tone it down—maybe if you are selling caskets to the bereaved, or perhaps weapons to the Defense Department. But unless you are in one of those businesses (or a few others), your point of view should have an element of fun. And what's more, you should be having fun doing it. If you aren't having fun creating content, you're doing it wrong.

Approaching your content with a sense of fun and personality doesn't mean you don't sell something dead serious, or even what some might consider boring. Consider Eloqua, a company based in Vienna, Virginia, that makes marketing software. (See Figure 4.2.) Eloqua created The Conversation as an interactive sales tool targeted to companies that want to learn about how to make their online marketing more effective.

The Conversation set out to turn Eloqua.com visitors into prequalified, motivated leads. If that sounds boring, then you haven't seen the video, in which Eloqua educates its potential customers about its suite of marketing lead-generation products with a humorous, light, and engaging approach.

"All right, then," the video begins, after a visitor indicates that she works in marketing. "Obviously I'm not going to be able to use any of the typical marketing tricks on you (sex!), so allow me to just be direct (puppies!)." The video tool leads people through a smart, fun, interactive series of questions and answers—making the experience a two-way instead of a one-way lecture.

Be appropriate for your audience. Does "be appropriate" sound like something your prudish aunt might hiss at you through

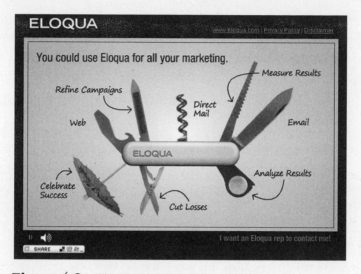

Figure 4.2 The Conversation by Eloqua
Source: http://illuminate.eloqua.com

pursed lips? Well, at the risk of sounding preachy, it's important to adopt an appropriate tone for your business purpose and for your audience. We said to have fun; we didn't say to be raucous.

In fact, there's a huge difference between having fun and being wild, silly, or (worse yet) inappropriate. As with anything, it's important to understand both your identity and your audience. It's great to take some measure of risk, but be careful to remain consistent with who you are. The voice you choose must sync with your purpose and the people you are writing to.

Build on your brand. Be sure that the voice and tone of your content reflect your brand and its attributes.

Brand is another one of those squishy marketing terms that's interpreted and applied in a thousand different ways. We asked the question "What is a brand?" to our Twitter followers and within 10 minutes we got a wide variety of answers. Here are a few:

- "It's a promise."

- "It's an expectation."

- "It's product and personality."

- "It's the full embodiment of a specific product or a service, including the company presentation and the consumer perception."

- "An impression, image, or personality that has to leave a long-lasting favorable emotional feeling in the consumer's heart."

- "A brand is what a brand does."

- "A brand is the emotional value assigned to a product or service by the people who want it."

- "The identity of a service or product that arouses different senses within [the] market."

- "The distinguishing mark or image used by customers as a mental shortcut to sum up who you are and what you represent to them."

- "The DNA of a product, [a] coding of uniqueness."

- "The sum of all conversations."

- "A product is something you buy. A brand is something you have a relationship with."

- Or this, from ExactTarget's Jeff Rohrs: "The mark left after a red-hot iron is applied to a steer's hindquarters." (*Wiseguy!*)

As defined here, brand is simply the image people have of your company or product. It's who people think you are. Or paraphrasing Amber Naslund of Radian6, quoting Ze Frank, it's the "emotional aftertaste" that comes after an experience (even a secondhand one) with a product, service, or company.

"Know who you are" is another way of saying, "Align your voice with your brand." But the result is the same: You have to make sure that the voice you use is completely in line with who your audience thinks you are.

Consider *Pawn Stars*, a popular show on the History Channel, and compare it with *Antiques Roadshow*, which airs on PBS. Both shows are essentially the same: appraising antiques, memorabilia, Americana, and the like. But the approaches are vastly different, and so are the brands: *Pawn Stars* is colorfully gritty and blunt; *Antiques Roadshow* is highbrow and well-spoken. Which brings us to our next point, handily. . . .

Differentiate from the pack of bland. Just as each of us has a unique personality, each company has a unique perspective. Or it should, anyway. Rohit Bhargava effectively argues in *Personality Not Included* (McGraw-Hill, 2008) that being faceless doesn't work any longer.

"Personality is the key element behind your brand and what it stands for, and the story that your products tell to your customers," Rohit writes. "Every element of your business, from your interactions with your customers to the packaging of your product, is an element of your brand personality, and these are the elements that inspire delight or indifference among your customers. In short, personality matters."

Personality is particularly critical in the age of social media, which "requires focusing less on marketing your products and benefits, and more on understanding how to use the personality behind your brand to build a relationship with your customers," Rohit adds later.

Let your originality—your specialness, your brand personality—come through in your online content. Give your readers or visitors a sense of a person or point of view, just like Emma does. So does Young & Free Alberta, a web site launched by Edmonton-based Servus Credit Union in 2007 to connect the large ($10 billion in assets) financial institution to the 17-to-25 crowd in hopes of winning their business.

Young & Free Alberta (www.youngfreealberta.com) is an ambitious program that includes a separate web site, an annual marketing campaign and spokesperson search to find the Alberta "spokester" of Generation Y, as well as videos, Flickr photo feed, Facebook group, and more. But you get a sense of its voice by browsing through its videos and on its blog, where an entry on budgeting ("Budgeting Can Be Easy . . . Really!) clearly aims to make finances less intimidating for young adults[6]:

---

[6] www.youngfreealberta.com/blog/budgetingcan-be-easy-really.html

One of the toughest things about budgeting is that it takes a LOT of work—work in the form of will power ("I do not need the $150 pair of shoes. . . . I do not need the $150 pair of shoes") and also in the form of just sitting down and writing up a budget! That's why, my Young and Free friends, I thought that I would share with you a nifty little tool that makes budgeting a piece of cake!

Know who you are talking to. . . . As explained in Chapter 3, your content—and all of your marketing, really—is the start of a relationship with your customers, right? So who are you talking to? Who are you trying to attract? You'll want to broadly identify the types of buyers you want to reach. Marketers call that process *developing buyer personas* for the stuff you sell.

A buyer persona essentially represents a type of buyer you think will be interested in your product or service, and the idea behind creating buyer personas is to understand customers' specific wants and needs. Knowing your audience is particularly important for creating content, and buyer personas can help shape your content to make it more relevant to your prospective buyers, especially as you are using words and phrases your potential customers use.

Most businesses will be speaking to more than one persona. For example, Ann is on the board of trustees at her local public library, and its customers are any of the some 10,000 card-carrying patrons who visit to check out any of the 250,000 items in the library collection. That sounds like one persona, right? It's not, because the library actually serves vastly different constituents:

- Those who access the library's collections both online and in person

- Those who live in neighboring communities (the library is a key member of a regional lending consortium)

- Other libraries that borrow from its collection

- People, foundations, and a local Friends of the Library group that support the library with donations and fundraising

- Local community groups that partner with the library on programs

- Public school teachers

- Genealogy researchers who rely on the library's extensive genealogy materials

- Nonprofits that use the library's meeting rooms

- Parents of young children who frequent the busy children's room and bring their children to story hours

- Teenagers who hang out in the teen room and participate in library programs like Wii tournaments and library lock-ins

- And finally, other people who live in the community and rely on the library as a resource for community programs and information—like recycling programs, senior classes, or summer programs for kids

Just as thinking about these various personas can help the library better serve its community, buyer personas can help shape your content to make it more relevant to your prospective customers. It's important to think about how your personas might shape the voice of your company, and specifically what words and phrases and tones your personas relate to.

How do you figure out what words and phrases your personas use and relate to? Broadly, by listening before you talk. Ideally, you can interview those people you are trying to reach in your marketing. But you can also gain insight by listening online: by reading the same publications or blogs that they do; by listening in on conversations in social outposts like Facebook and Twitter; and by using online keyword research tools like Google Adwords, Wordtracker, and Keyword Discovery to see what keywords related to your business people are searching for.

That last point brings up another reason to literally speak the language of your customers: You want to appeal to them, certainly, but you also want your content to appear in search results when your would-be customers are looking for what you have to offer. How do your customers describe your product or service? What words do they use? Lee Odden, CEO of Top Rank Marketing in Minneapolis, Minnesota, relayed a story about a client who described its business as "telemarketing outsourcing." But through keyword research, Lee's client discovered that its customers typically searched on "call center outsourcing" instead.

"The language used on social sites is like the canary in a coal mine," says Lee. "It can tell you an awful lot about your customers, and how you can engage them."

... *And how to talk to them.* In literature, and in business, people seem to imbue the notion of voice with some mystical quality: By tapping into it, or uncovering it, or finding it (or however it is supposed to magically reveal itself to you), you'll find your higher, truer self, or the essential nature of your company. There may be some truth to that. But more often than not, in art (and in business), that voice is deliberately crafted, not something you stumble across like you might stub your toe on something you've been missing.

The audience you are developing the material for plays a role in developing the voice. "It's not about us; it is about them," says 1938 Media founder Loren Feldman. Author Steven Pressfield says the "critical fact to remember is that the writer's voice is artificial," because the voice can change from one piece of work to another.

"The writer's voice (or director's, choreographer's, photographer's, entrepreneur's) arises from the material itself and acts in service to that material," Pressfield writes on his blog. "It can, and often does, change from book to book, dance to dance, album to album, business venture to business venture."[7]

Your intended audience plays a role in how you think about developing your voice, and the role you want it to play in your marketing.

---

[7] http://blog.stevenpressfield.com/2009/08/the-writers-voice

Communicative Health Care Associates, mentioned earlier, might adopt a more expert tone when it addresses institutions, and another, warmer tone for families that need its services. It might not always be necessary to adjust your voice (companies with a very narrow market may have only one voice). But if you serve several specific audiences, consider tuning your content voice to each.

Take a stand. Voice isn't just about how you write, but the perspective you bring. It's important to communicate a position, or an attitude, about a subject. Let your readers know where you are coming from, or how you feel about a topic or focus. Doing so communicates both who you are and the unique perspective you bring to whatever you are writing about. It also helps protect you from being a me-too blogger who simply regurgitates what others are already saying. "Successful bloggers have something of their own to say," says Problogger's Darren Rowse.

Consider the Church Marketing Sucks blog (www .churchmarketingsucks.com), published by the Center for Church Communication, a nonprofit founded to help its member churches market themselves more effectively. From the name of the blog itself to the post titles ("Other Churches Suck: How Not to Market Your Church," "Your Church: Is There an App for That?"), you get an immediate sense of the nonprofit's perspective, which is that although church marketing efforts are usually replete with lousy communication practices, cheesy logos, and bad clip art, it doesn't have to be so. And the nonprofit can help.

"We've got the greatest story ever told, but we don't know how to tell it," says founder Brad Abare. Everything about the organization's blog underscores the idea that "we help the Church tell that story," Abare adds.

HubSpot, which sells what it calls "inbound" marketing software, takes a stand when it says that so-called interruptive outbound marketing methods (like trade shows, e-mail blasts to purchased lists, telemarketing, and advertising, among other things) are old school. Instead, it insists that all the hip kids know what works, which is inbound marketing that attracts customers to you (and includes producing killer content, by the way). In countless blog posts, videos, and other content, HubSpot is unwavering.

A few years ago, on his On Startups blog, HubSpot founder Dharmesh Shah articulated the angst that taking a strong stand can create for business leaders. He was speaking about a video that HubSpot produced, starring CEO Brian Halligan[8]:

> *When building this video we had to decide: Are we really advocating that companies throw away all of their old marketing methods (including telemarketing) so they can switch to our way (inbound marketing)? It's just not practical. If we asked people to do that, we'd risk losing a bunch of prospects that just wouldn't take us seriously. We'd risk a bunch of our prospective customers thinking we were a whole lot of clueless [marketers]. But we did it anyway. Then, we went a step further. When we created the associated blog article, we gave it a controversial title "Dude, Cold Calling Is for Losers." Now, not only are we making fun of people that are doing cold calling, we're actually calling them losers. Remember, we have 5,000+ people that are subscribed to this blog[;] many of them are marketers, and most of them [are] likely do some sort of telemarketing.*

Does HubSpot take some heat? Sometimes. But Marketing Vice President Mike Volpe says it's a calculated risk. "If you try to please everyone, you end up being bland and no one talks about you," Mike says. HubSpot frequently takes a stand in many of its blog articles, such as announcing its decision not to exhibit at live trade shows and events. "Sometimes we even get beat up in the comments over our point of view," Mike adds. "But, by taking a stand, we are stimulating conversation."

As Guy Kawasaki says, "Don't be afraid to polarize people. Most companies want to create the holy grail of products that appeal to every demographic, social-economic background, and geographic location. To attempt to do so guarantees mediocrity."[9]

---

[8] http://blog.hubspot.com/blog/tabid/6307/bid/4333/Dude-Cold-Calling-Is-For-Losers-Video.aspx

[9] http://blog.guykawasaki.com/2006/01/the_art_of_inno.html #axzz0jzBQj7gI

And finally, your voice should be authentic. Authenticity is one of those soft, amorphous words that's tossed around quite a bit these days—like *transparency* and *being genuine*. It's hard to understand what *authenticity* really means, as the idea is open to wide interpretation.

When we say to be authentic, we mean you should make it clear that your stuff has the stamp of an actual person or actual people, and that person or those people have the qualities (a point of view, a personality, a sense of enthusiasm for the subject, and suitability to your audience) that make for a compelling approach to content as a solid foundation for the start of your relationship with your audience.

You should also be comfortable being who you are, which is pretty much where we started this chapter. It's about not forcing your voice or style to be what it's not; it's about fostering a voice that best represents you, your company, and your goals, and that will resonate with your intended audience.

Does that sound hopelessly New Age-y and squishy? It's not. As John Jantsch, author of *The Referral Engine* (Portfolio, 2010), says, "You don't always have to try to catch the latest fad. Just capture what's real about your product or service. Honesty sells because you can usually pull it off. . . . Be just what some target market wants and be it all the way."

When John said that, in 2006, he wasn't talking specifically about voice. But it applies as well to your company's communication style as to anything else.

Eighteen Business Buzzwords We Need to Ban Because They Make Us Sound Like Tools

Ann got an e-mail press release from a technology company the other day crowing about a partnership with another organization. It read, in part: "We believe the alliance . . . represents a synergistic win-win with significant value add for both solutions, allowing each to utilize and leverage their unique strengths in the market."

(Continued)

(Continued)

Huh? If the news was worth covering, she couldn't tell, because the press release was stuffed to the seams with jargon-filled corporate-speak. She deleted the e-mail almost immediately, sat back for a minute, and thought about E.B. White.

E.B. White was, of course, the author of *Charlotte's Web* and *Stuart Little*. But he was also the co-author, with William Strunk Jr., of *The Elements of Style*. (Actually, in 1959, White edited and updated Strunk's *Elements*, originally published in 1918. Strunk had been one of White's professors at Cornell.)

The Elements of Style is considered a classic playbook for writers, and you'll find it in full view on the bookshelves of most writers in the way that—as the writer Richard Ford has said—you'll find the Gideon Bible in most hotel rooms, as a beacon to the hapless: "In case your reckless ways should strand you here, there's help."

The Elements of Style doesn't teach anyone how to write, of course. But it does school you about critical fundamentals of the art and science of writing: Clarity. Brevity. Boldness. E.B. White has been dead for almost 25 years, and it's been 50 years since White's version first hit the streets, yet the brief (85 pages!) volume is newly relevant . . . more so, in fact, for us and you and businesses struggling to find their way as media companies in this newly social world.

In the 1980s, when Ann was a student at Simmons College in Boston, her first journalism class was with a professor named Charlie Ball, who assigned *The Elements of Style* as the only required textbook for the course. Professor Ball did his best to impart the fundamentals of reporting and writing the news—conveying the "inverted pyramid" approach to reporting that puts the meatiest, most important stuff at the top of the news article. Especially in pre-Internet days, when print newspaper editors were necessarily stingy with column inches, journalists needed to be able to churn out clean, accurate, and (most important) *brief* prose.

"This is how direct and brief I want your lead sentence to be," Professor Ball said to the class one day: "Dead. That was the condition of the body of a Caucasian male found in the park. . . ." He was joking, of course. But you get the point.

In those days, Ann's sentences were painfully long and unfortunately overwritten, and they tended to weave a tale versus cutting directly to the chase as good reporting should. As Professor Ball handed her embarrassingly marked-up copy back to her, he invariably said, "Do not be tempted by a twenty-dollar word when there is a ten-center handy, ready and able." He was quoting *The Elements* (*Number 14: Avoid fancy words*) in his characteristically direct way.

And so Ann clung to Strunk and White that semester like an infant lab monkey to its wireframe mother, depending on it to survive. Walking across the quad, she repeated the rules like a prayer: *Number 4: Write with nouns and verbs. Number 7: Do not overstate. Number 10: Use orthodox spelling.* She took to carrying the slim volume around in her pocket as a kind of talisman, like the way a superstitious bride carries something blue: for luck, or perhaps at least as a simple gesture to not tempt fate.

She passed Professor Ball's course, and even worked for a time as a reporter for the *Boston Globe.* But her heart wasn't in news reporting, and her editors quickly assigned her to Features, which suited her storytelling spirit. She eventually forgot about *The Elements of Style.* But later, when she had moved into online business writing and editing, she itched for the old talisman again: She was faced with what E.B. White had discussed in *Number 21: Prefer the standard to the offbeat.*

"Another segment of society that has constructed a language of its own is business," White writes. And so we end up with words or treatments those of us in business know quite well: long, Latinate words like *formalize* and *utilize* and *monetize.* Words created to make the individual

(Continued)

(Continued)

who uses them sound clever and smart, but they really are nothing more than weird, bloated versions of themselves. (The writer Matthew Stibbe says they suffer from "word obesity." We love that phrase.) E.B. White recognized the pretense, too, when he sniffed, "Usually, the same ideas can be expressed less formidably, if one makes the effort."

A tenet of ClickZ.com, a company Ann co-founded in 1997 as one of the first Internet marketing-focused web sites, was that the writing be conversational and that the contributors write from the *I*, from their direct experience with the then-nascent idea of marketing or advertising a business on the Internet. At ClickZ, based on the set of reminders and rules set forth by Strunk and White, she corrected Frankenspeak, jargon, indirect phrasing, qualifiers, passive voice, overwriting, overstating, unorthodox spelling, and awkward and unclear or pretentious phrasing, and, yes, she preferred the standard to the offbeat. *Good-bye, monetization.* And in doing so, she applied *The Elements of Style* again, in a newly digital world: She saw the work she did with the writers at ClickZ as almost a calling to strip the *corporate* from the *speak*: business writing *could* sound human!

In his day, E.B. White seemed to hold a low opinion of writing done for business or marketing. But he lived in a different world: an age of billboards people paid attention to and jingles they would hum. Yet interestingly, today, in the world in which we do business—ostensibly marked by an allegiance to authenticity, and engagement, and trust, and personality, and all that—White's core message now newly applies to businesses, too.

E.B. White likely couldn't have fathomed that something like the Internet would one day buttress his rationale for good, clear, interesting content. Yet, almost 25 years later, well . . . here we are.

Inspired in part by *The Elements*, here are 18 words and phrases we'd like to ban from marketing, sales, corporate communications, business schools, blogs, and boardrooms.

On second thought, let's just go ahead and ban them from everywhere. Entirely. Forever. You should never feel compelled to use any of the following words in any situation, including in all of the amazing content you are going to create after you've read this book. Banning these words is a step toward creating great stuff that sounds human, and speaks to us because it's written for humans by humans.

1. *Impactful*

   This is a terrible word that many people in business and education like to toss around to describe things that make an impact. But the word does not appear in most dictionaries and, if it does, it should be banished.

   Instead: Try *influential* or *substantial. Powerful* is good, too.

2. *Leverage*

   This word is the poster child of words that began life as nouns and (perplexingly) find themselves now used as verbs.

   Instead: Try, depending on the intended meaning, *influence*, *exploit*, *enhance*, *rely on*, or just plain *use*.

3. *Learnings*

   Another one of those sorry souls that began as one thing and morphed into something unfortunate: in this case, *learning* (as in *knowledge*) has been made plural, and I'm sure it's plenty upset about it, too. (Play this out: *knowledge* becomes *knowledges, information* becomes *informations,* and things quickly become more of a mess than they already are.)

   Instead: Use *lesson.*

4. *Synergy* (Also: *Synergistic. Synergism. Synergize.*)

   All of these are used when a combined result is thought to be greater than the individual parts. When this happens, everyone wins, so there is no need for a snazzy word to describe it.

(Continued)

(Continued)

Instead: Try *cooperation*, or *help*, or *joint*, or *pooled*, or *combined effort*.

5. *Revolutionary*

People often use this in business to describe things that really aren't. Unless you just invented an escalator to the moon, don't use this word to describe it.

6. *E-mail blast*

Businesses often use this phrase to describe an offer they've e-mailed to their subscriber list. The problem is that it suggests a certain disrespect. Are you a spammer? If so, then you've *blasted*. Legitimate businesses mailing a legitimate offer to an opt-in subscriber list? Not so much.

Instead: How about *newsletter*, *e-mail offer*, or *subscriber update*?

7. *Proactive*

The opposite of *reactive*. We know that businesses want to seem like they're cutting-edge and confronting every issue they face even before the issue occurs. But this word just sounds pompous and should not be used, unless perhaps you are in marriage therapy.

Instead: Try, depending on the intended meaning, *active*, *anticipate*, *forestall*, or *foresee*.

8. *Drill down*

Used to convey when people are getting into the boring little details of a topic. Related to this one is *deep-dive*, although apparently one happens in soil, the other in a swimming pool or ocean.

Instead: Try *in-depth* or *detailed*.

9. *30,000 feet*

A high-level view of a situation. Reserved for people who don't have the patience or capacity to drill down or dive deep (or sometimes both). In other words, those with short attention spans or (possibly) your boss.

Instead: Use *overview* or *executive summary.*

10. *Incenting/incentivizing*

Sales folks and midlevel managers love these darlings. You shouldn't. You should kill them.

Instead: Try *encourage* or *provide an incentive.*

11. *Almost any word that ends in* -ize

Including the preceding one as well as *productize, monetize, budgetize, utilize, socialize,* and *operationalize.* The sole exception is *optimize,* but only in the content of search engines, and only because it's so ubiquitous.

Instead: Find a word that doesn't sound like it was first uttered by the robot on *Lost in Space.*

12. *Solution*

Businesspeople often use this word to describe a product or service they can't otherwise explain.

Instead: How about actually explaining exactly what the product or service does and allowing the customers to decide whether it solves their problem?

13. *Users*

A dehumanizing word that strips people of any individuality and humanity. Online marketers and drug dealers are the only two industries that refer to their customers as *users,* says Gerry McGovern, author of *The Stranger's Long Neck: How to Deliver What Your Customers Really Want Online* (A&C Black, 2010).

Instead: How about *people? Customers? Friends?* Or how about calling out the specific group of people you want to engage—crafters, movie buffs, dog lovers, swimming pool installers, or what have you?

(Continued)

(Continued)

14. *Almost any word rooted in technology but applied to humans*

    Including: *ping* to mean *follow up*, *bandwidth* to mean *capacity*, or *offline* to mean either *not working* or *outside of this already horribly long meeting.*

    Instead: Use words that describe what humans do, not machines.

15. *Overused words*

    A whole bunch of words that used to be good, solid words, and now have been overused to the point of meaninglessness: *Robust. Granular. Box* (but only when you are *outside the —*). *Strategic. Space* (as it applies to the market you are in). *Traction.*

16. *Mashed-together words*

    Another class of words that individually are harmless, but mashed together become horrid: Buy-in. Mission-critical. Dial-in. Best-of-breed. End-to-end. Value-add. Next-generation. Face-time. Push-back. Net-net. Win-win. And low-hanging (as it applies to fruit when you aren't talking about an actual tree or orchard).

17. *Silly phrases*

    There are a zillion of these corporate-speak silly phrases: *Run it up the flagpole. Eat your own dog food. Out of pocket. When the rubber meets the road. At the end of the day. Peel back the onion. Open the kimono. Open the kimono at the end of the day while you are peeling an onion.* But two we find particularly silly are *moving forward* (as opposed to what? Standing still? Spinning our wheels? Slamming it into reverse?) and *touch base* (because I'd like you to keep your hands off me. Can we just talk?).

18. *Offensive phrases*

Finally, here are two more we dislike: *Nazi* when applied to business concepts (as in *brand Nazi*) or *drinking the Kool-Aid* as applied to accepting ideas or concepts (sometimes, without understanding). Since these two phrases are rooted in unfortunate and regrettable events in history, using them seems offensive or (at the very least) in bad taste.

Special thanks to those helpful people on Twitter who helped compile this list (and made us laugh):
@Brainzooming, @seemills, @jkgala99, @KellyeCrane, @AnthologyMonica, @adamkmiec, @followlinus, @mbbunnell, @debmaue, @useglobalreach, @alambchop, @irenekoehler, @kpedraja, @laceyhaines, @FromChristina, @johnmccrory, @evengenius, @2020_Innovation, @maddiegrant, @DawnPappas, @jmrichmond, @zoziku, @JenKaneCo, @tamadear, @jblock, @klingaman, @jamiewalker19, @patrickstrother (via @betsyschro via @LornaLyle).

CHAPTER 5

Reimagine; Don't Recycle

Anatomy of a Content Circle of Life

Here comes the fun part: What content are you going to produce? What formats are you going to use—ebooks, white papers, blog posts, videos, photos, podcasts, tweets on Twitter, Facebook status updates, customer case studies, or iPhone apps? The short answer is, "Yep."

We're not being flip. Rather, we're suggesting that you always keep an open mind when you think about the material you want to create. Instead of a "one and done" approach, treat anything you develop as pieces of a larger whole. View all of the pieces of content you plan to create as expressions of a single bigger idea. Or, alternatively—if you are starting with something larger, like a white paper or ebook—think about how you can create smaller chunks of shareable content from that single content asset.

Adopting a broader approach to creating content requires a shift in thinking. Most organizations are accustomed to approaching marketing as a single campaign or initiative, and less as an ongoing, long-term model—as content requires, points out Jeff Rohrs, vice president of marketing at ExactTarget, an Indianapolis-based e-mail marketing company. "Taking a holistic view requires thinking differently, because organizations are programmed otherwise," he says.

This is also a good time to point out that the responsibility of creating good content does not fall solely on the shoulders of the marketing department. With the rise of the social web, the lines between marketing, public relations, and customer service are blurring. Your customers do not care which department's responsibility it is; they look at your company as a single entity. So as you develop a content strategy, it is critical to include the voice and input of everyone in the company if you hope to be successful.

You certainly can create a killer blog or an amazing podcast as the cornerstone of your content. And maybe if you're a sole proprietor or a small shop, that's enough to drive business your way. But it's more efficient and effective in the long term (and necessary for larger organizations) to take a broader view: to create content that can come to life in various formats, across many different platforms, and that can address multiple audiences. Creating a system—wrapping it around a regular schedule or so-called editorial calendar—can make its creation a whole lot more manageable, too.

"It's hard work to develop content," says Stephanie Tilton, who produces ebooks and case studies (among other content) for business-to-business (B2B) companies. "The key is to reuse and repurpose. Ask yourself, 'How can we repurpose content development efforts to yield as many assets as possible?'"

You could think of it as Stephanie suggests, like you are *repurposing* that larger piece of content into other formats, or slicing or *atomizing* it into smaller bits to share, as our friend Todd Defren terms it.[1] But *repurposing* suggests something that might happen as an afterthought—like you might reuse an old Cool Whip container to store leftovers—whereas we're talking about something far more intentional, as something that happens in the first phase of your content plan development. Rather than *repurposing*, try *reimagining*.

The idea is to "deconstruct that white paper and create an array of info snacks that you can sprinkle across the Web, or to package smaller pieces of content," says social media consultant Jay Baer. Jay calls this "getting more bait in the water"—or creating opportunities to reach as wide an audience as possible, but using the same source material, repackaged and reimagined.

---

[1] www.pr-squared.com/index.php/2008/06/atomize_your_content_share_in

In doing so, you create a sort of content ecosystem, or a Content Food Chain, because it implies a logical sequence of re-creation and rebirth—a content circle of life, if you will.

A food chain, as you know, is the sequence of who eats whom in a biological community or ecosystem. A food chain starts with the primary energy source—usually the sun or boiling-hot deep-sea vents—that feeds the organisms in the mud, which fertilize the grass in the field, which feeds the rabbits, which feed the snake, which feeds the owl, which feeds the alligator.

In the Content Food Chain, your content is not literally feasting on other content; rather, you are creating an overall content plan fueled by a single Big Idea, or core message, which is a rich and robust source that can act as the energy source for feeding and sustaining the rest of the stuff you reimagine.[2]

The ensuing material can rely on that fuel as source material, allowing for new distribution and new channels (figuratively giving it new legs), reaching new audiences along the way (or at least reaching audiences again), and propagating your ideas through social media channels. What's more, search engines will index each effort separately, multiplying your ability to be found by customers.

So, for example, you could use your Big Idea as the source material to develop a larger piece of content—perhaps an ebook, a collection of case studies, or a best-practices white paper—that would then feed the development of smaller, snack-sized, reimagined content (perhaps blog posts, video blog posts, newsletter articles, and so on).

Seizing the White Space (Harvard Business Press, 2010), a book on business-model innovation written by Mark Johnson,

---

[2] Attention biologists, environmentalists, and other earth scientists, as well as literalists and purists: analogy is intended for illustrative purposes only. This explanation is both intentionally vastly simplified as well as slightly massaged to suit our purpose in the issue of content creation. Please refrain from letters or comments or supporting documentation that explains any nuances of the food chain that you fear may have eluded us.

co-founder of Innosight, based in Watertown, Massachusetts, serves as the foundation of the content strategy for this boutique business consulting, training, and investment firm. The book itself is prominently featured on Innosight's home page, and although Johnson didn't write it solely as a marketing piece, it has nonetheless become the Big Idea that has fueled other content, according to Renee Hopkins, Innosight's publications editor. Examples include a series of posts on Innosight's blog, articles in its *Strategy + Innovation* newsletter, and guest pieces in the *Harvard Business Review* blog and various trade publications that target aspects of the health care industry.

"The book gives us a number of foundation concepts we can subsequently publish as blog posts or longer articles," Renee says.

MarketingProfs did something similar with its *State of Social Media Marketing* research report, published in December 2009. Based on the information contained in this weighty 242-page survey of 5,140 marketers, MarketingProfs subsequently produced its own webinar ("The Naked Truth: Insights from Our Social Media Marketing Research"), article ("The State of Social Media Marketing, by the Numbers"), as well as various smaller articles and blog posts that featured individual charts or highlighted some interesting research nuggets. The heft of this research also earned MarketingProfs some press mentions on 102 business-related blogs and gave MarketingProfs staffers plenty to talk about at various marketing events and non-MarketingProfs webinars.

Similarly, e-mail marketer Constant Contact each month develops a content theme—perhaps list building, social media integration, learning from metrics, and so on, says Martin Lieberman, who heads up content development at the Waltham, Massachusetts–based company. "We try to package our content across the platforms around that theme," he adds. "So you'd likely see similar messages in our *Hints & Tips* newsletter, our blog posts, and our bylined contributions to external publications, for example. We also repackage our newsletter articles and blog posts into guides and white papers."

Like Constant Contact's, all of the content you create can be loosely based on the same message or ideas, but it won't look exactly the same. Your webinar doesn't have to look a whole lot like a blog post, for example, just like a rabbit doesn't look much like a snake.

Here's how to create your own efficient, sustained Content Food Chain.

First, Look toward the Sun

Start by seeking out and researching your primary energy source (the Big Idea) that will feed the rest of the ecosystem. Your Big Idea is your fuel source, and what it is depends on, of course, are your goals and objectives from Chapter 3 (*Who are you trying to reach? What do you want them to do when you reach them?*) matched with the wants and needs of your buyers (*What do your prospects and customers care about? What can we create that they'll value?*).

For example, are you trying to reach health care information technology (IT) buyers to get them to demo your software? Perhaps your Big Idea is to develop content around how to survive a compliance audit. Are you trying to reach mothers to get them to enroll their children in your learn-to-swim class? Perhaps your Big Idea is pool safety, and you plan to write a series of blog posts on how to avoid backyard accidents and on which swim rules are myths ("Do you really have to wait an hour after eating?"), as well as publish Flickr photos, a video series of games to play in the pool, and so on.

Tip: You might already have a library of content you've previously created. In that case, it's a good idea to take inventory so you know what you have, as mentioned in Chapter 3. Aggregate all you've created—articles, white papers, ebooks, webinars, PowerPoint presentations, speeches, or what have you—in a central location. A simple spreadsheet will do; on it, capture information (a page title and URL) on where each lives on your site. Cull and categorize each according to the various themes, topics, or key messages. Discard the stuff that's obsolete; keep the stuff that's timely or evergreen.

Create a Publishing Schedule

A publishing schedule, also called an editorial calendar, allows you to plan, produce, and publish content. A publishing schedule is critical for a Content Food Chain, because it'll help give your content consistency and make it easier to manage. Russell Sparkman of Fusionspark Media, in Langley, Washington, advocates a publishing schedule he calls "1-7-30-4-2-1."

With Russell's model as inspiration, we've slightly modified and annotated his formula here. This is, of course, a comprehensive and ambitious plan. Modify it to suit your own needs, ambitions, and resources.

1 = Daily

- Twitter updates that offer something of value to your constituents

- News items you read elsewhere that are relevant to your core content, posted to Twitter or your Facebook fan page (Russell recommends using Google Alerts to provide you with a steady stream of news relevant to your product, service, or cause. You can also curate stories produced elsewhere; see Chapter 6.)

- Responses to blog comments on your own blog, or left on other industry blogs if you can manage it

- User-generated content (UGC) on your site, through your own site's submission functions, or dynamically fed through sites such as Flickr

7 = Weekly

- At least one new blog post; two or three if you can manage it

- A short video (one with simple production values—of someone on your team giving a presentation, for example)

- A how-to article

- Participation in related forums, or discussion groups on LinkedIn

- Update of your primary web site's pages or sections

30 = Monthly

- Write a meatier blog post or article based on deeper research, or an interview with a subject-matter expert. (Q&As are great!)

- Create and mail an e-mail newsletter.

- Produce a short video (two to three minutes, with increasingly greater production values—with script, location shooting, multiple cameras, and so on).

- Produce a video of one of your executives speaking at a conference.

- Produce an audio podcast.

- Create a PowerPoint presentation and post it to SlideShare (or other sharing site).

- Organize and promote a cocktail or coffee hour meetup, or a similar gathering offline.

- Contribute a guest post or article to another blog or publication.

- Produce a webinar.

- Publish a case study or customer success story.

4 = Quarterly

- Publish a research-based white paper.

- Create a case study collection and distribute it in PDF format.

- Create an ebook (again, distribute it as a PDF).

- Produce a video series.

- Produce a special issue of your e-newsletter.

- Make an announcement of contest or sweepstakes winners.

Russell also recommends creating biannual and annual content (that's where the 2 and 1 come in): bigger events that can also feed the development of content throughout the year.

"If done correctly, a biannual event would be something worth videotaping, so that you can use the video to fill weekly, monthly, or quarterly needs," says Russell. So, once or twice a year, think about content marketing activities that are more of "a celebration, an event, an announcement," he adds. Some suggestions[3]:

- Produce a live or virtual event, and record the sessions for later use in your weekly, monthly, or quarterly content needs.

- Host an executive roundtable and record the proceedings.

- Produce an annual industry white paper or ebook.

- Produce a best-practices guide.

- Speak or present at an annual conference.

- Announce and launch a contest or sweepstakes.

- Update your web presence with a new story feature, a new tool set, or new functionality.

- Create and launch an iPhone app, or a Facebook app, tool, or widget.

- Produce a game.

---

[3] Russell Sparkman, "Content Marketing Secrets, Part III: Easy as 1-7-30-4-2-1" (www.fusionspark.com/blog/2009/10/13/content-marketing-secrets-part-iii-easy-as-1-7-30-4-2-1).

Does that sound like a lot of production, a lot of coordination, a ton of writing, and a boatload of content? You bet it is, which is why you'll want to modify it to suit your capabilities. Ottawa-based Kinaxis, for example, develops a regular publishing schedule based on a Big Idea it develops from top keywords gleaned from its search engine optimization (SEO) analysis.

In 2008, Kinaxis set out to engage its intended audience—the supply chain community—with the goal of increasing web site traffic, driving sales leads, and generating positive word of mouth, all with the underlying goal of improving natural search results. "Thought-leading content development and subsequently SEO are at the very core of everything we do," says Kirsten Watson, director of corporate marketing. "Our aim is to invest in creating compelling content about the burning issues that matter to supply chain experts today."

Using a multipronged, content-driven approach that includes Twitter, community building, blogging, and video, Kinaxis says it was able to build and sustain an active community and triple its number of web-based sales leads to 42,000 in 2009. Specifically, Kinaxis says it recorded a 2.7-fold increase in traffic to Kinaxis.com, a 3.2-fold increase in leads generated online, and a double-digit increase in paid subscriptions to its RapidResponse software-as-a-service product.

Its content machine is particularly well oiled: once a month, Kinaxis produces a keyword-inspired white paper, which it then reimagines into daily, weekly, and monthly content in various formats. Then it starts the cycle all over again. Based on source material from the white paper, its publishing schedule looks something like this:

1 = Daily

- Twitter updates
- Facebook Fan Page updates
- Responses to blog comments and comments elsewhere

7 = Weekly

- A series of related blog posts (Kinaxis usually updates its blog with new posts three or four times per week.)

30 = Monthly

- Video interview with the white paper author

- Audio from the interview published as a podcast

- PowerPoint presentation posted to SlideShare

- Case study

4 = Quarterly

- Webinar

Kinaxis "creates 10 things out of one thing," Kirsten says. The specific variety of what content you develop will vary greatly, depending on your marketing objectives, your expertise, your interest, and your budget, she adds. But the approach is the same whether you are trying to reach moms or geeks or supply chain managers (like Kinaxis is). "Be a resource for them, or solve a problem for them. Don't simply push your product," Kirsten says (allowing us a handy opportunity to underscore another Content Rule: *Share or solve; don't shill.*)

Feed the Beast

Should you create a larger piece of content first—like Innosight, MarketingProfs, or Kinaxis—and then atomize it into smaller chunks of content like blog posts, podcasts, and so on? Or should you do the opposite: begin by creating a collection of smaller chunks, and then collect or compile them into a larger ebook, white paper, or best-practices guide?

Either approach is fine. The important point is that your content is all part of the same circle or continuum, right? So it doesn't matter where, exactly, you begin. In our experience, most B2B companies like to create the larger pieces of content first, and then reimagine them into smaller chunks. Meanwhile, sole proprietors and businesses that sell to consumers tend to take the opposite approach.

Wherever you jump in, remember that it's all about that single Big Idea or a specific theme. Whether you start small or large, your idea or theme is always the foundation, and each piece of content you produce should have a place in that larger picture. It might be easier, then, to start by producing smaller blog posts or podcasts—to start small by writing a series of pieces that expound on a chosen topic—for two reasons:

- *First*, starting small is less scary than starting big. It's easier to create and publish a few posts about a given topic than it is to conceive, write, and produce an expanded 50-page ebook.

- *Second*, starting small allows you to test your ideas or concept and gauge your audience's reaction to your ideas before you invest the time, energy, and budget into producing a larger piece that might fail to resonate with your target audience. It gives you more flexibility, in other words. For example, you might create a few blog posts and share them through social channels like Twitter and Facebook, only to realize (based on feedback or watching clicks) that you should take another approach, or perhaps swerve in a slightly different direction.

Aim for Variety, and Do Something Unexpected

Express your content ideas in various formats, lengths, and media. Think text and video and photos and PowerPoint, for example. But also vary the *kind* of content you are producing within each format: Mix longer blog posts with shorter posts, timeless evergreen topics with time-sensitive commentaries, personal topics with professional ones. (See Chapter 24 for a helpful blueprint of how one company, HubSpot, mixes up content on its blog.)

The idea is to create compelling stuff that your audience will want to read, and here it pays to surprise them a little by mixing up what they otherwise expect—even every once in a while. Kinaxis, for example, produces a whole series of YouTube videos on supply chain management and enterprise software humor. Some of its comedy videos—such as the *Late Late Supply Chain* talk show and the sitcom short *Married to the Job*, starring Damon and Sibley, a husband-and-wife supply chain team—are produced in-house; others are scripted and acted by an outside production company. (*Married* is a joint production between The Second City Communications and Kinaxis.)

We can guess what you're thinking: Supply chain management and enterprise software jokes? Sounds funny—as in funny-*strange* and not funny-*ha-ha*, right? Well, you couldn't be more wrong. The comedy is actually funny, and it's unexpected. Check it out at http://kinaxis.com/supplychaincomedy.

Adding an element of surprise both drives viral sharing and gives your company some personality.

Imagine New Creatures

In the real world, the alligator doesn't feed the rabbit. But here's where the content circle of life deviates: You can also use a webinar to feed new and smaller pieces of content again. For example, the Q&A sessions from the webinar might be turned into a blog post or newsletter article; or you might interview one or more guest webinar speakers for a podcast. Thus, your larger chunks of content also feed your smaller efforts.

And by the way, if your organization serves several industries or verticals, you can tailor any of your content to separate audiences by inserting a few customized PowerPoint slides at the beginning, tweaking the title, and developing targeted messaging that speaks directly to the audience you are trying to reach.

Feeding the Content Food Chain

Bust your content silos! Do you have a print newsletter? Do you produce a regular podcast? Run a version of a print article on the blog, upload the best headlines to Facebook, post transcripts of your podcast online, and chat everything up on Twitter. Many of the ideas here reinforce the notion that you should not silo your content. Rather, you should sprinkle it freely across any of your platforms.

Whatever you create, be sure it's optimized for search engines. The content you reimagine should be refined to include the universe of keywords that will help your site rank high in search engine results. In other words, always be mindful that you're not only creating different kinds of content but also optimizing each for the search engines that pull your audience to you.

Be sure that all of your reimagined content also gets all the other stuff that should be in there, such as social sharing capabilities and a clear call (or calls) to action that will drive sales. By social sharing capabilities, we mean adding "social bling"–like buttons to share and "like" content across social platforms such as Twitter, Facebook, and LinkedIn, as well as subscribe buttons (for more, see Chapter 8).

The possibilities for reimagining your content across channels and platforms are nearly inexhaustible, limited only by your (and your audience's) preferences, abilities, and objectives, and (of course) your budget. Here are 13 ideas to get you started:

1. *Think small.* Is creating a white paper or an ebook a daunting task? Create smaller chunks of content instead. A series of smaller blog posts will be easier to produce and more digestible for readers short on time and attention, and it will multiply your search love.

(Continued)

2. *Think really small.* Ask your Twitter followers or Facebook fans for their take on a specific theme or topic related to your business, and create a blog post from it (with credit to them, of course). Something open-ended that solicits personal suggestions or advice works best, such as: What's your favorite must-have iPhone app for business? What's your must-read book on widget management for 2011? What's your favorite social media tool? As C.C. says, "Think acorns, not trees."

3. *Bundle.* Conversely to Number 1, bundle existing blog posts around a central theme into an ebook or white paper. Give it away freely (not requiring users to register to download it), or not. See which approach works best for you in Chapter 13.

4. *Create a content chop shop.* A white paper or position paper can become a series of blog posts, or a bunch of informative audio podcasts that your audience can listen to during their daily commutes, suggests C.K. Kerley, a New York City–based marketing consultant (www.ckb2b.com). A conference where you videotaped several speeches by your company's subject-matter experts can become a series of online videos.

   Or: "Findings from a recent study you commissioned can become a set of tweets and wall postings . . . that link back to a blog post on the study . . . that links to an audio podcast that discusses the study's biggest surprises . . . that links to a video interview of various subject-matter experts discussing the study's implications . . . while you also provide a 'quick read!' synopsis of the study's findings for mobile viewers," C.K. says.

(Continued)

(Continued)

5. *Ignite conversation.* Categories, themes, and challenges addressed in your content can give rise to (or bolster) a LinkedIn or Facebook group that you create and monitor. *Tip:* Instead of founding a group that bears your company name, create a group that unites members around a common challenge or theme. People are more likely to join a group if it has such broader appeal.

6. *Tell client stories.* The customer success stories that you've published as articles or PDFs can become a best-practices webinar series or they can be upgraded into a series of video testimonials.

7. *Record presentations and speeches.* Record the speeches or presentations your team gives and post them on YouTube. Capture your CEO delivering an overview of your annual report on video, and publish it with the executive summary text. Repurpose as needed to your blog, or Twitter, Facebook, or other social sites.

8. *Go mobile.* The industry data that your team regularly tracks can become a stream of mobile SMS alerts that your market can subscribe to and remain informed of industry developments while working remotely. *Tip:* Be sure that you optimize your content for mobile. "The best practices of social media content are vastly different from the best practices of mobile media content—because the devices from which your audience views your content are completely different," says C.K. Just pull up the same web content on a laptop and a smartphone and you'll understand exactly what we mean. Optimizing for screens large and small requires more effort, but it's worth going the extra mile if you want your content to be accessed via smartphones. (And you do.)

9. *Post presentations and ebooks on SlideShare.net, and post white papers on Scribd.com.* These free services allow you to upload PowerPoint or keynote presentations to share on SlideShare, and subsequently share freely on Twitter, your blog, and so on. A PowerPoint slide show presented at an industry event can become an online slide show perfect to view on screens both large (desktop, laptop) and small (smartphone). Consider adding voiceover to the slides to make the presentation even more dynamic.

10. *Same stuff, different way.* Interviewing someone for a blog post or article? Capture it on video or audio with a few extra key questions to differentiate it from your story, then post them separately.

11. *Go behind the scenes.* Give readers or followers an insider's view of your company. Share a photo on Twitter from a podcast or video in progress. Share what content you're working on to Twitter or Facebook.

12. *Remake the news.* Take a recent news release from your company and write a short blog post on its significance. Don't just repost the release: Give the audience your take on why it matters.

13. *Curate Twitter posts* on a common theme and create a SlideShare presentation. This is particularly effective after a shared experience, such as an event. Want it to be even cooler? Mix in the quotes with candid photos from the event itself.

CHAPTER 6
Share or Solve; Don't Shill

Good content shares or solves; it doesn't shill. In other words, it doesn't hawk your wares or push sales-driven messages. Rather, it creates value by positioning you as a reliable and valuable source of vendor-agnostic information.

As we said in Chapter 2, your content shares a resource, solves a problem, helps your customers do their jobs better, improves their lives, or makes them smarter, wittier, better-looking, taller, better-networked, cooler, more enlightened, and with better backhands, tighter asses, and cuter kids. In short, it's of high value to your customers, in whatever way resonates best with them.

Consider Procter & Gamble's approach. The brand's Pampers division launched a series of web-based videos called "Welcome to Parenthood," featuring real parents talking about the stuff new parents love to obsess over (diapers, potty training, nighttime, and naptime). The 14 episodes were made available on Pampers.com and on the brand's Facebook page. The project was co-sponsored by pharmaceutical company Abbott, which makes infant products Similac and Beech-Nut. Rather than simply shilling diapers, P&G is sharing parenting advice and helping parents navigate those consuming early years of parenting. It is creating content parents care about.

Similarly, the Wisconsin Cheese Board created innovative microsites called the Grilled Cheese Academy (http://grilledcheeseacademy.com) and the Cheese and Burger Society (www.cheeseandburger.com).

The sites offer a variety of interesting combinations of sand-wiches in an entertaining, interactive format, and also encourage visitors to submit their own creations and share them on social networks such as Facebook, Twitter, and so on. The Wisconsin Milk Marketing Board—a nonprofit funded by dairy farmers that promotes the more than 600 varieties, types, and styles of Wisconsin cheese and other dairy products—wanted to find a fun, personable way to ignite the passion so many people already have for cheese, said Patrick Geoghegan, senior vice president of corporate communications.

"We wanted to give our visitors something to interact with, with personality and passion," Patrick says. "It's not only a fun way to market [our] product, but a great way to teach [the] market something about [our] products." The sites expand customers' notions of how they can use cheese in unique recipes, such as The Sheboygan, a beef-and-bun setup piled with Wisconsin cheese curds, beer mustard, split bratwurst, sautéed onions, and sauerkraut. "It's aspirational," Patrick says.

The approach has worked so well for the Wisconsin Milk Marketing Board, Patrick says, that it has spawned Cheese and Burger Society parties in 70 countries worldwide, inspiring a kind of real-world club from what was conceived as a fictional society.

"No one cares about your products or services," says Brian Kardon, who heads up marketing at Eloqua, a marketing services company based in Vienna, Virginia. Far better, he says, is for companies "to start viewing themselves as sources of information." Such altruism, he adds, pays you back.

So what about you? What is your audience genuinely interested in reading, seeing, or knowing about? Your job is to generate new ideas and pull compelling stories out of your own organization. And by *stories*, we don't mean yarns or fairytales; we mean how your business (or its products or services) exist in the real world: how people use your products, how they add value to people's lives, ease their troubles, help shoulder their burdens, and meet their needs.

Here are six characteristics of a good content idea or story:

1. *True.* "The very first thing I tell my students on the first day of a workshop is that good writing is about telling the truth," writes Anne Lamott in the first sentence of the first chapter of *Bird by Bird* (Anchor Books, 1994). "We are a species that needs to understand who we are. Sheep lice do not seem to share this longing, which is one reason they write so very little."

   Anne is speaking to people who write for a living (or want to). But you, too, have to make truth the cornerstone of anything you create. It should feature real people, real situations, genuine emotions, and facts. As much as possible, it should show, not tell. It should show your product as it exists in the world, through customer stories, case studies, or client narratives. It should explain, in terms that people can relate to, how it adds value to the lives of your customers, eases their troubles, meets their needs. Your content is not about storytelling; it's about telling a true story well.

2. *Relevant.* What's the purpose of your content? What is its key message? Why are you telling it and what do you hope to accomplish? One trick from journalism school is this: Try to express the gist of a piece of content in a single sentence. Doing so will help you focus what it's about and what your reader will take away from it.

3. *Human.* Good content must have a human element to it. Why? Because your readers are people, and so will better relate to the story if you relate to them on their level, rather than talking above their heads. This is true of B2B companies, too: Even if you are a company that sells to other companies, focus on how your products or services touch the lives of people. By the way, when you are writing about people, a good rule of thumb is this: Be specific enough to be believable, and universal enough to be relevant. (That's another journalism school gem.)

4. *Passionate.* This one is simple: You have to care. If you don't care about what you are writing about, neither will

your audience. To quote blogger Johanna Hill of The Mercurial Wife, "Nobody cares until you start caring."[1] In other words, passion is contagious. Encourage your customers who are most passionate about your business to share your story in their own unique and genuine ways. In their voice!

5. *Original.* Your content should give a new and fresh perspective on your topic. What's new about it? Why is it important? As Ann's former journalism teacher, Charlie Ball, would say (quoting veteran *New York Sun* journalist John B. Bogart), "When a dog bites a man, that is not news, because it happens so often. But if a man bites a dog, that is news." (But please don't bite a dog. Thank you.)

6. *Surprising.* Good stories have an element of the unexpected. They arouse curiosity or surprise your readers. Your story must engage before it can be expected to do anything else. Later in the book, we'll talk about companies (even B2B companies) that are adding an element of surprise to their content fare to help drive viral sharing and enhance a company's personality.

Content that has all or most of those six elements will attract your audience and appeal to them on a fundamental, emotional level. In essence, creating stories that have these elements allows your audience to connect with you as one person to another, and view your business as what it is: a living, breathing entity run by real people.

But where do you find these stories? How do you tap into them? It's not especially complicated: You have things to say. You have people who want to hear them. The key is to find the angle that makes your story appealing and then frame your true, relevant, human, passionate, fresh, and (occasionally) surprising content in terms of why it matters to your customers. So ask: *What's relevant to my customers? Why should they care? What's in it for them?*

---

[1] http://scribnia.com/blog/2010/07/14/behind-blogsjohanna-hill-mercurial-wife

If you sell accounting services or circuit boards or another B2B product, you might be feeling at a disadvantage here. You might be thinking that you don't have human, passionate, fresh stories to tell. But (with all due respect), you're wrong. There are plenty of examples of B2B companies with ostensibly boring products that are proving otherwise. Read the case studies in Part Three to see how Boeing's content pulses with life or how Kadient adds an element of fun to its software products, among other examples.

Here are 25 more ways to uncover the stories within your own organization.

What Do I Talk about When There's Nothing to Say?

Are you wondering how you are going to create all this content when you don't have breaking news to share on a regular basis? Previously, companies were expected to talk to the world only when they had something newsworthy to share. Those days are over. If you want to remain relevant and top of mind, you need to find a way to converse much more frequently than only when you have big news.

So what might you talk about when there's nothing to say? Consider these 25 approaches to developing relevant content.

1. *Chat with customers.* Arm your sales staff and other customer-facing folks with micro-video cameras to capture face time with prospects or customers. Bring a camera along the next time you attend a networking event. Not sure what to say? Try asking customers a single question to unify their answers and string them together for a compelling video. Ask something like, "What's your biggest marketing challenge? Name one business goal for 2010." Or, "What's a strategy you're using to grow your business this year?" *Bonus:* You can do this with employees or others you meet at an event or gathering, too.

2. *Interview luminaries.* Q&A interviews with thought leaders, strategic partners, or flat-out interesting or creative thinkers make for compelling text, audio, or video content. They also raise your profile with them, and they will most likely link to the interview from their own, better-read sites. And don't forget the thought leaders in your own organization, too. *Tip:* A simple Q&A chat via Skype is easy to do and allows for back-and-forth banter that gives an interview more energy and makes it more fun to read. Capture the text, edit for clarity, slap on a headline, and you're done!

3. *Share real-time photos.* Configure your blog to work with Flickr so that you can upload photos from industry events, meetups, or other gatherings. Snap photos to share on Twitter via Twitpic or other Twitter photo-sharing services. Having fresh content matters here, so consider posting photos straight from your mobile phone, or invest in an EyeFi card that fits most digital cameras and will upload photos to the Web instantly. *Bonus:* The faster you can get your photos up, the more likely it is that people will use them to refer to, share with others, and drive traffic to your content.

4. *Ask customer service.* The front line is a great source for content, so ask them: What are customers contacting us about? What problems do they have? How might you help them resolve their issues? This approach is great for regular content with a recurring "questions from our customers" theme. Blogging expert Mack Collier suggests that you also mention the customer who asked the question you're answering, as well as link to her site or blog if she has one. "This just increases the chance that she will comment on your post *and* promote the post to *her* social network!" Mack says.

5. *Monitor search keywords.* What keywords are people using when they land on your blog? Monitoring those

keywords can inform your content stories and suggest new opportunities, because the keywords tell you what your would-be customers are interested in and actively looking for, suggests Lee Odden of Top Rank Marketing. *Bonus:* You'll notice that some pretty strange or humorous search words or phrases may be leading people to your content. Share some of them in a blog post.

6. *Monitor social media keywords, too.* Monitoring social conversations and trending keyword topics on Twitter, blogs, and social status updates can be a rich source of content ideas, adds Lee. Doing so gives you a sense of what people are talking about in real time and what matters to your customers now. For example, if people are talking about a certain topic that maps into what you do, it's an opportunity for you to piggyback publish and give them what they're looking for. Offering a contrarian view or a more complete picture is often a way to capture some of that attention, Lee points out. That "complete picture" part is important: research the facts ("Tell a true story well."); don't just spew opinion. *Bonus:* Choose trending topics that your audience might never connect to your business. This is a great way to surprise your community, and often leads to more conversation and interaction. (More on this later.)

7. *Research online.* Use something like Google AdWords Keyword Tool to determine what people are searching for. If you sell rubber ducks, for example, you might be interested to know that 750 people have searched for "bride and groom rubber ducks" in any given month, 501 for "yellow floating ducks," and another 460 for "cheap rubber duckies." Those might suggest topics to create content around. Bonus: Google Predictive Search is great for this, too, because how Google auto-completes your search query suggests what people are actually looking for. Another great place to research content ideas is Yahoo! Answers or LinkedIn Answers; the questions people post related to your own searches or queries can reveal a

treasure trove of information. And finally, SlideShare presentations are great for delivering B2B prompts.

8. *Trawl industry news.* Share an opinion about a recent news story that's affecting your industry or audience. Whenever possible, be timely; you could benefit from the extra boost of being one of the first to comment on the topic, because latecomers might reference and link to you. *Bonus:* Embed a video and give your take on why it's relevant.

8½. *Related to the preceding: Trawl nonindustry news, too.* Play off a popular general news story and relate it to your own industry. In journalism, this is called using a news hook. What did the 2010 FIFA World Cup have to do with growing your small business? Nothing, really. But in an article at American Express OPEN Forum, Rohit Bhargava offered four lessons that small businesses could glean from South Africa's hosting of the games.[2]

9. *Get inspired by your own passions.* Consider these recent blog posts: "What World of Warcraft's Patchwerk Can Teach You about Recovering Morale" (by Christopher S. Penn) or Brian Clark's "Ernest Hemingway's Top 5 Tips for Writing Well." On the surface, they may make you tilt your head, doggie-style, and wonder how those combos came about. It's exactly such piqued curiosity that draws in more readers. *Bonus:* Film a video or write a blog post interview with a person far outside of your industry whose insights and concerns might parallel your audience's. When Loren Feldman had stand-up comedians perform and speak at his Audience Conference (www.theaudienceconference.com), an annual event on audience and community, many attendees were initially confused. But they eventually realized the challenges of building community apply to show business just as well as to traditional business.

---

[2] www.openforum.com/idea-hub/topics/marketing/article/marketing-lessons-from-south-africas-world-cup-playbookjohn-jantsch

10. *Go behind the scenes.* Show things that your readers or followers don't usually get to see. Share photos that give an insider's view of your company. Consider using these as teasers of some new, compelling content, product, or event that you'll be sharing soon. *Bonus:* Encourage your customers to also share their photos of or stories about favorite staff members they have interacted with, or how they use your products in their lives. Have your employees join in the fun by sharing pictures of their workspaces.

11. *Go to an event.* Actually, this one is a three-fer. Before an event, talk about what you hope to get out of it, why you are looking forward to it, and so on. Then, during the event, share your impressions, session notes, interviews, or candid photos. Better yet, do real-time blogging or tweeting of sessions that your community will get value out of. Finally, follow up an event with more substantive thoughts on whom you met; what you did, learned, enjoyed, and were surprised by; and so on. *Bonus:* Take event photos and videos and use something like Animoto (www.animoto.com) to create an above-average slide show. End it with a call to action for viewers. (Animoto will make anyone's still photos into something a world apart from your grandparents' vacation slide show!)

12. *How-to content.* Any type of content that helps someone create something or solve a problem has value for others, like "Ten Steps to Getting Your Podcast Off the Ground" or "Five Tips for Having a Weed-Free Lawn by June." For example, a freelance photographer might create a video about "Eight Things You Must Know to Take the Perfect Picture," or a chiropractor might create a blog post about the "Top 5 Ways to Eliminate Back Pain during Long Car Trips." "People love how-to posts, and they are frequently shared on social media sites like Twitter, which only means more traffic and exposure for you," Mack Collier says. *Bonus:* For companies, this is also the perfect way to promote

products in a way (indirectly) that won't offend your readers, but (as always) adds value.

13. *Best practices or productivity tips.* Do you have tips or tricks to be more effective in an area? Do you have best practices to share? People are always looking for efficiencies, and this type of content is always highly useful and shareable. Position yourself as an expert, since you are providing solutions to dilemmas commonly faced by many.

14. *Reach into your community.* Create content that showcases your readers, viewers, commenters, and other active members of your community. If you notice that Maisy and Simon consistently comment on your blog posts, for example, write a post thanking them; also point out who they are, and link back to their blogs or businesses. You might even highlight some of your favorite posts from their blogs. *Bonus:* Once you start highlighting your audience members, you might well spark more participation by others who hope that they too might get a spotlight shone on them.

15. *Dig in the archives.* If you've been creating content for a while, what have you done that you might revisit or update? Quite often, something you've written about in the past could be updated and become useful again.

16. *Invite guest posts.* Give your readers or employees the chance to create a guest post for your blog. (For a blog post template to share with novice bloggers, see Chapter 11.) Don't limit yourself to only written content, of course. Many of your readers will be excited to participate, because it means more exposure to and interaction with another audience.

17. *Check out your competitors.* What are your competitors creating content around? Is there anything you'd like to say in response? *Bonus:* It's okay to compliment when a competitor creates something you find well done. Praise them for creating it—and link to them, because you need to walk the talk about being authentic and human.

18. *Create a regular content series.* A themed series is a great way to help you create regular content. Pick a day of the week, say every Thursday, and post the same type of content on that day. A regular, scheduled release of content will engage your audience; they will come to expect it and look forward to it. Come up with a catchy, fun title for this regular feature to make it easier for others to talk about and share with their audiences.

19. *Mine Facebook, LinkedIn, SlideShare, and other social networks.* Find a LinkedIn question you'd like to address and answer it; then invite your readers to offer their two pesos. Find a cool presentation on SlideShare to share with your own audience, and then offer your take on it. Talk about the Facebook groups you participate in (or don't), and explain why. Ask a question on Twitter and share the results on your blog.

20. *Start a meme.* What's a meme? In its simplest form, a meme is simply an idea that is spread from individual to individual, culturally. In a practical sense, this means that you might pick a topic to discuss and then call out (or tag) a few other bloggers to post on the same topic.

21. *Offer your two pesos.* Review a book, iPhone app, favorite news sites, wallpaper sources, whatever. Create a list of your favorites, or dig into just one. Yes, everyone has an opinion, but your audience wants to hear yours. Never be scared to share it. *Bonus:* Use this approach in conjunction with number 18 and share your favorites on a regular basis. For example, with his Digital Dads Watch (www.digitaldads.com/tag/digital-dads-watch/), every Friday C.C. highlights the writing staff's favorite online videos from the previous week.

22. *Channel your inner surly teenager.* Take the opposing or contrarian view on an issue that's on your mind or in the news, or is being talked about in your industry (see number 6). Is there an event everyone goes to but you're not a fan of? Is someone in your industry getting a bit big for their britches and needs to be knocked off their pedestal? Never shy away from kicking the hornet's nest a bit if you are passionate about your feelings. ("Take a stand," remember?) *Bonus:* Taking a stand might spur others to create content agreeing or disagreeing with you, so be prepared.

23. *Host an event.* Though we love online interactions as much as the rest of you, nothing beats face time with others. Schedule after-hour drinks, lunch, or even morning coffee around a topic or theme and invite everyone who might want to come. Encourage people to document and share the event in whatever medium they use to create content. *Bonus:* Be ready for success and embrace it, as Dave Delaney discovered when he started Geek Breakfast in Nashville, Tennessee, to get to know the local technology lovers. What started out as a handful of people has grown into a monthly gathering of close to 100. To accommodate everyone, Dave now has to split the event into two sittings at the restaurant where they gather.

24. *Curate the voices of many.* Are your employees creating content of any sort? Maybe the content they create isn't directly related to your business, but showcasing the people who make up your company shows the human side of your business. For example, check out twitter .zappos.com, where you can read the tweets and view photos of every employee at Zappos. This effort is a perfect fit for the company's unique culture. *Bonus:* Embrace all the successes of your employees: Your office manager completes her first marathon. The vice president releases his first music album. Shine a spotlight on the people who make your company what it is, even if their achievements aren't directly related to business.

25. *Curate from elsewhere, too.* Curating content and news from several must-read sources into a central location can help you create a valuable destination site for readers. You can curate manually (by using RSS feeds, for example) or consider software systems that can do it for you,

like Curata, Eqentia, Lingospot, or Loud3r. (For more on content curation, see the next section in this chapter.) *Bonus:* Think beyond the obvious industry news sources and instead curate based on your passion or location. For a small business, church, or organization, consider becoming the go-to source of curated local news.

One final note: Leave stuff undone. Every piece of content you create doesn't have to be perfectly crafted, nicely argued, or well said. In fact, sometimes it's okay to look a little untidy—it's downright preferable. We aren't advocating sloppy work. Rather, we are suggesting that you leave room for your audience to step in with their thoughts and ideas on a blog post. Don't get hung up on production values when it is the message *in* the content that is more important.

What I Really Want to Do Is Direct: Hiring Content Creators and Sourcing Content from Elsewhere

We wrote this book to empower you to create killer content. But we don't mean to suggest that you yourself have to be the one doing the creating.

Depending on the size and structure of your organization, you may choose to hire people to create content with you, or *for* you. Or perhaps you need to augment your own content with content that's aggregated or curated, co-created, licensed, or user-created. Clearly, in a larger organization—including some of the companies we've profiled—there isn't simply a single person tasked with developing the content, reimagining it, amplifying it, and then getting up again the next morning to shave, shower, and do it all over again.

So where do the content creators fit into the organization? And if you hire writers or editors or other creators to produce content for you, what should you look for? And what about other sources of content—like curating material published elsewhere? Licensed content? Co-created or user-generated content?

Original content created by you or for you is—hands down—an organization's BFF. It's the richest and most valuable kind of content you can publish. No other kind of content pays off quite so handsomely as that which you've developed yourself. "[W]hen you take the time to really understand your audience, create content specifically for and about them, in a voice that's uniquely yours; then deliver your content in formats that engage and motivate; you're delivering the kind of user experience that will bring people back for more," writes Kristina Halvorson in *Content Strategy for the Web* (New Riders Press, 2009).

That's true whether you are doing the actual creating or providing incentive for someone else to do it for you. (And by the way, even if you never scratch a single word onto a single page, the rules you absorb from this book will help you articulate to others what you want them to create as well as more effectively manage how the content creation gets done.)

WHO OWNS YOUR WEB SITE CONTENT?

Who owns your web site content? In other words, who has ultimate responsibility for conceiving it, producing it, managing it, and (maybe sometimes) killing anything that's not working? In a tiny organization, that's an easier question to answer. But the answer gets exponentially more complicated for a larger organization.

"I'd say that nearly 100 percent of the time, when we first start talking to a client about their content challenges, it doesn't take too long for us to realize that the core of the problem isn't even content-related," says Kristina Halvorson, who is the CEO and founder of Brain Traffic, a content strategy consultancy in Minneapolis. "It's a people problem. People are creating content in silos. They're launching content and then forgetting about it. They're publishing content online without any real, measurable objective."

So the content piles up. Without a plan—without real editorial oversight of what's happening—content quickly becomes redundant, outdated, unnecessary. And then you're stuck with a bunch of content no one cares about.

The problem, Kristina says, is that organizations still see content as a sort of commodity, something that's easy to create, something they already have too much of. But, as you're learning, *good* content isn't something that comes easy.

"Creating and caring for quality content takes dedicated resources, especially time," says Kristina. "And no one's being given enough time to deal with content and all its inherent complexities. So they push it off. They procrastinate; they delegate; they do everything they can to avoid being responsible for Web content."

Considering that most people are dealing with web site or social media content on top of their regular jobs, this isn't a surprise. "When there are content problems and people say, 'That's not my job,' the biggest problem is that it's probably not." And so, Kristina concludes, "That lack of content ownership—accompanied by a lack of content policies or guidelines—effectively ends up landing organizations in a Wild, Wild West of content."

The solution is to deputize someone (or a team of someone's) and charge them with achieving all of the things we discuss in this book: defining and overseeing the content agenda and strategy for the organization. In a larger organization, that person might be someone such as a chief content officer, whose job is it to establish and manage all web content development and publishing efforts. In such an organization, the chief content officer might be an executive function, overseeing a content team of web editors and writers and interfacing with other business units. In a more modest-sized organization, the chief content officer might act more as a functional editor, producing content herself as well as working directly with internal or outside contributing writers.

The person who heads up your content might not necessarily carry the moniker of chief content officer, of course. Depending on the scale of your web site and your publishing efforts, and the culture of your organization, perhaps it's more fitting to staff the lead content role with a director of content, managing editor, editor-in-chief, web site editor, or content editor—or even chief blogger.

Maybe that person is you. The point is to put *someone* in charge and deputize that person with enough power so he becomes an essential part of your online strategy. Someone on your team has to be ultimately responsible for creating and overseeing the rules and guidelines that will shape your web content, whether on your company web site (or web sites) or on social media platforms, and anywhere else your company shares or publishes online content.

Here are some possible responsibilities of your top content person:

- Leading the web content strategy initiatives in consultation with other key players

- Creating web content standards (like voice, tone, timeliness, relevancy, and so on)

- Deciding what you'll publish (and for whom, and where, when, and how)

- Participating in operational discussions about resource planning and management, content management technology, and so on

- Creating content and grooming, training, and motivating content creators

- Making sure that everyone in your company owns and reads a copy of this book (a shameless plug)

What to Look for in a Writer (or Any Kind of Content Creator)

Your lead content person might hire staff writers or tap in-house content creators. Or you might choose to work with outside contract writers or producers and adopt a model of hiring or contracting with content creators who function within your company as embedded brand or corporate journalists (see Boeing, Chapter 26).

The phrase *embedded journalist*—coined by Albert Maruggi of Provident Partners in St. Paul, Minnesota, at least as applied to business—is not unlike a journalist embedded with a military unit. Whether they are on staff or they are contract hires, full-time or part-time, embedded journalists work inside the company, writing articles or blog posts or producing videos or podcasts to attract a specific audience.

"Brand journalism is not a product pitch," David Meerman Scott writes in his blog. "It is not an advertorial. It is not an egotistical spewing of gobbledygook-laden, stock-photo enhanced corporate drivel." Rather, the person you hire will convey your company's true story in a compelling way, by doing all of the things this book lays out: uncovering the stories about your brand and how your customers are using it; narrating them in a human, accessible way; and sparking conversation about your company, its customers, or its employees.

Hiring someone trained as a print or broadcast journalist is a good option, because journalists are trained in how to tell a story using words, images, or audio, and they understand how to create content that draws an audience in. Their innate understanding of audience also gives journalists a critical outsider's perspective—a nuance that marketers can sometimes miss. They might be on your payroll, but they are better at expressing neutrality, which is a distinct advantage in creating marketing content. (Of course, passion counts for a lot, too. Some of the best content creators have more passion than formal training, and they have learned by trial and error how to channel that passion to engage an audience.)

Ideally, by the way, you'll find a journalist or other content creator with a bit of a sales streak, someone who understands the business goal of content, who has a passion for online tools, and who (at least on the Web) is a bit of a social butterfly. Whether you call it *brand journalism*, *corporate journalism*, *business journalism*, or (borrowing from the Dutch) *bedrijfsjournalist*, here are qualities to look for in content creators you hire:

1. *Nose for a story.* The best content creators are the ones who can smell a good story. They also recognize

the bones of a story easily, and they instinctively know how to develop the content to make it human and interesting.

2. *Digital intuition.* Rick Burnes, who creates content for HubSpot (see Chapter 24), says good content creators understand how the Web works. In a post on his blog, RickBurns.com, he writes, "The Web is an ecosystem, and if you don't intuitively understand the dynamics of this ecosystem—how Twitter can drive traffic to a blog; the kinds of headlines that attract attention; the simple things you can do to build blog subscriptions—you won't be able to help your company attract online visitors."

3. *An amateur passion.* Look for people who are already online and creating content, even as amateurs—writing a personal blog, sharing photos on Flickr, creating videos or podcasts, and the like. The root of *amateur* is the Latin word for *love*. Someone who creates content for the love of it will likely have the necessary passion to do the same for your company.

4. *A salesy, social streak.* This is also from Rick, who points out that the best content creators "promote their own content. They build and nurture relationships, and they know how to use these relationships to spread their own content, without abusing them." In other words, look for folks who are social butterflies online, even if they may not be in the real world.

5. *An open mind.* Most of the journalists Ann worked with in the past would sniff at the idea of an embedded job, because they think doing so is demeaning or equates to selling out, compromising themselves, marginalizing their talents, ruining their reputations, smiting their families, bringing shame, or permanently installing themselves on the dark side. The key is to find people who understand and embrace the fundamental thesis of this book, which

is that businesses now have both an imperative and the incentive to produce top-shelf content.

As Rick points out, "For businesses, content is a means to an end, not an end in and of itself. Every article, tweet, and video is assessed based on its ability to generate visitors, leads, and customers, not on any subjective judgment of content quality." The flip side of that, of course, is that only quality content ultimately succeeds in meeting the necessary business objectives. In other words, terrible, biased, advertorial-type content has no place in your business. (Also, a side note to journalists who might be wrestling with the notion: You'll make more money on the dark side. Just sayin'.)

6. *ADOS.* This stands for Attention Deficit ... *Ooh! Shiny!* We're mostly kidding with this one, but these are the folks who have a passion for new digital tools. They are always looking for the newest and shiniest object. They always have (or covet) the latest gadgets, they are experimenting with the most cutting-edge technologies, and they have the coolest apps on their smartphones. They can be handy people to have on your team, because they can help you figure out how those technologies apply to growing your business. Thanks to Peter Shankman, author of *Can We Do That?!* (John Wiley & Sons, 2006), for this term.

SOURCING CONTENT FROM ELSEWHERE

Sourcing content from elsewhere is another way to augment or feed your content machine.

Bear in mind, however, that any content you choose to republish on your site should adhere to your guidelines and standards, so as to integrate seamlessly into your site and match your brand's voice, tone, and all that. And of course you'll still need a lead content person on your team tasked with the care and feeding of the sourced stuff, too.

You might consider one or more of the following options for sourcing content from elsewhere.

Curated Content

Content curation is the act of continually identifying, selecting, and sharing the best and most relevant online content and other online resources on a specific subject to match the needs of a specific audience. Such content and resources include links to articles, blog posts, videos, photos, tools, tweets (or what have you) published elsewhere on other web sites.

Just like gallery curators collect the best art to house in their museums, content curators uncover the more valuable and relevant content to share on their sites. Of course, unlike gallery curators, content curators collect and share *links* to that content; they generally don't lift and repurpose the full content outright, inasmuch as it applies to text. (The rules are sometimes different for video and photos. As always, when it doubt, seek permission.)

Content curation isn't necessarily anything new. Content aggregation—or the automated harvesting of links to content—is what powers services like Yahoo! News and Google News. Finding extraordinary stuff (or extraordinary deals) to share online with an audience is what sites like Cool Hunting and Likecool .com do, what bloggers have long done, what so many of us do on Twitter already, or what aggregators and social sharing sites like Alltop, Digg, StumbleUpon, and Delicious have been doing.

But recently, content curation has been emerging as a field of its own. Unlike pure aggregation, curation includes a human element: Human editors add their own organizing and filtering skills—and, well, *judgment*—to the services that gather the content. And unlike StumbleUpon or Digg or the rest, curation services like Curata, Eqentia, Lingospot, and Loud3r offer the ability to intelligently and quickly aggregate real-time content based on specific search terms—kind of like a hunter-gatherer on steroids.

Content curation can fit into an organization's content strategy nicely. By finding, filtering, and sharing the timeliest, most relevant, and most stimulating online content, curation can further establish an organization as an authority and thought leader, and a resource to its audience. Sifting through a pile of web content and finding the tastiest, choicest bits for your readers is a great way to build trust and authority with them, and to become a valuable resource for them on any particular topic. They'll rely on you to filter the best stuff, so they don't have to hunt it down themselves.

What's more, for organizations just getting into generating content and publishing online—say, for those just starting a blog or a micro-site—curated content allows ramping up quickly, both from a search engine optomization (SEO) perspective as well as from a content perspective. Something is always better than nothing, so don't hesitate to share the content if it is relevant.

Content curation is effective—assuming, of course, that you have the strategy and budget to support it. That said, we have two cautionary bits of advice before you dive in:

1. *Content curation isn't a shortcut.* If you are thinking that you can rely on content curation rather than creating and publishing original content, here's a recommendation: *don't.* Don't rely exclusively on either handpicked or auto-mated content curation services to feed your own hungry belly. Curated content is a perfectly good way to extend the content of your own site, but it is only that: an extension of your own publishing efforts.

   There are sites that rely on only curated stuff—Novell's Intelligent Workload Management (www .intelligentworkloadmanagement.com) is one—but, in general, curation should be used in addition to and not instead of your original content, for many of the reasons outlined in this book. Figure 6.1 is an example of a cloud computing security site called Trusted Cloud, which demonstrates that kind of content mix. It is, interestingly, also published by Novell.

   Ultimately, you'll want to produce your own origi-nal content rather than adopt a "what she said" content strategy. Think of it this way: You can't always forage for wild berries; you occasionally have to plant your own crops, too.

2. *You still need a human at the helm.* Using curated content doesn't mean you have an automated machine spewing out content like Dr. Seuss's Eight-Nozzled

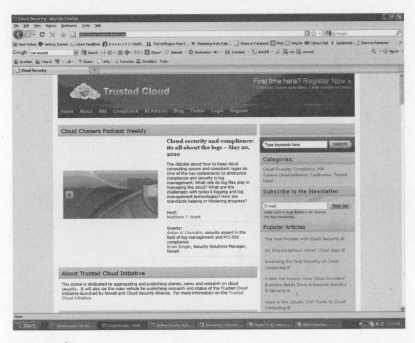

Figure 6.1   Trusted Cloud Web Site
Source: www.trusted-cloud.com

Elephant-Toted Boom Blitz[3] (although that machine spewed "sour cherry stone pits," not blog posts). Curated content still requires the deft touch of a real, live, human editor to pick and choose and order (and occasionally comment on) the best stuff for your audience. As with any kind of content, warm-blooded humans make all the difference.

Co-Created Content

For this discussion, we are defining co-created content as content sourced from established content creators, some of whom might already have some notoriety or a built-in audience in their area of expertise.

The MarketingProfs Daily Fix group blog (www .mpdailyfix.com), which publishes marketing commentary from a wide variety of industry contributors, is an example of a co-created site. So is OPEN Forum from American Express,

---

[3] Dr. Seuss, *The Butter Battle Book* (New York: Random House, 1984).

Figure 6.2　OPEN Forum Web Page

which publishes a wealth of resources for small to medium-size business owners—including videos, articles, blogs, networking capabilities, and so on (www.openforum.com). (See Figure 6.2.) The site taps influential bloggers, industry leaders, and savvy entrepreneurs to provide practical, actionable information and insights. The only advertising or branding on the site, of course, is that of American Express.

For brands, co-created content is a great way to quickly establish expertise by partnering with those already in the business of creating content that meets your needs, and then publishing it on your own site or a branded content site (like OPEN Forum). So a company that sells all-natural baby products might tap a well-known mommy blogger, a wine store might partner with a high-profile food blogger to contribute recipes or upload photos, or a local economic development agency might identify a successful local business leader to create video. Contributors are paid in various ways: sometimes with cash, or sometimes with the notoriety or glory of producing content for you, and with the access you offer to a new audience.

Co-creating content can allow you to tap into a built-in audience and gain some high-profile, unique perspectives. But be sure you are clear about the rules for contributors prior to publication. For example, what's the desired frequency of your contributors? Will you allow your contributors to repurpose or republish the content they create for you elsewhere? Who will retain copyright: you or the author? If the copyright remains with the author, can you secure permission to reimagine that content elsewhere, at a later date?

User-Generated Content

User-generated content (sometimes called UGC) is content that is produced by your customers or by people who visit your site, as opposed to professional writers or content creators or production companies. In other words, rather than creating your own content, you can invite your audience to do it for you (that's sometimes called crowdsourcing). This seems like an awesome solution to getting lots of great content for your site—and it can be. But like most things in life, it's not a magic bullet.

Consumer-generated product reviews and ratings can add a sense of community, interaction, and liveliness to e-commerce sites: Epicurious.com visitors rate recipes with a fork system and submit reviews with tips and suggested changes or substitutions. Golden Retriever Rescue of Wisconsin allows visitors to share personal stories on its web site, giving a human (and canine) face to its cause, building community,and—as a result—generating donations.[4]

Ford Motor Company has done an amazing job encouraging its fans to share their stories on The Ford Story (www.thefordstory.com), which runs articles by Ford fans as well as news and interesting features and updates about Ford products. (See Figure 6.3.) For example, a story about one woman's touching reaction to the Ford Mustang edition that supports breast cancer research runs alongside a story about how Ford is developing a digital model of an employee, Santos, to improve ergonomics at its manufacturing plants.

By allowing users to post additional details or insights, or to upload their own content, UGC adds interactivity while adding

---

[4] www.grrow.org/grrowi/success+stories/default.asp

Figure 6.3   The Ford Story Web Site

a depth and breadth that's hard for staff writers to replicate. (Of course, social media strategies—like simply allowing comments on a blog, using tools like TweetMeme to capture Twitter responses, or installing Facebook's Like button—encourage audience interactivity and participation, as well.)

If you do encourage UGC on your site, you should:

- *Plan for engagement.* There's nothing worse than building a forum designed to entice your audience's interaction only to have it flounder, after some initial excitement, into an online ghost town, with the virtual equivalent of tumbleweeds gusting through the deserted streets. If you do launch a UGC component, be sure you have the engine to moderate, respond to, and encourage participation there. You get only one shot at building a successful community site.

- *Be prepared for the undesirable.* Your audience might participate on your site in ways you might not expect, or want.

For example, Chevrolet's attempt to generate positive UGC backfired when the carmaker launched a web site inviting visitors to use video clips and music provided by Chevy to create their own ads for the Tahoe. Unfortunately for Chevy, the site attracted environmentalists and others who hate Chevy, who created their own kinds of ads critical of its gas-guzzling behemoths.

Of course, fear isn't a reason for *not* doing UGC (frankly, if people have negative things to say about your products or company, they are probably already saying them somewhere), but it can be hard for a company to stomach criticism. There are some ways to counter the negative stuff, or the worry about it, such as crafting *community guidelines* (which is preferable to *terms and conditions*) with clear, specific rules; using human moderators and automated filters against truly offensive or litigious content; and empowering your audience members to ensure that the UGC remains pertinent and its quality high. Most people want a friendly atmosphere and positive experience, so you can enlist and empower your top users to help you. (At MarketingProfs, we lovingly refer to this tactic on our own UGC-powered Know-How Exchange Forum as the "inmates running the asylum.")

Licensed Content

As the name implies, licensed content is content that's licensed from content producers—sometimes for a fee, or sometimes in exchange for attribution (see AskPatty.com, Chapter 22). It might be articles or blog posts, in addition to a wide variety of other content, such as online audio, video, and images.

Since you are licensing it from elsewhere, the content likely won't be unique to your site. But licensed content might be an option if you want to create an exhaustive, deep library of online information for your audience. And (as with the benefit of curated content) licensed content can reinforce your position as a credible and authoritative source of valuable information, because you've successfully collected the good stuff in one place for your audience.

CHAPTER 7
Stoke the Campfire

Have you ever had the joy of building a campfire and then sitting around it with friends and family, enjoying its warmth, the camaraderie, and the instant community? It is the perfect place for giggles, sharing stories, and forming lifelong friendships. It doesn't matter if it is at summer camp or in your backyard; since people first discovered how to make fire, campfires have brought us together.

Are you wondering what exactly setting wood on fire has to do with the subject of this book? Well, a campfire is an apt metaphor to embody the step that so many companies skip over. When they do, they are left wondering why no one is engaging with their awesome content.

Just because you create welcoming content does not mean that people are going to immediately sit next to it to be warmed. Even when people start gathering, you will need to keep their attention so that they don't leave. If you are still skeptical about the metaphor, stick with us for a few more pages and it will become clearer.

How to Build a Fire

Before you can embrace the metaphor, you need to know the basics of how to build a real fire in five steps. Content *and* survival techniques in one book? Bet you didn't expect that!

> *1.* Start with small, easily ignitable branches and twigs (tinder) and pile them in the middle of where you want to build a fire.

2. Surround the tinder with bigger sticks in a teepee fashion, allowing plenty of space for air to circulate. (Don't forget that fire needs fuel *and* air to continue burning.)

3. Light the fire from multiple sides and allow it to grow slowly. A quick flare-up is exciting, but it also burns out very quickly.

4. Once the fire is going, add larger, longer-burning logs that will provide continual warmth without needing much tending.

5. Adjust the logs in the fire every so often to keep it interesting; add fuel as necessary.

Your Content Campfire

Now that you know how to build a basic campfire, we can move on to helping you build one for the content you are creating. As you know, content comes in lots of different types, styles, formats, and sizes. It is essential, therefore, to establish a solid foundation for your content strategy rather than randomly gathering content and hoping it all ignites in the end.

Campfires give both warmth and an instant community. Cowboys on the open plains would start a campfire and everyone would gather around it. Some might come for supper, others to sing songs, others just to be with other people in the lonely prairie. Similarly, you need to welcome others to your content campfire, however long they initially stay. The more welcomed your visitors feel, the longer they will stay, the more they will invite others to visit, and the more often they will come back. And that is your main goal.

Start with the Small Stuff

Remember the tinder you needed to get a fire started? Small, highly combustible items that catch on quickly and help ignite the bigger stuff?

There is no magic prescription that will point you in the right direction, but here are some ideas to get you going:

- *Go off and search for tinder.* Visit other blog posts, videos, or other online content that's related to your industry, keywords, or topics, and leave appropriate comments on them. Don't be spammy, of course. The key is to leave thoughtful comments on what's been created and to invite readers to check out your stuff as well.

- *Create tinder on your site.* Create a series that is highly shareable. Perhaps it is about a current issue that everyone has an opinion on, some breaking theory about your market, a top 10 list of some form, or a series of interviews with luminaries.

The goal is to raise awareness and traction for your content. So think about what you could create that people would find value in and immediately want to share. Ask yourself, "Would I retweet this, or share it on Facebook?" If you can't answer yes, others won't, either.

One caveat: Avoid link baiting. UrbanDictionary.com defines *link bait* as "content placed on a web site specifically for the purpose of enticing people to link to it."

You must strike a balance between fanning your own would-be fire and relying on link baiting to gain what is at best a temporary audience. Use nuance: It may be perfectly appropriate to include the names of industry influencers in your content just so you get on their radar. But always make sure that you are doing it with purpose and substance: a reason beyond just getting their attention. (Remember what we said about a quick flare-up. Style is pretty, but substance sustains.)

Ultimately, you want as much of your content as possible to be shared around the Web. You want people talking about it, commenting on it, and sharing their reactions to it. Even though any press is good press, it is better to get attention because of high-quality content rather than link bait consisting of a gratuitous new top 10 list of influencers.

Finding the Bigger Sticks

So the kindling is ignited. You've got something going, people know about it, and some are visiting your site regularly. Now it's time to give them something more. In other words, you must continually feed the fire for people to want to keep coming back to it. A steady stream of good content is necessary. Here's where you need to create a publishing schedule or editorial calendar, as we discussed in Chapter 5. The plan doesn't have to be set in stone or scheduled further out than the next three or six months. If it is easier, lay out by quarter or season how you plan to attack your content stream.

This is also where you begin to build momentum, based on what you will be creating and when it's scheduled, as we also discussed in detail in Chapter 5. If you've determined that you are going to do a webinar next month, what are you going to put in place in the weeks leading up to it to generate interest, conversation, and sign-ups? After you've conducted the webinar, what are you going to do to reimagine that content for further use to keep the attendees and others engaged?

So while each piece of content is reimagined within the content food chain, it's also tossing fuel on the fire. Regularly dependable, reoccurring, reimagined content is the key. This is how you should be thinking about each piece of content you create, every time.

Singing Campfire Songs

The best part of building a campfire is having friends and strangers gather around it, creating a sense of community.

While you most likely won't have anyone with a guitar strumming out "Kumbaya" and other camp favorites on your site (although that could be strangely cool in today's YouTube world!), you do want to build up and foster your community as much as possible. One key consideration (which needs to be communicated to executives at your company) is that community takes time to develop.

A community cannot be forced, manipulated, or magically conjured. And, as with most other things in life, quality trumps quantity. It's better to build a smaller community of people who actually are interested in you than it is to build a huge community of *meh*.

Why Doesn't My Content Have Any Comments?

People revisit a site for numerous reasons:

- They find the content compelling and interesting.

- They like the conversation that happens in the comments or discussion forums.

- They enjoy, as experts, helping others.

- They want to be seen, for their own gain, as members of a community.

Some of your most committed followers might be the most silent because they are simply there to learn. With social platforms like Google Buzz, Twitter, and Facebook increasingly fragmenting conversations, the number of blog comments might not appear as robust as in the recent past. Never judge the success of your content solely on the number of comments, likes, or thumbs-ups you get. That feedback is part of the story, but it is certainly not the whole story.

The key to keeping them coming back is new, fresh, and relevant content. The moment you stop publishing is the moment you start losing your community. "If you aren't out there consistently, you'll get left behind," says Frank Days, director of social media for Novell.

Telling Stories by the Campfire Light

You, as the host, have the job of leading the stories around the campfire you have built. Just like the spooky stories we remember from our youth, the best stories are those that connect with the people listening so that they can then take them and share with others.

"Campfires of today are DNA deep. They are not where all the people are, because all the people are not in one place anymore." Chris Brogan, co-author of *Trust Agents* (John Wiley & Sons, 2009), said this in his BlogWorld 2009 keynote speech. He then reminded the audience, "Your awesome site isn't awesome. Getting your stories into the hands of the people who need them is awesome."

We said earlier that passion is contagious. Your passion will shine through in your content. And if it triggers an emotional reaction from your audience, then they are more likely to share it with others.

Sharing does not mean plagiarizing or pirating your content. Rather, when your story is good enough, people will share it with their own communities. Thanks to the nature and etiquette of the Web, whenever someone quotes or talks about something you've created, that person will link to the original source. They can also directly embed your video or photography content on their own site in addition to adding a link.

So instead of viewing your story or content as a static and pristine object owned by your site, think of it as a social object that can be taken, retold, and shared by others.

What's a social object? That leads, handily, to the next chapter!

CHAPTER 8
Create Wings and Roots

Every single piece of content you create should of course live on your web site, or in your content library, pages, and other ports of call (like a landing page) you establish. But that's not the whole story, which brings us to Content Rule Number 10: Create wings and roots for your content.

This advice is usually applied to parenting: Give your children roots to keep them grounded and levelheaded and offer them wings to explore new worlds and have new adventures. But it also applies nicely to content: Ground your content solidly in your unique perspective, voice, and point of view, but give it wings to soar freely and be shared all across the Web as a social object.

After all, a powerful component of social media and online business is the fact that everyone is a publisher, right? And this includes your readers. Everyone is empowered to share, link to, and comment on every piece of content that sparks his or her interest. This is why we have stressed that each piece of content should be viewed as a social object that also exists beyond the platform it is published on.

"The engine in great social objects isn't in the mechanism itself; it's the fuel—the content—at its heart. Identifying and focusing more effort on high-octane fuel will do more to win friends and influence people than anything else," says Campfire creative director Steve Coulson. "Just produce great content, and it'll speak louder and travel further than you can imagine."

To use another analogy: You cannot have the mentality of survivalists who hoard everything they grow for themselves. Rather, be like Johnny Appleseed, spreading seeds to allow everyone to enjoy the fruits (metaphorically). Sow your content seeds to nurture awareness, spread positive sentiment, allow your audience to spread your message for you, and, ultimately, grow your customer base.

Wings for the Web: Findable, Accessible, Shareable

FINDABLE

When people search on Google or Bing, can they find your content? If you have video content on YouTube or Vimeo, how easy is it for someone looking for the type of video you shared to find it? How can you know? Try it yourself: How quickly can you find your own stuff?

There are many search engine optimization (SEO) strategies to boost your search rankings. But fundamentally, be sure you've provided as much information as possible in the context and description of your content. Include keywords you want to be found for (including long-tail keywords or terms you are trying to own as your own; see Chapter 1). Is your content answering a specific question? Then make sure that question is in your content somewhere.

Establish profiles on all the leading social networks. Search for your company or its products on the social web, too: on Twitter, Yelp, Facebook, LinkedIn, or any other networks you or your customers participate in. It's important to establish profiles, even if you only use your presence there as a landing page for redirecting visitors to sites you are active on. You don't want to be invisible or, worse, have someone else claim your name or your company's name.

ACCESSIBLE

Every day, people are interacting with content on a variety of screens, so it is critical that you make sure that what you are creating is available to as many different platforms as possible.

Just a few years ago most of us didn't have to worry about our sites being viewable on phones; now it is critical for all of us to ensure that they are. If you are now wondering whether your site is available to mobile phones, ask a handful of friends with different devices to surf your web site. The results may surprise you.

We are also in the midst of a bit of a battle in the browsing wars, with Apple declaring that it will not support Adobe Flash on its devices. This means that if your video files (or entire site) are built in Flash, they will not be viewable on the popular Apple iPad or iPhone; you could thus be missing out on new customers.

Always test your content on as many browsers, phones, and devices as time and resources allow.

Accessible also refers to making a deliberate decision whether to gate your content behind a registration page (and if you do, what information to collect). For advice on whether to require registration in return for access to your content, see Chapter 13.

SHAREABLE

Why do you e-mail articles to friends? Or like a post on Facebook? Or share things on your own networks? In a study of the most e-mailed *New York Times* articles, researchers at the University of Pennsylvania[1] found that readers wanted to share articles that inspired awe.

What's more, stories that triggered an emotional response were more likely to be e-mailed and positive articles were shared more often than negative ones, the researchers found. Moreover, longer articles generally did better than shorter articles, according to the Penn researchers (although they theorized that it was just because the longer articles were about more engaging topics).

So-called surprising articles, like one about free-range chickens on the streets of New York, were also more likely to be e-mailed. But articles that evoked a response that went beyond surprise to awe, or what the Penn researchers defined as an "emotion of self-transcendence, a feeling of admiration and elevation in the face of something greater than the self," were

---

[1] "Will You Be Emailing This Column? It's Awesome," www.nytimes.com/2010/02/09/science/09tier.html.

among the most shared. An "opening and broadening of the mind" is how one of the researchers described the effect of such articles.

What does that research finding mean for you, the content creator? It means you should definitely create content that adheres to the Content Rules, paying special attention to Number 8: Do something unexpected. It also means you should both subtly and actively encourage your audience to share.

Make sharing across all social networks as effortless and easy as possible. Encourage your audience to Buzz your content via Google, retweet it on Twitter, or like it on Facebook. Feature the major buttons prominently on each piece of content you create. Consider using a centralized service like ShareThis.com, which allows you to place just one button that expands to offer buttons for various sharing services for users to click on. (The good thing about using a service like ShareThis is that as new social networks evolve, the company will add the new platforms to the mix, so you don't have to.)

Also, when you upload video, audio, or photography content to other services, ensure that your settings allow the sharing of that content. Creative Commons (www.creativecommons.org) licensing allows you to clearly set the terms for what others can and cannot do with your content, in addition to sharing it. (Will you allow others to use your photos for corporate brochures with attribution, for example?)

Making content shareable also includes making it easy for others to embed some of your content in their own sites or blogs. Business blogger and *Trust Agents* co-author Chris Brogan calls this giving your content *handles;* an example might be a widget, tool, game, SlideShare presentation, or almost anything that can be manipulated or interacted with. An interactive quiz widget that your customers can embed directly onto their blogs, to share on your behalf, is a good example. One from ExactTarget is shown in Figure 8.1.

And finally, consider publishing any research or charts you produce in both PDF and PowerPoint format. Doing so allows your audience to use your charts in their own presentations—with your company name or logo intact, of

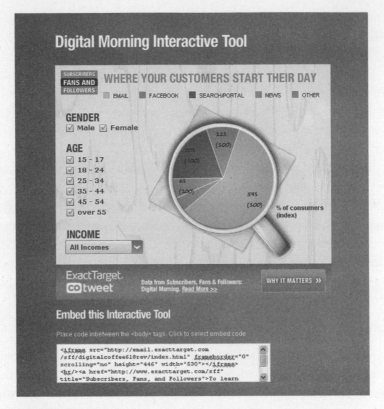

Figure 8.1   Make Your Content Shareable
Source: http://email.exacttarget.com/sff/interactivetools.html

course—making it another case of your audience spreading your message for you.

Fishing for Attention in the Activity Streams

An *activity stream* refers to interactions happening (including content sharing) across various social media platforms. You can see it in real time by visiting the home page of Twitter, for example; notice how quickly the stream refreshes there. Activity streams aren't monitored constantly; people pop in and out of them throughout the day, which means that something you shared has likely disappeared soon thereafter. Activity streams are exponential, however, and by that we mean something noticed by one person has the potential to be shared many times over—exponentially.

So what are some practices for publishing and sharing in social activity streams?

- *Engagement is the goal.* Engaging with people on social networks is key, because when someone retweets you on Twitter or comments on a status update in Facebook, it shows up in that person's activity stream. So the more people who engage with your content, the more times that content is disseminated to each of their community of friends and fans. More engagement means more exposure to new people.

- *It is okay to share more than once.* This is especially true in the Twitter and Facebook streams, which are far more real-time than in a blog or elsewhere. If you share a link to your latest content in the morning, it's okay to share it again at the end of the day. (Clearly, don't annoy your followers. Common sense should prevail.)

- *Move beyond words.* Photos and videos break up the text and instantly get attention. Add variety by including various content formats.

Ann's Take on Twitter: Everything I Need to Know about Twitter I Learned in J School

In journalism school, I learned that news stories work best when they are simple and direct, at least in any given story's lead sentences. And simplicity (and other tenets of good journalism—like brevity, clarity, and immediacy) is now a cornerstone of how so many businesses, brands, and individuals communicate on Twitter, Facebook, LinkedIn, and other social networks.

Of them all, Twitter can be the most challenging. In part, there's a limit on how many characters (140) you can share in each post to Twitter. What's more, though, it's hard to know exactly how to be most effective and, well, social there.

Here's how some of the mantras from my undergrad days now inform the best tweets.

(Continued)

(Continued)

Make every word count. In traditional news journalism, and on Twitter, you have only so much space. On Twitter, of course, it's a mere 140 characters. As I learned in journalism school, writing short is a lot harder than it looks. It's a lot more work to choose your words wisely, to be concise, than it is to ramble on luxuriously. For example, I love how Tim Siedell communicates so much in a single tweet:

Figure 8.2 (http://twitter.com/badbanana/status/1942761348)

Keeping a tweet *really* short—like close to 85 to 100 characters—also makes your tweet more retweet-friendly, since it allows a little wiggle room for forwarding:

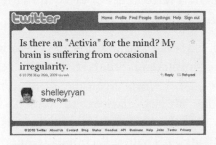

Figure 8.3 (http://twitter.com/shelleyryan/status/1928645623)

Keep it simple. Like my journalism professor Charlie Ball's directive to avoid 20-dollar words, the best news reporters tell a story simply and clearly. Similarly, don't try to cram too much information into a single tweet. On Twitter, less is often more.

Also, link directly to blogs or other online sources, and always link to the full story rather than trying to juice up page views by, for example, linking to the home page. Shorten URLs through bit.ly or similar services. Twitter will usually condense your links, but I like bit.ly's rich click-through and retweet stats. For example:

Figure 8.4 (http://twitter.com/ karenswim/status/2030492891)

Finally, avoid the temptation to fit more into a tweet by the liberal use of abbreviations. Such shorthand might maximize your character count, but it makes your tweet read like a teenager's text message.

Provide context. News reporters do this by plugging in some of the back story on a given news item. On Twitter, offer context by using keywords and hashtags, when appropriate, so that readers can more easily get the gist of a conversation, thread, or topic. Like this:

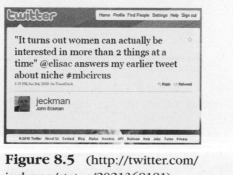

Figure 8.5 (http://twitter.com/ jeckman/status/2021368181)

(Continued)

(Continued)

Or this:

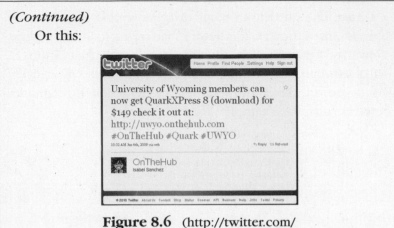

Figure 8.6 (http://twitter.com/
OnTheHub/status/2030095622)

Lead with the good stuff. In journalism, the inverted pyramid style places the most important information at the top of any story, and then the ensuing narrative explains and expands on it. In other words, the first paragraph should contain enough information to give the reader a solid overview of the entire story. Approach sharing links or information on Twitter similarly, giving the strongest and most compelling bit in the tweet and then linking to the rest of the story elsewhere. For example:

Figure 8.7 (http://twitter.com/
MackCollier/status/2030444385)

Write killer headlines. Headlines sell a news story or a blog post much like a great tweet invites a reader to click. Tweets that are short, punchy, and compelling are so either because they tell the reader precisely what you are offering

("How to . . ." or "27 Ways . . .") or because they are clever or funny.

I like how John Haydon tweets a punchy headline and then adds his take on why it's a good read:

Figure 8.8   (http://twitter.com/ johnhaydon/status/2030125905)

. . . and how Cameron Moll makes his tweet clever and funny:

Figure 8.9   (http://twitter.com/ cameronmoll/status/2029925794)

Graphics expand on the story. A good image or graphic complements a news story. Similarly, linking to a picture via Twitter tells a story with far more impact. For example:

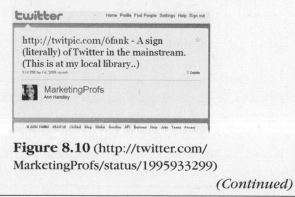

Figure 8.10 (http://twitter.com/ MarketingProfs/status/1995933299)

(Continued)

(Continued)

   People make things interesting. News reporters often focus on how people are affected by a given situation or event. On Twitter, similarly, it's the people who keep it interesting. That means talking to (or "@ing") folks liberally, as well as adopting a conversational tone and community spirit. For example:

Figure 8.11   (http://twitter.com/ swoodruff/status/2019336221)

And that applies even when you are representing a brand:

Figure 8.12   (http://twitter.com/ LLBeanPR/status/2005525875)

   Consider the reader. Journalists spend a lot of time coming up with the right angle for a story. On Twitter, be similarly thoughtful in your approach. The immediacy of Twitter might tempt you to dash off a tweet with little forethought. But if you respect your audience of followers similar to the way journalists consider their readers, you'll spend more time thinking about what to tweet than you'll spend actually tweeting it. Believe me, your followers will appreciate your effort.

Source: A version of this article originally appeared in Mashable, http://mashable.com/2009/06/05/twitter-journalism-school

How to Make Your Content Go Viral

Let's get this out of the way right now so that there is no confusion. *Viral* means your content catches fire, earning tons of views, retweets, and likes, and is shared globally in the remotest villages and biggest cities. It's huge! Epic! Sounds great, huh? How do you get yourself some of that? How can you make your content go viral?

You can't.

Are some of you convinced otherwise? Although there are techniques that can enhance viral sharing (as we talked about earlier in this chapter), and you can certainly nudge, poke, and pray for it as well, the truth is that viral is a largely happy accident.

The sooner you realize that you are not in control of what goes viral, the better. What you *can* control is the form your content takes and whether it is compelling. You've heard us say more than once to make your content as good as possible for your audience and the rest is up to them. That mantra applies to viral content. It might happen, or it might not. But it's largely not up to you.

CHAPTER 9
The Care and Feeding of Fans

You've got a web site, a Facebook page, and a Twitter account. You are feeding all of them on a regular basis with new, interesting, and engaging content. But do you know whether doing so is helping you at all? What do customers think of what you are publishing and sharing?

In addition to creating content, you are also building a community of fans and customers around you. It's critical to take care of your community by listening and responding to them when appropriate.

Recall the steps to building a campfire. What happens when you ignore a fire for too long? It either burns out or burns out of control. Neither is what you want.

Setting Up a Listening Dashboard

Listening is one of life's most important skills. If you have kids, you know how often you have to tell them that they need to listen closely. The last thing you want your community and customers to think is that you lack listening skills. Luckily, you have various listening tools at your disposal to help you pay attention to your audience.

As with many things online, free and premium (paid) tools of varying quality are available. We are going to focus on a few free ones, because the premium services constantly add new features and require investigation by you to determine which feature set is appropriate for your needs and budget.

Having a central location for coordinating your listening efforts is important to success. That location is your *listening dashboard*, which may simply consist of a new folder in your RSS reader (if you use one)—or an entirely different setup.

- *Google Reader*

    You have many options in RSS readers. Google Reader is one of the most popular, and it's easy to set up. If you have an information technology (IT) department, ask them what they recommend and support so that you can get help from them if you need it. Don't have an IT department? (Did you just laugh at that notion of having one?) Then consider signing up for a free Google Reader account, which will give you all the features you need. It's a cinch to figure out and begin using right away.

    Whichever RSS reader you use, you'll want to fill it with the feeds and searches that make sense to you. More about that in a bit.

- *Google Alerts*

    This service allows you to enter search terms, phrases, and URLs into a profile; Google will then e-mail you whenever its search engine indexes something new on the Web that matches your search. At a minimum, you should set up searches for your company name, your web site URL, any major product names you have, and perhaps your name or (if you work for a company) executives' names.

    You'll have the option to adjust the settings to have the e-mails arrive either immediately as Google finds a match or in a daily digest. You can mix and match options for each search, and it is up to you to determine what frequency is optimal for your needs.

    Also consider setting up alerts for your competitors and the industries you work in as daily digests. These are not as critical as the searches that directly concern you, but they will help you stay on top of what is going on around you.

- *Search.Twitter.com*

  Twitter's search function allows you to key in a word or phrase to see all mentions of that word or phrase by anyone on Twitter in the previous two weeks. This is a great way to get a quick snapshot of what people are saying about you or your product, but it's not the most powerful use of this tool.

  After you perform a search, on the results screen in the upper right you'll see a mention of subscribing to a feed of that search. You'll want to copy that URL and add it to your listening dashboard so that any new search results thereafter show up automatically; you won't have to come back to the site every few days to see whether anything is new.

  Don't get discouraged if your searches don't turn up any results right away. With all the new content you'll be creating, that will soon change!

- *Relevant blogs*

  No matter what your business is, there are likely blogs out there that you should be reading—those that cover your industry or are otherwise relevant. Add them to your listening dashboard so that you can stay current on what is going on around you.

Of course, all of these methods focus on social media and people who might be talking about you but are not contacting you directly. For those who are ready to contact you directly, though, be sure to offer options for doing so on your site and social media profiles.

Provide a detailed Contact Us page on your site that clearly lays out all the ways someone can get in touch with you: phone numbers, e-mail addresses, mailing addresses, Twitter handles, and so on. Don't leave someone confused about the best way to contact you! (Does that sound like obvious advice? You'd be surprised how often it is overlooked.)

Responding Quickly, and with Sincerity

How you respond to a potential customer or an upset current customer is critical. You should begin thinking about it right now, before either situation actually happens.

Although there are innumerable scenarios that you might be confronted with, the following sections highlight some common types of people you might encounter. Any response, by the way, should occur quickly. How quickly? As quickly as you reasonably can.

COMMENTERS

Almost every piece of content you create—from the video showcasing your latest speech to the blog post about your new product rollout—has the possibility of generating comments. Show your community that you not only read their comments but also appreciate them. Be sure that at least once a day you read through your comments and respond to them individually.

Sometimes that response will be a simple thank you to someone. Often, though, a question will be asked or something said that you'll want to respond to more substantively. In both cases (and really with anything you write online), be sure to reread your response before hitting the Publish button.

PASSIVES

Once your listening dashboard is set up and you begin to be more active online, you are sure to cross paths with people who might be perfect customers for you. They haven't actually come to you yet, and they may not even know about you, but they might have posted something on Twitter or another social site such as "I'm looking for a new cheese grater"; and you, as it happens, sell cheese graters with a comfort grip handle!

When that happens, be careful that what you say or do does not come off too aggressive, so as to scare them off. Be direct and helpful, but don't dive in with the hard sell. Take a softer approach. Let them know that you saw that they were looking online and that what you offer might be a good fit; then tell them how they can get in touch with you to get more information.

You've now shown them that you are listening, that you are trying to be a part of the community, and you have given them a clear path to your door. You've done your part, and the next move is up to them.

TROLLS

No longer does the term *troll* refer to angry creatures that live under bridges in children's fairy tales. Today, trolls are people who get a misplaced sense of accomplishment from stirring up trouble online.

UrbanDictionary.com defines *online troll* as "one who posts a deliberately provocative message to a newsgroup or message board with the intention of causing maximum disruption and argument." You can spot trolls because they say things that have little to do with the topic at hand, in the hope of getting people to focus on them rather than on the discussion.

Never feed the trolls! As hard as it may be, do not respond to them; do not acknowledge them in any way.

PASSIONATES

You might hear the world *passionate* and imagine rabid fans and ambassadors. But keep in mind that angry people can be passionate, too. More than one business has been confronted with a passionate consumer who has written an anger-fueled blog post attacking the brand's product. Someone who is willing to write such a post is also likely to write an overly positive one if you can address and resolve the problem at hand. Social networks amplify; people increasingly realize they have a megaphone online and will use it to be heard.

You won't be able to fix every problem that customers run across, but at a minimum you must respond to let them know that you are listening. If you don't know whether your response might be appropriate, you might discuss it with your legal or public relations team.

But that said, it's key to not sound like a lawyer or a flack. Be sincere and honest. Let the customers know that you are glad they expressed their frustration, because now you can make improvements. Assure an irate customer that you both want the same thing: a seamless customer experience. So (1) apologize for the malfunction or disappointment, and (2) thank the customer for bringing the issue to your attention so that the business can make this right and help future customers avoid the same frustration. As quickly as possible, take the discussion offline, away from a public forum.

Of course, the same approach applies when the passion is positive. If you give passionates a form-letter response of thanks, they may view you as insincere. Offer a heartfelt thank you and let them know how much you appreciate their kind words. These are the people to get know better, because they could quickly become some of your best customers—and even more important, your biggest advocates online.

CHAPTER 10

Attention B2B Companies: This Is the Chapter You Are Looking For

Whenever we give presentations or keynote addresses, there's always someone who raises a hand and asks: *Wait a sec. How does this apply to B2B?*

So we're anticipating that there are a number of you B2B business owners or marketers reading this book now, who might be formulating the very same question in your own heads right now. Here's the thing: Everything covered in this book applies to businesses that sell to other businesses—or to any other kind of organization out there, for that matter—whether you sell routers, HVAC systems, swimming pools, or ice cubes or are charged with marketing your synagogue, swing band, accounting services, hospital, zoo, oil paintings, candidate for school committee, Pop Warner football league, pizza shop, or PTA group. In other words, the Content Rules that make for good content apply broadly, which means they apply to you, too.

That said, we know that organizations selling to other businesses face some unique challenges. So we're dedicating this chapter to creating content in the B2B world, condensing the lessons elsewhere in the book and packaging them specifically for you. For help, we turned to our friend here in Boston, Stephanie Tilton of Ten Ton Marketing (www.tentonmarketing.com), who works extensively with B2B companies to develop their own brands of killer content. What follows is Stephanie's account of how to create B2B content that ignites.

Here's what you'll find in these pages:

- A brief overview of the specific trends compelling B2B organizations to adopt content marketing

- A concise overview of content and what it can do for your B2B organization

- Seven steps you can take to develop a solid B2B-focused content strategy

Your Prospects Are Avoiding You

Prospective B2B customers spend significant time researching their options before making a purchase. B2B companies know this better than anyone, of course. What's more, you are typically not dealing with just one person in the organization; you're dealing with a committee of buyers.

After all, your service or product will likely be used across many areas of the company. That means that each person with influence over the purchase decision typically wants to research, evaluate, or vet the alternatives. Most of these buyers turn to the Web to access information—whether to solicit opinions from peers through Facebook, Twitter, LinkedIn, or other social venues or to sift through content on your site and others.

This affects B2B companies in interesting ways: Because your prospects are making decisions based on these online interactions and their own research, they can avoid contacting your company until they are closer to actually making a purchase, or quite late in buying cycle. And who can blame them? We all know we'll get inundated—*harassed!*—with e-mails and phone calls the minute we raise our hand and say we're in the market to buy.

That said, according to an IDG Communications survey of IT professionals conducted in December 2008, a majority of the time, buyers aren't finding the information they need while researching their options.[1] And if your company isn't delivering relevant information, it's not going to make the short list of possible vendors.

The flip side, of course, is that your company can win big-time by offering up the information your prospects are seeking. In fact, in a survey conducted by DemandGen and Genius.com, 66 percent of respondents indicated the *"consistent and relevant communication provided by both the sales and marketing organizations"* was a key influence in choosing the company they ultimately made a purchase from.[2]

Marketers Need to Pick Up the Ball and Run with It

So what does this mean for your business? First and foremost, there's a lot more pressure on you to produce valuable content that replaces the interactions your salespeople used to have with prospects throughout the so-called buying cycle—or the length of time it takes someone to make a decision to purchase. (In the B2B world, of course, that decision period can be many months, or considerably longer than it might be to choose a flavor of ice cream from the freezer case.)

In fact, according to Forrester Research, *"Long sales cycles and complex purchase decision making challenge B2B marketers to find the most qualified prospects and to build relationships long before the first sales call."*[3] As a result, you need to embrace a new mind-set—one focused not just on generating leads but on developing a strategy to keep prospects engaged until they're good and ready to talk to your sales reps.

---

[1] MarketFusion, "Technology Vendors May Be Losing Close to 50% of Their Potential Sales Due to Inadequate Online Information," IDG, December 18, 2008.

[2] *Inside the Mind of the B2B Buyer,* DemandGen Report and Genius.com, March 2010.

[3] Laura Ramos, "B2B Lead Management Automation Market Overview," Forrester Research, September 22, 2009.

Content Marketing Is the Key

This is where content comes in. If you can deliver content that your prospects find interesting *and* informative *and* entertaining, they'll see you as a trusted source of information—an adviser, an enviable position for any organization.

Let's say your prospects see your solution and your competitor's solution stacking up fairly evenly. If you provide the information that answers your prospects' questions and concerns, and engage them throughout the decision period—and your competitor doesn't—you've increased the likelihood of winning the deal. Let's face it: while many companies strive to be thought leaders, the truth is that only a handful can do it well. But the beauty of content marketing is that any company (of any size) can excel at it—and set itself apart.

Additional Steps to Getting Hitched: Content and B2B, True Love Always

The Content Rules and the fundamentals of developing great content we talked about in Chapters 3 through 6 of this book—the why, who, what, when, how, and where—still apply, but with some notable additions we outline here.

WHY: CLARIFYING OBJECTIVES FOR B2B CONTENT

It is critical to measure the results of your efforts; you know *someone* is going to be asking for the reports. Besides, you want to know which content is—and isn't—working so you can prioritize going forward.

For B2B companies, the job of each piece of content is more nuanced: Each piece of content you produce should be tied to a short-term goal, such as "encouraging the reader to sign up for the XYZ webinar." Plus, it should be associated with your company's strategic objectives, such as "increasing sales by 15 percent in North America." With clear objectives, you can understand how well you're hitting your mark. If the objective of one white paper was to move prospects from general awareness to more specific interest, how well did you do? And if your overall objective was to produce 400 sales-ready leads within six months, how did you fare?

Once you have this insight, you can strengthen your content marketing efforts, putting into play what has worked to date and leaving lackluster content by the wayside.

WHO: UNDERSTANDING THE NUANCES OF YOUR B2B AUDIENCE

Who is your audience? What are their issues? You can't deliver relevant, valuable content unless you understand what makes them tick, and can fully grok their concerns and objectives. (See Chapter 3.)

That's easy enough for most organizations to figure out, but B2B organizations often have a more difficult time of it. The problem is that many B2B organizations paint portraits of their prospects in broad brushstrokes—and as a result, they fail to paint a clear picture of just who it is the company is trying to reach and engage. While you may think titles and roles are sufficient for targeting your content, they're not. Here are two examples of why this approach is flawed.

Take a look at Table 10.1, from a 2010 Forrester Research survey. You might be tempted to lump the titles of *application*

Table 10.1   In Other Words: You Can't Assume People with Similar Titles Approach the Buying Process in the Same Way

Top Five Influences, Application Developer	Top Five Influences, Enterprise Architect
Peers and colleagues (word of mouth)	Peers and colleagues (word of mouth)
Vendor, industry trade, or professional web sites	Your direct vendor salesperson
Technology or business publications, magazines	Consultants, value-added resellers, systems integrators
Consultants, value-added resellers, systems integrators	Vendor, industry trade, or professional web sites
Your direct vendor salesperson	Technology or business publications, magazines

Source: Forrester Research, "For B2B Tech Companies, Demographics Shape Adoption," January 2010.

Table 10.2   CIO Archetypes and Focus

Archetype	Focus
Function head	Achieving IT operational excellence
Transformational leader	Creating enterprise-wide change
Business strategist	Driving business strategy

Source: "State of the CIO 2009," *CIO*, January 2009.

developer and *enterprise architect* in the same category of those responsible for developing enterprise applications. But by assuming these two variations on an application developer fit into the same tidy box, you wouldn't understand the best channel for reaching either of these distinct roles. After all, they consult resources in different ways during their decision-making process.

Here's another example. Many organizations tend to think that all chief information officers (CIOs) are created equal. But findings from *CIO* magazine's "State of the CIO 2009" research report illustrate otherwise. The report summarizes three CIO archetypes, each with very different focuses and goals (see Table 10.2). If you assume all CIOs are alike, you're going to produce content that isn't relevant to any of them.

To connect with your would-be buyers, you need to understand who they are—what they care about, what makes them tick, and what's the best way to bond with them. You do that by developing buyer personas—profiles of the ideal customer—based on what you know of your current customer base and prospects. While you don't need personas for every single person you sell to, you should develop buyer personas for all major roles involved in the buying process. For example, develop personas for the individual(s) who will use the product or service, the one who will implement or manage it, and the one who will write the check.

For each role, learn as much as you can about how that person goes about making a buying decision. What is this person's role in the purchase process? What questions does this person need answered at each stage of the buying process? Here are some additional questions you should try to answer:

- What work issues keep this person up at night?

- What motivates this buyer to take action?

- What sources does this person turn to for information and daily news?

- How does the prospect go about making business decisions?

- What types of organizations does he or she belong to and what events does she attend?

- Does this buyer seek advice from colleagues, industry peers, and/or unbiased third parties?

- How is this person dealing with the problem today?

- What specific words or phrases does he or she use to describe the issues he or she is facing?

- What might prevent this type of buyer from choosing your company or offering?

- What are this prospect's content preferences throughout the buying cycle?

To gather this information, consult your customer database and customer-facing folks; conduct polls and surveys of your customer base; and monitor the online conversations where your customers are, such as on Twitter, blogs, Facebook, private discussion groups, or LinkedIn groups. You can supplement this data with industry research that tells you a bit about general trends in particular industries.

What: Map What You Know to How They Buy

Once you've gotten to know your audience, you need to understand the steps they take on the way to making a purchase decision. You can map out the buying process at a very basic or more complex level. The key is to understand how your prospects and customers think of the buying cycle, who is involved, and what their information needs are at each stage.

Next, you can create a grid or spreadsheet that maps the questions and concerns of each buyer at each stage of the buying process. Map these information needs to the content formats your prospects prefer. You should have uncovered these preferences for content as part of developing your buyer personas. But if you need some outside assistance—and you happen to sell a technology service or product—you can tap into outside research conducted by the likes of TechTarget and the *InformationWeek* Business Technology Network, to name two.

While you work on nurturing new customers and forging new relationships, be sure not to neglect your existing customers. (See Table 10.3.) Be sure to create content that helps deepen the relationships you've already built with customers. Your current customers have different needs from your prospects; if nothing else, they want to understand how to get the most out of the products or services they are already using. (See other ideas in the Loyalty column on the far right of Table 10.3.)

Now you're ready to begin creating, or finding, or reimagining content to fit the specific needs of buyers at certain stages. A good place to start is to conduct an audit to see which of your current content you can reimagine in various formats and on various platforms (see Chapter 5).

WHEN: WHAT'S SPECIAL ABOUT THE B2B EDITORIAL CALENDAR?

In addition to producing relevant information, the next most important thing you can do is provide it consistently, at every stage outlined earlier. Keep in mind that your content is largely taking the place of the interactions your sales reps would otherwise be having with prospects. Because of that, it's critical for B2B companies that each piece of content be considered not as an ad hoc exercise, but as an element of a larger whole. Follow the ideas presented in Chapter 5 and create an editorial calendar with major milestones for creating and delivering content. And develop a production schedule for the project team to follow for each individual project. The beauty of this approach is that you avoid fire-drill mode and instead develop efficient processes for continually pumping out content of interest to your prospects and customers.

Also critical is to include a call to action that points buyers to the next logical piece of content. In other words, your call to

BUYER STAGE/ PROSPECT TYPE	RECOGNIZE PROBLEM		UNDERSTAND OBJECTIVES/ POSSIBILITIES		COMPARE SOLUTIONS/ VENDORS		MAKE SELECTION/ PURCHASE		LOYALTY
	Concern	Content	Concern	Content	Concern	Content	Concern	Content	
USER	• Is this an industry trend? • What could happen if I don't address this?	• Blog posts • eBook • White paper	• How are others dealing with this? • What are the options for addressing this?	• Podcasts • Analyst reports • Webinars • Videos • Best practice and how-to guides	• What do I get with this solution? • What results have others seen?	• Solution brochure • Case studies • Videos	• Are other customers satisfied with their decision?	• Testimonials	• User guides • Newsletter • Best-practice guides • Online community • User conferences
BUYER					• How much does it cost? • Is it worth the investment? • Is this vendor stable? • How does this vendor compare with others in the industry?	• Price list • ROI studies • Case studies • Company brochures or fact sheets • Analyst reports	• Can the vendor match all my requirements?	• Proposal	• ROI measurement
TECHNICAL					• What are the technical details? • How will this integrate into our environment? • What deployment issues should I expect?	• Technical white paper • Case studies • Webinar • Demo • Datasheet			• Installation manuals • Implementation best practices • Tutorials • New product/ feature releases • Online forum

Table 10.3   Map Out Your Prospects' and Customers' Information Needs and Content Preferences

action should guide the prospect further along the decision process. And ideally, each content asset (or reimagined set of content) you offer will be associated with a unique landing page; this helps prospects find exactly the information they're interested in.

How: Craft Interesting, Informative, Entertaining Content (Yes, You Can!)

Much of this book is about how to do just that. But for B2B companies, special attention must be paid to Content Rule Number 8: *Do something unexpected.*

There are lots of examples in this book of companies that sell dead-serious products that nonetheless have figured out a way to market them in a way that both drives viral sharing and enhances the company's personality. Using a little humor or entertainment is also a great way to drive awareness about invisible services or products that exist in the background of business infrastructure—say, technology products or security services.

Check out ideas from Kinaxis (Chapter 5), ExactTarget (Chapter 4), or Kadient (Chapter 23) (see Figure 10.1).

Figure 10.1   Kadient Produces Humorous Videos to Connect with Its Audience

Figure 10.2   Marketo Created an Interactive Game to Build Relationships with Qualified Prospects

Or perhaps you have the resources and initiative to produce something like the witty interactive game and quiz from Marketo (see Figure 10.2).

Or consider Cisco's campaign for its ASR 1000 router. Rather than soliciting real-life customer testimonials about how Cisco equipment helps them meet their technical challenges (which would likely be stuffed full of language detail like the buzzwords that appear in our list in Chapter 4), Cisco sought testimonials from the likes of Santa Claus and the Easter Bunny, talking about how dependent they are on the network. Can you imagine what would happen if Santa had reliability issues on Christmas Eve? Christmas would be doomed!

In other words, Cisco was able to drive home the same point, but to do so in a funny, intriguing way. How might your company develop its messaging to add an element of the unexpected?

Four Content Ideas You Shouldn't Miss

Competitive comparisons. Create a downloadable document that offers a feature comparison of your product to your competitor's, or reviews pricing details. TechTarget's 2009 media consumption report[4] revealed that a majority of technology buyers want

---

[4] "TechTarget 2009 Media Consumption Benchmark Report 2: Closing the Gap between IT Buyers and IT Marketers," TechTarget, 2009.

content comparing a vendor's offering to the competition as they get further along in the decision process. Yet few companies put out competitive comparisons for public consumption. Don't forget—this is information your sales reps would have handed over during meetings with prospects in the past. Now that buyers are delaying interactions until the last possible minute, you need to deliver this information online. If you *don't* offer it but your competitors do, guess who'll make the short list of potential vendors.

Consider the approach of one Vancouver-based company: RitchieWiki (www.ritchiewiki.com) is a collaborative web site created and maintained by Ritchie Brothers Auctioneers (www.rbauction.com) as the go-to source for industrial equipment specs and everything else anyone could ever want to know about heavy machinery and the manufacturers, people, uses, projects, and history of it (did you know that the Caterpillar 535B skidder—one of about 900 made in the United States—produces 180 net horsepower?). Ritchie Brothers curates information for its industry in a central, accessible source. How might you be a go-to resource for those in your industry, including your would-be customers?

A more nuanced approach to case studies or success stories. Use case studies or customer success stories for more than just demonstrating the value of your solution. Rather, position them to overcome objections early in the buying cycle. First, you need to understand why your customers were initially skeptical of your offering. Let's assume your company is Docs-R-Us and sells document-management software. Perhaps during interviews, you discover that many of your customers were initially hesitant because your solution is offered through a software-as-a-service (SaaS) model. Companies were concerned that users without Internet connections would be unable to access electronic files—a fear reinforced by their talks with other SaaS providers.

If enough of your customers shared this concern, you've got good reason to try to preempt the objection before it scares off other (potential) customers. Find out what turned these current customers' views around. In this case, let's assume it's because you enable users to access files while offline. Then present a story that highlights one customer's concern with this issue and why your offering ultimately won that customer over. Instead of producing a case study entitled "Docs-R-Us Helps XYZ Corporation Locate Records in Half the Time," you could publish one entitled "Assessing Your Document Management Options: Why All Software-as-a-Service Offerings Are Not Equal."

You can also use success stories to address the needs of different stakeholders in the buying process. Scott Vaughan of UMB TechWeb polled a group of CIOs about what marketers could do better. It turns out that the standard problem-solution-results case study formula doesn't resonate with IT evaluators and decision makers. One case study element these CIOs said they'd like to see is a section on lessons learned while implementing the solution. Deliver that information and you'll stand head and shoulders above the competition.

Reimagined content. Chapter 5 gives you a framework for reimagining your content assets in various formats and across various platforms. Bundling related products together in a downloadable how-to tool kit is a great way to interest and engage your buyers. MarketingProfs packages various types of its content on the same theme into kits; a kit might include a how-to webinar, an assortment of tactical articles, worksheets or checklists, and a collection of customer success stories, for example. The kit itself is a product landing page that links to existing content in the MarketingProfs library.

Frequently asked questions (FAQs). Create a list of the common questions and answers that will allow your would-be buyers to find answers to their questions on their own. For details on how to create a compelling FAQs section, see Chapter 15.

Producing the type of content your prospects and customers are looking for can be enough to set you apart; remember, they're not finding the information they want a majority of the time.

WHERE: SPREADING SEEDS

The more your information makes it into the hands of your prospects, the greater the likelihood that they'll ultimately get

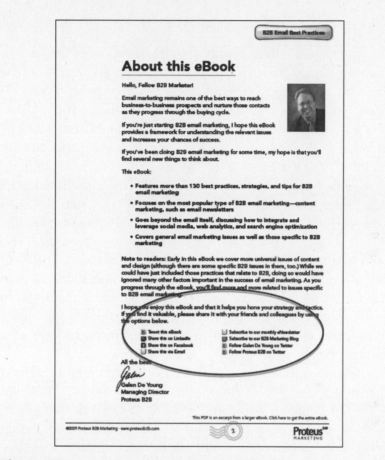

Figure 10.3 Embed Options to Facilitate Sharing

in touch with one of your sales reps, right? So make it easy to consume and share your content. If nothing else, embed sharing options in your PDFs. (See Figure 10.3.) As we explain in Chapter 13, Galen De Young of Proteus B2B wrote an article for MarketingProfs that details how his organization embedded e-mail and social media sharing options in an ebook on B2B e-mail marketing best practices. Using web analytics and data available from bit.ly—a URL shortener—he's been able to track and analyze the traffic from various referral sources. And Galen is certain that the PDF is getting shared much more than it would have had they not embedded sharing options.

To Register or Not to Register

Next, you should rethink registration (for more, see Chapter 13). Requiring prospects to register in exchange for your content should be a strategic decision, not a default option. If you do require registration, limit the amount of information you request: Don't ask for all the information under the sun. Instead, think of your relationship with the prospect like a dating scenario, and ask for a little bit of information during each successive interaction.

Say a prospect's first interaction with you is to download a white paper, ebook, or how-to guide from your web site. You might request the person's name and e-mail address in exchange for the download. You could then send an e-mail asking if she would like to receive useful information from time to time, In other words, see if she'll grant permission to be added to your database. At the end of the paper, ebook, or guide, your call to action could point her to another asset in your library—whatever makes sense for moving her through the buying process in a logical sequence.

Let's assume that you encourage her to sign up for the next paper in a series. When she requests the download, you could ask for her company name and role. At the end of that paper, you could point her to a one-hour webinar. When she signs up to attend the webinar, you could ask for her company size, time frame to purchase, and phone number—or whatever makes sense for your company.

The key is to ask for a bit more information with each contact so you can build the information up over time. That way you take the burden off the prospect while gathering the information you need. By using cookies, you can prepopulate your forms with the information you've captured to date. The prospect can see you're asking for just a bit of additional information with each interaction.

Also, don't be shy about putting out a press release announcing your latest content. Press releases aren't just for product or company news—they're a way you can make it easier for your prospects to find your content. Finally, be sure to post your content on relevant online communities, blog about it, and link to it through Twitter and in your e-mail signature (more about sharing options in Chapter 8).

Talking B2B Content with One of the World's Largest Software Businesses

SAS is not only the world's largest privately held software business—it has more than 11,000 employees in 50 countries and 400 SAS offices worldwide—but it's also an innovator in using content to grow its $2.3 billion business. Headquartered near Raleigh, North Carolina, SAS publishes an online magazine, white papers, blogs, and more to help advance its industry leadership as well as draw customers to its products and services. Here, Kelly LeVoyer, senior manager of external communications (KL) and John Mosier, SAS's integrated content manager (JM), talk about their approach. We particularly like how a company the size of SAS defines compelling content, and how SAS's approach is surprisingly similar to that of any smaller organization. (See what Kelly says about an organization's voice in her answer, for example.)

Q: Developing content to attract and retain customers in your organization is very different from what it might be for a small organization. What defines "compelling content" in the B2B space, particularly for a larger organization?

KL: I'm not so sure that the answer *is* very different from that of a small business, actually. Both current and prospective customers want content that helps them solve their problem, relevant to the buying stage that they are in—that is, whether they're early in the process researching vendors, or a longtime customer looking to use their SAS software (in our case) in new ways.

Of course, being able to deliver that content in a compelling way requires that you've done the research to identify the problems these audiences are faced with and that you have solid processes for developing the content. The complexity of those processes might be what sets us apart from a smaller organization.

(Continued)

(Continued)

But that aside, I think compelling content is timely (in that it reflects new thinking and responds to current issues), is easy to consume, is offered in multiple media, offers practical information, and sounds like it was written by a real person. I believe the voice of an organization is one of the qualities that can differentiate it from competitors. After all, at the end of the day, people want to do business with people—even more so when you're talking about committing to a significant financial investment.

Q: Where does an organization like yours begin?

KL: First of all, with more than 120 software products and more than 11,000 employees in 400 offices around the world, we have to set priorities so we can derive some concentrated impact. We typically set three to five global priority market areas, such as business analytics and risk management, and eight to ten priority industries that we concentrate our outbound efforts on. Our product marketing organization identifies the key issues or problems in those areas that our target audiences are facing, and from that point, content development happens in many different areas of the company, around the world.

I think what's key to your question, though, is how do we use content to *attract* customers—which is part of the new paradigm of inbound marketing. That's where our thought leadership strategy comes in.

We have dozens of subject matter experts around the world who share their knowledge with content in a variety of channels—via SAS blogs, e-newsletters, and magazines, as well as mainstream and social media. But they don't always necessarily talk about SAS. What's more important is that they offer thoughtful information, opinions, and predictions about that particular topic. By way of providing helpful information and contributing to the conversations, SAS will likely be top of mind the next time one of those readers is seeking a software solution.

Q: B2B organizations need to develop content that resonates at various stages of the buying cycle, right? For example, the content someone is looking for in the early consideration stage is different from what it might be down the line, when they are more committed and digging into more specific features. How do you know what will resonate with buyers at various points?

JM: From the metrics that our marketers share with us, from focus groups that we conduct, and from external research. We try never to miss an opportunity to gather groups of customers together at our conferences to focus-group test content strategies.

We have a complex matrix of target audiences, a lengthy buying cycle, and an evolving digital landscape, so we are always refining our approach.

Q: What are the challenges you face as a B2B company looking to produce content across your organization? Has it made marketing's job easier or harder?

KL: Honestly, the biggest challenge in my opinion is that we have so many ideas and simply not enough cycles to act on them. Related to that is the demand now for companies to be more agile with their content, and that can be a challenge.

The tech B2B market is a deep, wide, fast-moving river. There are issues, discussions, and announcements every day that impact us directly, and that we could develop timely, compelling content around. One of the challenges with agility at a company this size is the review cycles—but in my tenure at SAS, I've seen that improve. I think our foray into blogging, for example, has helped people realize that we have to move quickly and trust our experts more.

Q: How do you actually produce what you produce?

KL: We produce the majority of our content ourselves (including video, which comes from our high-end video facility at the corporate headquarters); some comes from partnerships with media companies, analyst firms, and research organizations. We have content producers all over the company, if you consider the PowerPoint presentations,

(Continued)

(Continued)

technical papers, marketing campaign assets, et cetera, that departments are constantly producing as part of their daily jobs. We consider all of that as fodder for content, including internal content that can be tweaked for external use—as long as it meets a priority need. The challenges, as we mentioned earlier, are to channel all this content into the right stages of the buying or customer support cycle—and identify and fill the gaps.

My team of writers are great at what I call merchandising content—that is, starting with something like a white paper or a webcast and repurposing that into a magazine article, a blog post, an interactive digital piece. Producing those shorter, more digital-friendly offshoot assets that we can promote easily via social media channels is a great way to see quickly what resonates with our audiences.

Q: Does SAS have employees dedicated to content?

JM: In 2008, we created two positions that SAS had never had before: a social media manager and the position that I ultimately assumed, the integrated content manager. I report in to our product marketing organization and focus on developing more disciplined processes that underlie our content development.

KL: And in 2009, I also created a new position called editor, blogs and social content. Our blog program is growing so rapidly, it needed a dedicated program manager, and that's what she's been spending the majority of her time on.

But the idea behind the social content part of the title is to create digital-friendly assets from our marketing content that can be easily shared in social media, and also to monitor the social media landscape and bring back to the team any trending topics that we should consider jumping into with new content.

Ready to get started? A good place to begin is with the Content Checklist in Part Four of this book.

PART TWO

The How-To Section

The first part of this book introduces and elucidates the rules for creating great content. Here, Part Two offers specific how-to steps to creating an array of things you might want to develop, beginning with blogs, which we consider your content front line.

CHAPTER 11
A Blog as a Hub of Your Online Content

Blog: A blog (a blend of the term *web log*) is a type of website or part of a website. Blogs are usually maintained by an individual with regular entries of commentary, descriptions of events, or other material such as graphics or video. Entries are commonly displayed in reverse-chronological order. *Blog* can also be used as a verb, meaning *to maintain or add content to a blog.*

—*Wikipedia*

A blog is a logical and appropriate first step if you want to create and publish the kind of content we discussed in Part One. A blog can serve as your online home base or hub for content, including posts you write, curated content you pull together, press mentions, and content created about your organization elsewhere that you want to share.

In other words, a blog can become the central location through which you can share your thoughts, words, and ideas with the world. There is no one right type of blog out there, so take the time to figure out what works best for your company.

You have a variety of blogging platforms or content management systems (CMSs) available to you. Among the popular ones are WordPress, Squarespace, Movable Type, TypePad, and Blogger. They have similar features but are different enough that you need to take the time to look at them all to determine which will work best for you. Most have the ability to host your blog site for you, but it is best to work with a developer to integrate the blog directly into your own web site so that you have one central location where customers can find you on the Web.

Blogging Guidelines

Before you start down the blogging path, consider the following 12 guidelines:

1. Define your purpose.

2. Set a reliable schedule.

3. Mix it up!

4. Move beyond the written word.

5. Size matters.

6. Learn how to write killer headlines.

7. Design is important.

8. Create momentum.

9. Consider comment moderation.

10. Categorize and tag everything.

11. Write the way you speak.

12. Don't overthink.

DEFINE YOUR PURPOSE

The heart of your blog is your content, of course. In most cases, that means writing regularly. The voice and perspective of your blog are critical (see Chapter 4). The look and feel (the design) of your blog are also important (more on this in a minute), but the content really is, well, king. As your readership grows, more people will likely subscribe to your blog via RSS readers and e-mail, so they may never even see the design of the site after their first view visits. In short, what you say is more important than what it looks like. And to determine what you'll be saying, you'll need to know:

- Who is your audience?
- Who is your competition for your audience's attention?
- What is the focus of your blog? What is it about?
- What goals are you trying to achieve?
- Have you set metrics for measuring those goals?

SET A RELIABLE SCHEDULE

It's important to deliver blog entries (posts) on a reliable, consistent schedule. How often should you blog? That's entirely up to you and your ambition and calendar, but at least twice a week is optimal. Tuesday and Thursday are widely considered optimal, but experiment with your own schedule. Most businesses publish posts during the workweek, but toss in a Sunday post every once in a while to test your weekend readership. (As with anything online, your mileage will vary. Blogger Tom Martin publishes MyMardiGrasExperience.com—a blog with a mission to rebrand Mardi Gras into a family event—only during Mardi Gras.)

You can produce a few posts at once and then publish them throughout the week. Boston Pilates instructor Lisa Johnson usually hunkers down at her desk on a weekend afternoon for four or five hours to pump out three or more blog posts, or a week's worth of content for her own fitness blog as well as that of Modern Pilates, the studio locations she owns. "Don't set undeliverable goals," Lisa says. "Set your own schedule."

MIX IT UP!

Consider the variety of topics and how much attention each deserves. Mix short and long posts, meatier posts and less serious posts, timely posts and evergreen, timeless posts. Look at how marketing technology company HubSpot mixes up its posts (see Chapter 24) so as to offer its readers variety.

MOVE BEYOND THE WRITTEN WORD

Your blog might be mainly images, like Richard Smith's Dollar ReDe$ign Project blog, which seeks to rebrand the American dollar bill. But most blogs are text-heavy, so it's good to spice yours up with graphics and other embedded elements.

Use photos in your posts to add a visually pleasing element or help further your point. You can find Creative Commons–licensed photos on Flickr, or you can purchase inexpensive artwork from a variety of stock photography sites.

You can also include charts, infographics, and checklists. You might even embed ebooks or other documents, YouTube videos, PowerPoint or SlideShare presentations you like or produce yourself, and widgets or tools that your audience can interact with.

If you embed content, it's a good idea to include in your post some keyword-rich text from the embedded document or video so as to give both your readers and the search engines a sense of what the embedded item is about.

SIZE MATTERS

How long should your posts be? Long enough to say what you need to say, but not too long. Is that too vague an answer? Perhaps. But the miniskirt theory of perfect length also applies to blog posts. You want to make them long enough to cover the essentials, but short enough to keep it interesting.

LEARN HOW TO WRITE KILLER HEADLINES

The headline is the most important part of your post. Spend as much time on it as you would the whole post, if you need to (don't just slap it on as an afterthought), and learn to do it well. As with ebooks and white papers (more on those in Chapter 13), a good title for your post will pique readers' curiosity and entice them to read more. If you worry that a title based more on intrigue won't give enough context to entice a would-be reader, you can add a descriptive subtitle to spell things out.

(A descriptive subtitle is a good place to include search terms or keywords, too.)

Here are some ways to create an intriguing blog post title:

- Pique curiosity: "What's a Dry Cleaner Doing on Twitter?" (from the MarketingProfs Daily Fix).

- Use superlatives: Instead of "Getting What You Want from Your Vendors," try "The Best Way to Get the Right Price from a Vendor."

- Use surprising or odd analogies: "The Inigo Montoya Guide to 27 Commonly Misused Words" (from Brian Clark on Copyblogger).

- Be specific: Instead of "One Way to Dress for Success," try "The One Thing You Need to Wear to a Job Interview."

- Simplify a complex subject comprehensively: "This Is Why You're Fat: An Update" (from LisaJohnsonFitness.com).

- Be contrarian: "Why Richard Branson's 5 Tips for Success Are Really only 4.5" (from Tim Berry's Planning Startups Stories), "Why Too Much Money Is Worse Than Too Little" (from Guy Kawasaki on the American Express OPEN Forum), or "How to Be Arrogant, the Right Way" (from Thomas Edwards's blog, The Professional Wingman).

- Use numbers, especially odd numbers: "27 Blogging Secrets to Power Your Community" (from Chris Brogan).

DESIGN IS IMPORTANT

Your blog, including its design, should have style and personality. If you don't have the resources to hire a designer, though, don't fret. There are numerous templates for every publishing platform available online for free or at minimal cost. Templates will get you up and running in no time and are a great starting point. Spend a few minutes online looking at other blogs and you will quickly realize that each is unique. There is no wrong or right way to do it. These are items that should be included in the design, though:

- An RSS icon to clearly indicate a subscription feed

- The option for someone to subscribe to the blog by e-mail (Feedburner will do this for you, for free)

- A clear way for someone to contact you

- A search box

- An archive of recent posts by topic or title

- Social sharing icons (social bling) that allow each post to be shared, liked, and passed along on Twitter, Facebook, LinkedIn, Google Buzz, and so on

- Links and bling to where else online they can find you (Twitter, Facebook, LinkedIn, Yelp, and so on)

CREATE MOMENTUM

What action do you want your visitors to take? "Too many people believe that by just having their content out there, that's enough. It's not," says HubSpot's Mike Volpe. Include relevant calls to action or triggers on each blog post, as with all of your content, he suggests. Each HubSpot post (http://blog.hubspot.com), for example, has at least three triggers: one beneath the headline, one to the right of the content (in the sidebar), and a third below the post itself, usually in the form of some companion content (a downloadable webinar, ebook, etc.). Including multiple calls to action serves the company's objectives as well as giving the reader a richer experience, Mike says, "by creating a path to consume more."

CONSIDER COMMENT MODERATION

An inherent power of blogs is their ability to spark conversation with and among your readers. But, because of the nature of the

Web, there will always be spammers and trolls who will add nothing of value to the conversation and will only frustrate everyone else involved. For that reason, you need some form of comment moderation in place.

Moderating is not editing. Never edit any comment that is posted to your blog, even if you disagree. Your readers have their own voices and opinions that may differ from yours. Moderation should be used only to keep inappropriate or off-topic comments off your site.

There are plug-ins and settings for all blog platforms that will help keep some of the spam out, but other settings will allow you to place a hold on a comment the first time someone comments and then white-list them for future comments so that they are not held. Others will allow you to hold a comment that has several links in it, which is sometimes a telltale sign of a spammer.

If you do elect to moderate comments, monitor them so that not much time passes between when a comment is made and when it appears on the site.

CATEGORIZE AND TAG EVERYTHING

You should categorize every blog post, assigning at least one category to it. The intent is to allow readers to click on those category names to find other posts you've written on the same topics. Search engines love them, too. Think of several top-level categories that describe the content you'll be creating, and add those categories to your blog's back end. Don't worry about having to determine all categories up front, because it's easy to add or delete a category.

In addition, add relevant keywords—or tags—to each post. Of course, the actual text of the post should contain keywords, but you can also add them as tags to help search engines find your content.

Consider creating unique tags for your own unique content and perspective. For this book, for example, we created *reimagined content.* Citrix Online coined *workshifting* to describe what used to be called telecommuting.

WRITE THE WAY YOU SPEAK

Write the way you speak (but don't forget to edit.) The casual, informal nature of blogging means that you don't have to create a perfectly crafted post with pristine grammar. So write the way you speak: friendly, casual, accessible. In short, human.

That said, there's a huge expanse between pristine and sloppy. Keep an eye on the easy stuff, at least: spelling, typos, the butchered and bloated text. *Bonus:* Have an editor do it for you. Everyone needs an editor (even really amazing writers).

DON'T OVERTHINK

Blogs deviate from traditional journalism in some fundamental ways, and among them is that you don't need to feel compelled to tell the whole, balanced story with every effort. It's okay to leave a little room for development and for the opinions of others. It's okay not to overthink or overrefine. As we discussed in Chapter 6, it's okay to leave stuff undone. You want your audience to have room to add their voices and opinions, too.

The *Content Rules* Easy-Peasy Blog Post Template

Kodak's chief blogger, Jenny Cisney, provides a simple blogging template to every contributing blogger of Kodak's A Thousand Words blog (more on Kodak in Chapter 25). Having some kind of framework to pass along to would-be writers, she says, encourages contributions by demystifying the fundamentals of a solid blog post, and makes contributors more comfortable with the process.

Kodak's template is fairly spare—it's a simple Word document titled "1000Words.Kodak.com Blog Posting Template . . . and Other Helpful Advice." It offers space for a post title ("attention grabbing, but concise"), body, and images.

Inspired by Jenny and the Kodak team, we've created our own *Content Rules* version. (You can download it for free at www.contentrulesbook.com/extras.)

This framework is suggested for only limited, occasional use by nonwriters and those unfamiliar with blogging. It's most appropriately shared within an organization to entice contributions from a reluctant or reticent staff; it's not intended for use as a universal, absolute, and definitive framework. There is not one single way to write a blog post, just as there is no one way to write in general. But you'll notice that this blog post template is very basic; it's intentionally a straightforward post skeleton.

Those with a flair for the subject (or for writing) will be able to enliven those bones, adding flesh and blood to create something on the page that's truly alive. Others won't; and it's likely that any post that relies solely on this framework might be similarly straightforward and, perhaps, a little bare.

That's okay, because the real value in sharing a template like this with others in your organization (or using it yourself) is to help neutralize the natural angst of confronting a blank page. Everyone feels that kind of anxiety, but it's a real shame the way it paralyzes so many would-be writers, turning their creative juices to frozen concentrate, and making them feel that blogging is scary and hard and simply not worth the trouble.

You can also think of this template as blogging training wheels. It will get you going the first couple of times, but before you know it you will be cruising on your very own.

POST TITLE

Let readers know how the post will be useful for them, and add an element of intrigue. Some tried-and-true formulas are "How to _____," "Nine Ways to _____," "The Secrets of _____," "What You Should Know about _____," or "The Weirdest [or Best, Worst, Funniest, Most Ridiculous, and so on] _____ I Ever Had."

(Continued)

(Continued)

FIRST SENTENCE

Your goal here is to hook your reader. Ask a question. State something mildly controversial, or universally interesting to your readers, that might spark intrigue. For example: "Have you ever wondered what it might feel like to trade jobs with someone for a day? Even a really boring job—like a highway toll taker?"

It's important to keep it simple: one idea per post. The goal is to give your reader one key takeaway.

_____

_____

NEXT PARAGRAPH

Here's where you begin to answer the question you raised earlier, or to start to explain your initial statement. Begin to fill in the details related to your initial statement or question. Share why you've made the statement and back it up with what helped you get to that feeling. Always remember that when you mention other authors' sites or articles you should link to them.

_____

_____

_____

_____

BULLETED OR NUMBERED LISTS

Create a list of your key points. If you've been writing about trading places with the toll taker for a day, for example, you might create the following points:

- The job is surprisingly social.

- But you breathe in a lot of fumes.

You don't need to have more than a few of these points.

-
-
-
-
-

ADD AN IMAGE

Graphics add personality and interest. Include a relevant photo or graphic with your post. Sites such as Flickr.com allow you to search for images that are for public use under a Creative Commons license. Be sure to read the license closely and always give attribution to the photographer.

CLOSE WITH A QUESTION

End with something that invites interaction in the comments section below the post. Something as simple as "What do you think?" is fine, but even better is something more specific to entice your readers to share a bit about themselves. On this post example, you might ask, "So what's the job you always wish you could do for a day?" or "What's the worst (or best) job you ever had?"

_____

_____

_____

OTHER HELPFUL ADVICE FOR BLOG CONTRIBUTORS

Brevity is best. On the Web, short trumps long. Blog posts that meander tend to get tedious, so shorter is generally preferable. Your post should not have to be the blog equivalent of *War and Peace:* It need only to be long enough to

(Continued)

(Continued)

convey your message. (Sometimes even a single paragraph can work.)

Respond to comments. After your blog post goes live, keep an eye out for comments. Respond to them as quickly as you can. (Kodak suggests eight hours, but we recommend an hour or two, if you can manage it.)

Shout it! Spread the word! Tell your family! Your friends! Facebook! LinkedIn! Let your network know your post is live; generate excitement for the post and earn some well-deserved kudos.

CHAPTER 12

If Webinars Are Awesome Marketing Tools, Why Do Most of Them Suck?

Webinar (n): A kind of online conference that each participant experiences remotely at his or her own computer, connected to other attendees and the event via the Internet. It is typically one-way, from the speaker to the audience, with limited audience interaction.

First off, we apologize for the slightly crude headline. But it's a headline writ in frustration.

Here's why: Webinars are a wonderfully robust and lively marketing tool, and an effective way to reach your prospects or buyers. Or rather, they *can* be; a 2009 study by Business.com found that a whopping 67 percent of business leaders who rely on social media for business information seek out relevant podcasts or webinars.[1]

That stat screams opportunity. And at least some businesses are responding; research by Outsell shows that B2B companies plan to increase their spending to produce webinar-related

---

[1] www.marketingprofs.com/charts/2009/3254/howsmall-businesses-leaders-use-socialmedia

Figure 12.1   Most Webinars Look Something Like This

content by 26 percent, according to its survey of more than 1,000 U.S. companies.[2]

So if webinars are so awesome, then why do many tragically underperform? Why is it that so many webinars remind us of the sad visage of the middle-aged former high school valedictorian, now tending customers and his broken dreams at his hometown gas station? (See Figure 12.1.)

Webinars, of course, are web-based seminars for viewing or listening to online. They are typically a combination of audio and PowerPoint, although they sometimes incorporate video, too.

Webinars take place on web conferencing platforms, which can be either an application downloaded onto each attendee's computer or a web-based platform. The attendees access the meeting by a link or meeting invitation distributed by the webinar host.

Attendees and the businesses that host them love webinars because they can be:

- *Robust.* Webinars are fun, engaging, and dynamic. In other words, they act and feel more tangibly *alive* than, say, a white paper or case study. Attendees can hear the speaker,

---

[2] www.marketingprofs.com/charts/2010/3476/digital-marketing-spend-to-surpass-print-in-2010

watch the slides (or video), and, in short, interact with the content you produce in a whole new way.

- *Interactive and social.* Done right, webinars feel like real-world classrooms or conference rooms. Participants get a chance to ask questions, as well as chat with the speaker, the moderator, and each other. Outside of the webinar itself, participants can interact on social back channels like Twitter (which only amplifies their visibility, of course).

- *Less intimidating.* Maybe your prospects aren't quite ready to field a call from your sales team, but they are happy to hear what you are all about in a no-pressure webinar in which they are one of many.

- *Affordable.* As online conferencing technology has evolved, the cost of the platforms has increasingly come down. Webinars are especially reasonable when you compare the cost of an online seminar with the cost (not to mention hassle!) of holding an in-person event.

- *Broad-reaching.* which means you can accommodate far more people, too. Instead of inviting a few prospects to an in-person event, you can invite hundreds to a virtual one.

- *Geographically neutral.* It doesn't matter whether the people you are trying to reach are in Dubuque or Dubai. They can all be accommodated at a virtual event.

- *A team player in the content mix.* Webinars can be reimagined as many things, including podcasts, articles, blog posts, or on-demand events.

- *Effective.* Remember that earlier stat from Business.com? Further research from RainToday backs it up: Event or conference presentations rate second to referrals and personal awareness as the top method for how professional services companies initially identify the firms they work with.[3]

---

[3] "How Clients Buy: 2009 Benchmark Report on Professional Services Marketing & Selling from the Client Perspective," www.raintoday.com/howclientsbuy.cfm.

- *Door openers.* Webinars give you a reason to reach out to prospects by phone or e-mail both before and after an event.

Sounds great, right? But of course, all that is accurate and sustainable only when the content of the webinar itself really grooves. Unfortunately, webinars often suck, for various reasons:

- *They are free events focused more on lead generation than value.* Too many webinars promise great content, but the sponsors or hosts don't really push the speaker to deliver on that promise. Rather, the sponsors care more about getting names to feed the sales funnel, or they want to use the webinar as a platform to sell their products or services. (This is what our friend Sean Howard calls getting "pitch-slapped.") "In the end, that hurts the credibility of the sponsor [and] the speaker, and makes everyone suspicious of the value of any 'free' webinar," says Shelley Ryan, who was instrumental in growing the online seminar program at MarketingProfs and now runs KillerWebinars.com out of Houston, Texas.

- *Speakers don't understand that presenting online is not the same as being in front of a live audience.* It's harder to present online, to an invisible audience, than it is to present in person. You can't look people in the eye or feed off of the room's energy; you also have to have exceptional content, because the content itself is what will engage your prospects. You can't compensate for boring, unprofessional-looking slides or a monotone voice with your winsome good looks and personality. "Online, you must keep the attention of people's eyes *and* ears," Shelley Ryan says. "Otherwise, they're checking e-mail and reading their horoscopes."

- *No one asked, "What if we have to emergency-land in the Hudson?"* Live webinars are still vulnerable to technical glitches, or a no-show speaker, or a rough presentation style, Shelley says. Practice, test, rehearse, and plan for a possible disaster. *Just in case*.

MarketingProfs has been producing webinars since 2003, which is forever in Internet time. Since every Internet year is equal in time to a dog year—that's how quickly the technology evolves—a seven-year tenure installs MarketingProfs as a clear veteran in the business of creating, producing, and marketing webinars. What follows is a blueprint for generating webinars that ignite your business, based on the lessons learned by MarketingProfs—as gleaned from interviews with Shelley Ryan as well as Vice President Valerie Frazee—in addition to experiences of other leaders in the space.

How to Create and Produce Awesome Webinars

Here are 25 keys to creating webinars to ignite your business.

CREATE

Follow this prescription to conceive of a single webinar or a webinar program:

1. *Ask, "What's keeping our customers up at night?"* Like any of the content you produce, the first question of content development is always, "What information do our customers or prospects want? What problems are keeping them up at night? How can we help?"

   You probably already have a sense of what the burning issues are for your customers, but for some a quick assessment of other content you're producing—like popular blog posts or most downloaded white papers or ebooks—can confirm what resonates with buyers.

2. *Create momentum.* Your goal should be to educate or inspire your customers, to be a resource and educator, but also to make it clear that you are there for them when they're ready to buy. What do you want your audience to take away? What do you want them to do?

"A key advantage to a webinar is that it allows you to start turning content into a relationship immediately," says Patrick Cahill, a partner in Rally Point Webinars, out of Boston and San Francisco. "Ask, 'What topics will spark more conversations with would-be clients?'" Patrick says.

3. *Go big, or go tactical.* MarketingProfs produces two flavors of webinars: how-to webinars that offer specific, tactical information, and (alternatively) big-thinking, inspirational, or high-level strategic seminars, often featuring big names in business or marketing rock stars.

An example of the former would be "A Killer Facebook Fan Page: Building It, Keeping It Fresh, and Integrating It into Your Marketing" or "Today's Top 5 SEO Essentials"; in the second category would be a seminar like Jeremiah Owyang's "Scaling Social Business: How Brands Can Build Their Business Now (and Position for What's Next in Social Media)."

Similarly, many companies create broadly appealing webinars to generate broad awareness and leads, and then host smaller affairs to a more qualified base of prospects. (The webinar for this second group might include a product demo, for example. The first would likely not.)

4. *Create your webinar registration form wisely.* If you're focused on lead generation, select form fields that capture relevant information and start to flag the hottest leads, without making the form so long and cumbersome that the visitor will abandon registration. And think about your long-term goals. Do you, for example, anticipate making this webinar a series? If so, consider adding a check box for opting in to future offerings and webinar invites.

5. *Write the story.* In his book *Beyond Bullet Points* (Microsoft Press, 2007), Cliff Atkinson points out that starting to create your presentation in PowerPoint before you have your key points and logical flow worked out is like a movie director hiring actors and starting to film before there is a script in hand.

A really good webinar needs foundational structure and support. Don't start by firing up PowerPoint; start by mapping out an outline of both your story and quick ideas for accompanying charts and photos. You can use Word, a notebook, a whiteboard, or chalk on the sidewalk. The point is to write down key points and assemble them into some sort of structure. *Presentation Zen* (New Riders, 2008) author Garr Reynolds calls this "planning analog": "Though you may be using digital technology when you deliver your presentation, the act of speaking and connecting to an audience—to persuade, sell, or inform—is very much analog," he says.[4]

6. *Show; don't tell.* Webinars allow you to marry voice, images, and sound and create something that teems with life. This is a boon especially to B2B companies or service firms, which are often selling an intangible thing that a buyer can't easily connect with.

   So show; don't tell. Use case studies, client stories, or colorful anecdotes to express your ideas and thoughts. Show your products or services in action as they help customers do their jobs better, run faster, jump higher, or whatever. Doing so makes your business human and accessible, because it explains your business in a way people can relate to.

7. *Have compelling slides.* Telling a great story extends into the slides you create, so your PowerPoint should be visually compelling. Here are some easy but powerful PowerPoint tricks:
   - *Streamline your slides.* Don't crowd your slides with tiny text that's hard to read. It's far better to create a companion handout with detailed information than it is to deliver text-heavy, dense slides. A good rule of thumb is to use a font no smaller than 32 point (which is ginormous; the font you are reading now is closer to 11 point). With

---

[4] www.garrreynolds.com/Presentation/prep.html

a font that size, you won't have room to say much on the slide—which is, of course, the point.

- *Offer one idea per slide.* Don't toss too much at your audience at once. Package your story with one idea on one slide at one time.

- *Use authentic video and images.* Boring stock images on presentations (or in other marketing materials, for that matter) detract from your presentation. Don't let your slides look like everyone else's. Seek out images or video from actual customers or employees, or look for interesting public images—for example, search Flickr to find unique images. (Go to http://flickr.com/search/advanced and search only within the Creative Commons license that allows use with proper attribution to the original photographer. And then, of course, remember to give attribution in your presentation.)

8. *This is a really important, critical point!* You felt compelled to read this particular point, right? That was because it carries a compelling title, and titles are important! In fact, titles are as important on webinars as headlines are on blog posts or articles. Your webinar title is both the promise of what an attendee can expect the content to be and an indication of how it will be presented.

   For example, which of these two seminar titles draws you in? "Insights from Social Media Research" or "The Naked Truth: What's Hype, What's Not in Social Media." (For more on writing great headlines, see Chapters 11 and 13.)

9. *Find a compelling speaker.* Your webinar might rely on a guest speaker who will present to your audience for a fee or for free (in the latter case, usually in exchange for the publicity). You could tap the tried and true: recognized experts or high-profile thought leaders, legends, gurus, sages, teachers, web-lebrities, academic professors, or book authors. But sometimes those people work the circuit and so might not say anything that your audience hasn't heard before or couldn't hear elsewhere.

A great way to uncover lesser-known but equally compelling talent is to practice what Ann calls social prospecting on sites like SlideShare or YouTube. Search keywords relevant to your industry to find people who have something to say and who can say it in a fresh way. Whatever approach you take, establish clear expectations and guidelines with any speaker, Shelley Ryan says. Set expectations early, and don't give in (too much), she adds. (By the way, social prospecting on other platforms is also a great way to uncover people with a passion for creating content. That's how Ann finds many of the contributors to MarketingProfs.)

10. *Moderators matter.* Choose your moderator wisely. A good, responsive moderator can make the difference between an awesome and an awful webinar. "A good moderator improves the experience for the audience," says Shelley. That includes keeping things moving at an energetic, brisk clip; paying attention to feedback or audience chat (and responding both publicly and privately to specific audience comments); and managing the questions from the audience (knowing when to interrupt the speaker to ask a clarifying question, for example, or posting relevant links in the chat window from resources referred to during the presentation). That person also moderates the Q&A period at the end or throughout the presentation.

This isn't as easy as it sounds. Sometimes attendees ask unintentionally vague or inarticulate questions, and it's important to "get at the question behind the question," Shelley says. "Of course, you also have to ignore the stupid or inappropriate questions."

11. *What about video?* If your Eeb conference platform supports video, go for it *only* if the video is short and it's truly relevant to the topic. It's tempting to include video just because you can, even though it might not further the narrative. Also, be aware of how different formats of video are experienced by the audience. For instance, there are two kinds of Flash video files—SWF and FLV. With an SWF file, *you* have control over when it starts. With an FLV, the

audience has player controls. That can really throw off a presentation.

And one more thing: Even today there are still people with slow Internet connections. Keep in mind that your video might still be queuing up for them right when you're ready to move on to the next slide. Warn those people ahead of time.

12. *Practice and rehearse.* Schedule a rehearsal ahead of the live webinar date to run through procedures, and go over the flow of the webinar itself. Specifically, make sure the speaker and moderator are comfortable with the platform and controls, test that their Internet connections and hardware are stable, and check whether the speaker's slides look and perform as expected.

You don't have to run through the entire presentation, but it can help to have your speaker at least start the presentation, to be sure he or she is comfortable both advancing slides and speaking in a natural, conversational tone with that invisible audience. Be sure to avoid the dreaded bedtime-story type of webinar, in which a speaker reads the words on the slide rather than telling the story in his or her own words. That is particularly grating for attendees, who likely read faster than the speaker speaks.

13. *Reimagine your webinar.* Plan to reimagine your webinar in various ways, just as you would any other content you produce. The team at Rally Point Webinars lays out what a reimagined webinar might look like. Here are their thoughts, which we've amended slightly:

○ *Pre-webinar article.* Before the presentation, send prospects an article or publish a blog post that gives prospects an idea of what to expect and helps drive them to register for the event. *Tip:* Split your list and test two article titles to see which generates greater interest. The one that draws more interest is the one you use or adapt for the webinar title.

○ *Pre-webinar podcast.* Interview the speaker about the topic of his webinar. An interview feels more lively than an article, and it also becomes a teaser for the upcoming event. Pre-webinar podcasts also boost attendance: Avaya CMO Paul Dunay says that publishing a podcast on the registration page of a webinar can increase the conversion rate from 10 percent to up to 50 percent.[5]

○ *On-demand webinar*. Record your event and offer access to it, on demand, on your web site. Over time, your company can build a library of on-demand events.

○ *PowerPoint presentation PDF*. People like printing a hard copy of the presentation slides. We don't really understand why, but they do.

○ *Webinar transcript*. Consider having your webinar transcribed, and offer the text as a download from the site or as a special offer to those who attend. You can also use the transcript to create smaller pieces of content: one or more (or a series!) of blog posts, for example. You can inexpensively outsource transcription to a virtual assistant. Many of them will use voice recognition software for a first pass and then edit to clean it up. Or try a transcription service such as CastingWords.com, which charges $0.75 to $2.50 per minute.

○ *Post-webinar podcast*. Excerpt the Q&A from the webinar as its own separate podcast, or interview the speaker to get responses to unanswered questions from the Q&A.

○ *Post-webinar articles, or follow-up blog post*. Publishing additional stuff based on the webinar gives you another way to extend the life of the webinar online and keep it active.

PRODUCE

14. *Encourage audience members to interact*. You might have attended webinars that don't: An attendee types

---

[5] Social Media to Market and Sell Professional Services—An Interview with Paul Dunay," www.raintoday.com/podcastepisode14.cfm, via Rally Point Webinars).

a question or comment into a tiny box, then wonders whether anybody on the other side noticed it. Better web conferencing tools allow everyone attending the webinar to chat live during the presentation, using a window alongside the main presentation screen. This kind of webinar has a whole different feel, because it gives participants a sense of community and a shared group experience.

If it sounds a little scary to share everyone's comments and questions, you can usually moderate that Q&A chat, too. Most conferencing tools will let you moderate the commentary by selecting what to show and what to keep out of the stream, Shelley says. Some web conferencing tools even let you control callers who want to submit audio questions by phone, but more webinars rely on text interaction.

By the way, some audience members will find the chat an annoying distraction. When MarketingProfs surveys its audience, 85 percent generally love the interaction and 15 percent typically hate it. Eliminate the distraction for those 15 percent; suggest that they switch the slides to full-screen mode to hide all the chatter coming from the rest of the audience.

15. *Encourage speaker-attendee interaction.* Build some interaction into the presentation itself, too. Stop to answer incoming questions instead of saving them for the end. Add a relevant poll or two. "No one wants to have a one-way conversation in this Web 2.0 era," Shelley says.

Draw attendees out by reaching out to each of them during the webinar itself, via private chat (if your platform allows it). "Ask, 'Are you getting value out of this presentation? Do you have any questions for the speaker?'" suggests Patrick Cahill.

Depending on the size of the audience, that might necessitate more hands on deck. In a modest-sized 200-person webinar, for example, that might mean up to six staffers on hand to work the room and reach out to individual attendees. That sounds like a lot, maybe, but Patrick says it's worth the trouble: "It's a little thing, but it adds tremendous value to upping the level of response and engagement."

16. *Encourage chat on social back channels.* Make it easy for those active on Twitter to talk about it there, either before or during the presentation. Creating a short, searchable companion hashtag allows people to find and share nuggets of information about your webinar. A hashtag is a kind of Twitter shorthand that groups related tweets with a single phrase or word preceded by the hash symbol (#). Twitter hashtags like the well-known #followfriday (or #ff) or #marketermonday help spread information on Twitter while also helping to organize it. As you might imagine, it's an especially favorite tool of conferences and event organizers.

Some web conferencing platforms are experimenting with incorporating live tweets—for example, enabling attendees to post comments directly from the webinar to Twitter, LinkedIn, and Facebook.

17. *Record your event.* One of the biggest advantages of web conferencing software is that it allows you to record the live event, including audio, slide presentations, Q&A sessions, and polling results. You can then reimagine that recording in various ways to deliver maximum return on investment from your webinar.

18. *Optimize for sharing.* Upload your webinar presentation and slide notes to SlideShare, and make sure they are optimized for search there. Use keywords in the presentation title and transcript. Tag your slides with plenty of relevant words so that users can find your content during searches.

19. *Spread it around.* The SlideShare site (www.slideshare .net) isn't the only place you can embed your SlideShare presentation: Load the SlideShare application onto your LinkedIn profile. The same thing goes for your Facebook page or company fan page. Embed the SlideShare widget into your web site's home page or blog.

Two other ideas: Add narrative to your slides with Slidecasting (www.slideshare.net/faqs/slidecast). You'll have to record the audio MP3 separately; Slidecasting will synchronize the slides and audio. And finally, SlideShare offers businesses an option—for a fee—to set up custom, branded microsites (essentially, a company channel). Doing so allows you a central resource for PowerPoint presentations, white papers, and webinars.

20. *Carefully craft your final slide.* Your final slide is a kind of visual takeaway for attendees, so be sure the slide visually inspires whatever next steps you want attendees to take. Usually the final slides in presentations are among the lamest or ugliest. But think of your final slide as the last word in a book or final point in a blog post: Create a slide that either converts browsers into buyers or inches them closer to doing so.

For a simpler sale, give your audience a link with a compelling limited-time discount offer. For a more complex sale, offer related content that furthers engagement— perhaps a downloadable checklist or worksheet or a companion guide.

Online marketing strategist Bob DiStefano ends his webinars by offering attendees a link for a free web site checkup, which applies the concepts he teaches in a webinar in a specific, relevant, personal way.

21. *Plan for a disaster.* You might have rehearsed and planned to within an inch of your life, but still stuff happens, right? You may not be called upon to land a plane in the Hudson River, but you should plan for the unforeseen and mitigate where you can.

For example: Get your speakers' cell phone or emergency numbers in case they don't show; be sure they have their slides printed out so they can present from paper if they lose their Internet connection; have a message prepared in the unlikely (but still possible) event that there's a total crash of the web conferencing platform. As with any disaster, preparedness is key.

22. *Get feedback.* Create a short survey (five questions tops) to get feedback from attendees on the quality of the content and their satisfaction with the overall experience. Include a survey link on the final seminar slide but start mentioning it early, before attendees start signing off (or before Q&A ends). It's important to encourage attendees to click through immediately, while the event is fresh in their minds, rather than e-mailing the survey link later.

   A key question MarketingProfs asks, which serves as the basis for its five-star rating metric, is this: "Would you recommend this seminar to a friend?" It's important to do something with the aggregated responses quickly, so the audience believes you when you say you really do care about their responses. MarketingProfs posts the star rating on the webinar library page usually within 24 hours.

23. *Follow up promptly.* Follow up within a day of the event, either by phone or by e-mail (or both, Patrick Cahill says). Include any promised collateral, including copies of the presentations, the link to the recorded session, and so on. "Extend the relationship still in the teaching mode," Patrick says. In other words, the approach is not "Can we offer you a demo?" but rather, "Do you have any new questions that have gone unanswered?"

   It's also important to follow up with those people who missed the live presentation, too, and offer a link to the recorded session. (And by the way, capture the same registration information for the on-demand session as you would for the live event; you want to qualify these leads just as you would any others.) You can also include links to any postevent content you produce, like a podcast of the audio, an article by the author, or a transcript of the Q&A.

24. *Measure your event's success.* Watch your audience behavior in each webinar—are they logging out early or sticking around? (If the speaker isn't keeping their attention, you might not want to invite that speaker back.)

After the event, track the number of registrants and the attendance rate, the quality of leads generated, and the rate at which they converted to buyers. Compare them to past events or predetermined targets to gauge your event's success.

25. *One final thing*. . . . Notice how we got all the way through this list and didn't mention how to choose a technology platform? That's because this is a book about content, not technology. But here's some fundamental advice: You have many web conferencing technology platform options, including On24, Citrix GoToWebinar, Adobe Connect Pro, Microsoft's LiveMeeting, and Cisco's WebEx. Many are good, but none is perfect. Don't be intimidated by price or swayed by salespeople—find, test, and pay for only the features you actually need.

"A Rose by Any Other Name. . ."

Should you call your online seminar a *webinar*? Or should you call it something else—like *virtual conference*, or *online conference*, or *web seminar*, or another thing entirely?[6]

When MarketingProfs launched its webinar program in 2003, it intentionally avoided using the word *webinar* because it conjured up hard-sell, lead-generation events that focused more on harvesting names and less on providing any real value to any attendees. Because MarketingProfs webinars were not lead-generation vehicles, it termed them *online seminars* to emphasize the educational value and disassociate them from the hucksters and smarmy Ginsu salesmen.

---

[6] Avoid using webcasting or screencasting, however, which refer to slightly different animals: A webcast refers usually to a video broadcast that's streamed over the Internet. A screencast is a digital video of a series of screen captures, usually with audio narration.

In a test on Which Test Won? (http://whichtestwon.com/navigation-bar-test), Anne Holland shares the results of an A/B comparison test between two versions of MailChimp's web site navigation menus. One version of the site used the term *Webinars* as a header, while the second site used the phrase *Online Training*.

In the test, the phrase *Online Training* increased visitor click-throughs from the support page to the target webinar page 10.4 percent. The company also tested *Live Training* and *MailChimp Training,* as well. In those cases, too, *Webinars* lost, Anne writes, adding, "Obviously, although all these words could be used to describe the same thing, certain words resonated better with the audience."

So does that mean you should toss out the *webinar* moniker in favor of *online training*? Not necessarily, says Shelley Ryan. "I used to hate the word 'webinars' because it meant 'waste of time' with all the lame lead-gen events out there," she says. But of late, as more businesses have gotten into the webinar game (including MarketingProfs; it now hosts both lead-gen webinars and member-only webinars). As such, Shelley adds, the quality of programs has improved, and *webinar* has become useful shorthand that conveys quick, actionable, online learning.

"'Webinar' is being used like Kleenex already," she says, "and there's no turning back."

CHAPTER 13

What's the Difference between an Ebook and a White Paper? (And When Should You Use Them?)

> *White paper* (n): An authoritative report or guide that often addresses issues and how to solve them. White papers are often used to educate readers and help people make decisions.

> *Ebook* (n): Simply, a book published electronically, designed to be downloaded and either read on a screen or printed.

Mostly, the differences between a white paper and an ebook are in style and tone.

A white paper (sometimes called a *research report*, *summary*, or *technical brief*) plays it straight. It is usually a topical report focused on a single central issue—for example, an emerging trend. White papers tend to be longish (10 to 12 pages) and geared to a technically specific audience—and B2B companies love them.

Ebooks—like Kadient's *Dive Deeper into Your Sales Metrics: Four Ways to Discover Hidden Sales Treasure* (see Chapter 23) are looser, more playful, and wholly more novel (no pun intended). An ebook might be just as long as a white paper—or longer—but with an engaging theme, appealing design, and layout dominated by bold text treatments and callouts.

Jonathan Kranz, author of *Writing Copy for Dummies* (John Wiley & Sons, 2004) and owner of the Boston-based Kranz Communications, puts it this way: "I think of white papers as the man in the gray flannel suit: an official who wants to establish authority by demonstrating what he knows in a formal, even pedantic manner." The ebook, meanwhile, "is the colleague in a Hawaiian shirt who sits next to you at the hotel bar, eager to be helpful and willing to share insights hard won through experience."

Adds Michael Stelzer, the author of *Writing White Papers* (WhitePaperSource Publishing, 2006), which also publishes SocialMediaExaminer.com, sees little difference between today's ebooks and white papers, except that some publisher "dressed up a white paper and put some makeup on it, and called it an ebook!" They are more alike than not, in other words, because they "both address a specific problem or trend that your customers will care about," Michael says.

At a glance:

White Papers	Ebooks
Long and linear—a deep read	Broken into smaller chunks—designed for skimming and scanning
Data-centric, often based on formal research	Concept-centric, based on ideas and trends of interest
Text-heavy	Visually heavy; main text is supplemented with callouts, bulleted lists
Formal, impressive; expert talks down to you	Casual and collegial; a conversation among equals

"Keep in mind these boundaries are murky," adds Jonathan. "Many ebooks will be based on research, for example, and many white papers may include illustrations and graphs," as well as customer success stories or checklists or other callouts. "But in general, the ebook is designed to be reader-friendly, while the white paper is intended to be conspicuously 'authoritative.'"

(In the publishing world, of course, *ebook* is short for electronic book, or the digital version of a conventional printed book. Marketers have usurped the term for their own use, but be aware that the use of the terms might cause some confusion for non-marketers within your clientele or organization.)

In either case, either white papers or ebooks are most appropriate to organizations that[1]:

- Want to transform an invisible quality—such as expertise or intellectual capital—into a tangible value.

- Need to educate people before they can possibly become customers.

- Have a product or service that demands thoughtful consideration (and even research) on the part of potential customers.

- Manage long sales cycles between initial contact and signed contracts.

- Speak to multiple levels of influencers before convincing decision makers.

- Work within an industry hungry for new or high-quality information.

- Sit on a wealth of intriguing customer success stories.

- Will eagerly promote the white paper or ebook through multiple channels: web sites, e-mail, blogs and other social media, media kits, and so on.

Either may not be such a great idea for organizations that:

- Sell products or services that do not require customer research or deep thought: Do you sell nuts and bolts, lobster

---

[1] Adapted from Jonathan Kranz, *The Ebook Ebook: How to Turn Your Expertise into Magnetic Marketing Material* (2009), www.kranzcom .com/ebookebook.pdf.

rolls, or beer cozies? Neither a white paper nor an ebook is a good option.

- Compete primarily on price or convenience, not on quality or innovation.
- Depend on impulse buys or simple commodity sales.
- Lack ideas or stories to tell.
- Will not (or cannot) promote the finished product. (And if this is the case for you, I hope you are spending a lot of time on LinkedIn networking for a new job.)

Nine Steps to Creating an Ebook or White Paper That People Will Want to Read

Is one of the two (or both) right for you? Great! Here are nine guidelines to producing great work.

1. *Pay special mind to Content Rule Number 6: Share or solve; don't shill.*

Obviously, the subject of your ebook or white paper should be something of value for your audience. What do your customers care about? How could your brand help them in their daily lives?

An ebook or white paper, especially, gives you lots of room to position your brand as a reliable and value source of vendor-agnostic information. That last part about being vendor-agnostic is critical, because you want to solve a problem for them or share a resource or two—not shill. Tell; don't sell.

Robert Half Asia publishes a slick, helpful ebook, *How to Conduct Successful Interviews*, covering topics like how you might spot when someone is exaggerating or covering up the truth in a job interview and listing questions a hiring manager should *not* ask. As a staffing company, Robert Half wants to get on the radar of hiring managers, and its ebook is designed to help the managers be more effective in their jobs, while at the same time effectively positioning itself as a resource to them.[2]

---

[2] www.scribd.com/doc/28228809/eBook-How-to-conduct-successful-interviews

Pet Expertise, which sells dog training supplies and natural chews, wrote a very useful ebook called *Basic Manners for the Family Dog*.[3] As the title suggests, it offers simple, direct advice with plenty of checklists to help people enjoy their pets and eliminate annoying or destructive behaviors. In other words, it's not about the products they sell; it's about helping readers have more fun with their dogs.

2. *Have a little fun*.

With their concept-driven format and graphical elements, ebooks in particular cry out for a fun, relaxed approach. (Yes, even if you are a B2B company.) Write in a friendly, conversational style that ties into an interesting, engaging theme.

Blue Sky Factory's *Ultimate Guide to Email* ebook is built around a martial arts theme, offering e-mail marketing campaign strategies and tactics geared to e-mail newbies ("white belts"), casual e-mailers ("black belts"), or battle-worn ninjas who seek more advanced advice.[4]

3. *Show; don't just tell*.

So many ebooks and white papers are bloodless. There's no living, breathing characters for us to care about or relate to. Your ebook should tell the story of how your product lives in the world, based on examples and situations throughout.

Consider the approach *Saved by a Hard Cover* takes. (See Figure 13.1.) Published by Friends of the Los Feliz Library, the content powerfully but simply advocates sustaining funding for Los Angeles Public Library branches by celebrating the role city libraries play in the lives of families. Instead of quoting circulation stats or usage rates, the group chose to tell its story more powerfully by collecting first-person essays, poems, and drawings by the children whose lives have been enriched by the Los Angeles library system.[5]

4. *Give it an intriguing title*.

Title your ebook with something that piques readers' curiosity and entices them to read more. If you worry that a title based more on intrigue won't give enough context to attract a would-

---

[3] www.petexpertise.com/dog-trainingebook.pdf
[4] www.blueskyfactory.com/ultimate
[5] www.scribd.com/doc/33603271/Saved-by-a-Hard-Cover

Figure 13.1   Saved by a Hard Cover

be reader, use a descriptive subtitle to spell out what the ebook delivers. (A descriptive subtitle is a good place to affix search terms or keywords that your would-be readers are monitoring and searching for.)

Some ways to create an intriguing ebook title are to:

- Pique curiosity: *What the Bible Says about Sex*, an ebook published by Global Christians.

- Simplify a complex subject comprehensively: *How to Create Killer Sales Playbooks* (see Chapter 23); or Marketo's *A Definitive Guide to Social Media*; or Acxiom's white paper, *Losing Money in the Mail*, which talks about how flawed data lead to wasted opportunities.

- Tell a story: Ron Ploof's ebook, *The Ranger Station Fire*, isn't about an actual fire; rather, it tells the story of how Ford Motor Company used social media to extinguish a public relations "conflagration."

- Use unexpected or curious analogies: *Seven Infectious Diseases of B2B Marketing—and Their Cures*, by marketer Kathryn Roy, pairs the notion of disease with marketing mistakes; *Getting to First Base: A Social Media Marketing Playbook*, by Darren Barefoot and Julie Szabo, links social media marketing and dating, and the classic *Healthy Mouth, Healthy Sex!*, by Boston dentist Dr. Helaine Smith, explores the connection between oral health and sexual well-being.

- Challenge conventional wisdom: *You're* Not *Lifting Your Head*, by golf pro Charlie King (see Chapter 19), challenges the notion that golfers who lift their head or take their eyes off the ball will miss the shot.

5. *Design matters.*

The visual nature of both ebooks and white papers means you may want to consider a professional to give your documents an inviting, lively look. The best-designed ebooks orient to landscape format (horizontal); white papers tend to orient to portrait format (vertical). Landscape design actually works better for screen reading, as well as visually differentiating your ebook from a white paper or collection of case studies, for example. In either case, punctuate the document with plenty of visual points of interest; callouts, bullets, headers, shaded text boxes, sidebars, small images, and so on break up potentially dense text and make for easy skimming. Also, use plenty of white space to give your content breathing room, rather than packing it all in shoulder to shoulder, like a subway car at rush hour.

Many people find it easiest to use a presentation software tool such as Keynote or PowerPoint to lay out their ebooks. To find affordable images, look to online stock photography retailers such as iStockphoto.com.

Pay attention to interactivity, too. Because most documents will be read or skimmed on a screen, include a live table of contents, in which each chapter heading or section is hotlinked to the corresponding text. When referencing something else online, be sure to hyperlink to it so that your readers can find out more. And include plenty of social bling. (We talk about that next.)

6. *Encourage sharing with social bling.*

The Content Rule to give your content wings and roots applies to ebooks and white papers, as well. To encourage readers to share your ebook freely, slap a Creative Commons license on it. Doing so lets people know that, although the material is copyrighted, they can also pass it around.

Include various social media sharing icons to encourage readers to give it wings—figuratively, to share an ebook through Twitter, Facebook, LinkedIn, and e-mail. Just the mere presence of e-mail and social sharing icons on ebook PDFs subtly reminds readers to readily share when it might not have occurred to them otherwise, writes Galen De Young at MarketingProfs.

The more seamless you make that process, of course, the more likely a reader will follow through, Galen adds. So make sure that any sharing options you embed in PDFs populate in the sharing platform. In other words, if you want readers to post to Twitter about your PDF, set it to launch Twitter and populate the tweet for them. They can edit the Twitter post if they wish, but in any case it's a good foundation. Include a Twitter hashtag as well, so you can reach people who follow the hashtag. (For more detail on social media sharing options, check out Galen's post on MarketingProfs: www.mpdailyfix.com/do-your-pdfs-have-embedded-sharing-options)

Give some thought to the tweet you create, too. Just like your ebook headline, it should offer some intrigue to encourage others to download it, too. Finally, be sure to also include a shortened

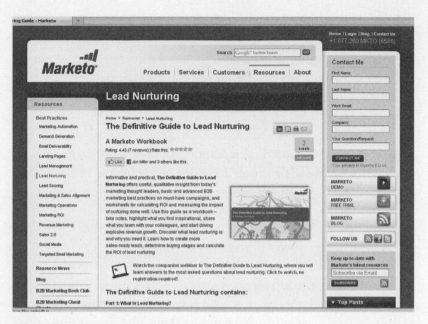

Figure 13.2   Ebook Landing Page

and trackable URL—through bit.ly or goo.gl—rather than making the sharer create one on her own. (For more on creating Twitter posts, see page 107.)

7. *Create a landing page.*

Create a landing page from which people can download your ebook. On it, you'll want to include compelling copy that sells the ebook, of course. Trick the page out with other bits of bling, too.

Marketing lead management company Marketo includes lots of elements that act as social validation for visitors who come to its ebook landing pages (and, actually, all of its content pages).

In addition to the standard explanatory content, Marketo adds a Facebook Like icon, TweetMeme's Retweet button, printing, e-mail, and other bookmarking and sharing options. (See Figure 13.2.) It also shows the number of views each ebook or other content has received, as well as a star-ranking system that allows users to rate content on anywhere from one to five stars. Marketo also includes testimonials specific to that piece of content from recognizable names or companies and allows others to comment, as well.

Finally, it relies on a tool called Box.net to embed a portion of the ebook on the landing page itself, allowing potential readers to flip through the first 10 pages to see if it fits their needs or expectations, says Marketo's Maria Pergolino. "We try to give readers as much information as possible on each ebook or other piece of content, to help them make an informed decision on whether it suits them," she adds.

8. *Promote like mad.*

You know what to do here, right? Feature the ebook prominently as a download on your web site, blog about it on your blog, tweet it on Twitter, and talk it up on Facebook and on LinkedIn; get the word out however you can. One tip: When you promote the ebook to your audience or to the press, analysts, or bloggers, send them a download link directly, rather than the PDF itself, so that you can track the number of downloads.

9. *What about requiring registration?*

So now you have an ebook or an online white paper that's compelling, well-written, informative, nicely laid out, and tricked-out with social bling. You've packaged it for download from a sweet-looking landing page, because the next step is to deliver it to your audience. But what's the best approach to get it into their hot little hands?

There are two schools of thought when it comes to delivery:

1. The traditional approach holds that, in exchange for the download, marketers collect names and pertinent contact information through some sort of registration roadblock. The idea, of course, is that they can use the names to market to later. You measure the success of your ebook or white paper by the number of registration forms you collect.

2. The second approach, encouraged by people like David Meerman Scott, says that collecting names is old school and shortsighted. It's better, David and others say, to "lose control" of your marketing and allow your ideas to spread virally, rather than hiding them behind a registration page. The impact of lots of people talking about you online ultimately pays off more handsomely, although you'll measure success differently: in the number of downloads or in the

number of bloggers or Twitter users talking about you as they pass your content around.

The first approach is difficult for many marketers to embrace, because they know that the number of downloads or views of their documents goes up exponentially when they don't require an e-mail address or other personal information in exchange. They know that bloggers or Twitter users will share compelling content freely, giving them loads of link love. Obsessing over sales leads is counterproductive, they say, when the real goal is visibility with your audience. "For decades, companies have offered web content as lead bait. But the goal should be to get the word out about your organization, not to misuse the Internet for the sake of an outdated technique," says David.

The second approach is also difficult for other marketers to adopt, especially in the B2B world. This is in part because it flies against the traditional way of capturing leads and doing business and in part because marketers are always anxious to produce some concrete evidence of their own department's success, and they link a definitive value to the return on investment (ROI) question.

So who is right? And which is the right approach for your business? The bottom line is this: It depends. Or rather, it depends on your goals.

If your goal is to amass a mailing list, use the first approach. You'll get fewer downloads than you would with losing control, so the number of folks you'll reach will be smaller, of course. You won't benefit from any social media sharing love, but you will wind up with a list of people to market to. By the way, collect information only if you actually have the capacity and a plan to do something with those names rather than holding on to a vague idea of marketing to them "someday"; otherwise, you risk losing credibility when that day actually rolls around.

If your goal is to cast a wide net, use the second approach. Requiring your potential viewers to provide personal information is an ineffective strategy for casting a wide marketing net, spreading your ideas and message, and generating awareness. Losing control will allow those ideas to spread and be shared easily and will allow your leads to be people who contact you as a result.

There is, of course, a hybrid approach for businesses, whereby certain pieces of content require registration, whereas others do not. Content that is intended to drive awareness of your products and services might not be behind a registration form (who are "top of the sales funnel," in B2B-speak). Content that is geared toward educating more serious buyers who are closer to making a purchase might be behind a registration form ("further down the funnel," in B2B-speak).

So there you go. Sorry to give you the classic consultant's answer of "it depends." But it does.

CHAPTER 14

The Single Biggest Secret to Creating a Compelling Customer Success Story

(Formerly Known as a Case Study)

Case study (n): An in-depth examination of a single instance or event: a case. It provides an approach to analyzing information, and reporting the results to gain a better understanding or insight into a particular concept or idea.

Does the beginning of that headline sound like a ShamWow infomercial on late-night TV?

Perhaps! But it's dead-on accurate.

Other sections of this book have given you exhaustive recipes for creating remarkable webinars, ebooks, video, blogs, and so on. But creating a really good customer success story—also known as a case study—is a far simpler task.

Most case studies are dry, dreary articles punctuated with stats and tedious information that bore rather than inspire. They focus on product features, not the human benefits. They tend to be stuffed with self-flattery, jargon, and Franken-speak.

The keys are to tell a story the intended audience wants to hear and to tell it with one simple imperative in mind. It helps to think of them less as *case studies*, which sounds clinical and detached and bloodless, and more like *customer success stories*, which sounds human and connected.

The simple secret is this: All you really need is to tell a good story that allows your organization to embrace the role of the cape-wearing superhero.

By *story*, we don't mean *fable* or *fairy tale*, despite the super-hero analogy. Rather, we mean a *true* story about how your company's products or services have solved a problem for a customer, eased its troubles, or met its gaping maw of a need. The idea here is to establish credibility, which means talking about what your organization's products or services accomplished for a client, not about your products or services in isolation.

Focus your case study on a company or client your products or services have helped, and cast yourself as the hero. That happy and satisfied customer gives a relatable, tangible example of how your products and services live in the world, allowing readers, viewers, or listeners (depending on whether you publish the story in text, video, or audio) the opportunity to imagine themselves in the happy customer's shoes, similarly enjoying the benefits of whatever it is that you sell.

In the meantime, you are the superhero who swoops in to offer the solution to a thorny pickle, threatening adversary, or annoying hitch and who, ultimately, saves the day, winning love and admiration and business. Done well, case studies have some drama and heat and create a human, emotional link between you and your would-be customers.

Here's how:

1. *The Setup: Give some fundamental facts.*

Present—in an easy-to-scan, bulleted list—the facts of the company or customer you are profiling. If you are focusing on an organization, you might include some or all of the following. Doing so grounds your story and begins to give your readers something to relate to:

- Organization's name
- Contact person

- Location (city and state)

- Industry

- Annual revenue

- Number of employees

Keep written case studies short, or no more than one or two pages. Include a summary or a "Quick Read" header in this first section to convey the gist of the case study in a sentence or two.

2. *The Challenge: Focus on the human story.*

Tell your story from the perspective of a main character or human being—in other words, talk about actual people. Let your audience get to know and begin to care about that person (and of course, always seek permission from clients before using their names, company names, or stories). Introduce him or her by name, and set the scene right away.

State the problem or challenge that will set your story in motion: What challenge does this person have? What kind of problems is it causing in his or her life? Flesh it out a little for your audience: What does that problem cost in stress, worry, money, lost opportunities, failure to succeed?

In an article at MarketingProfs, Gail Martin describes how to craft a story that will connect with your readers ("The Secret to Creating Compelling Case Studies," MarketingProfs, February 2008).

We've borrowed shamelessly from Gail to illustrate our point: A 52-year-old woman is told that she has a myocardial infarction. The reader is informed about a series of recent surgical developments. Medical science saves the day and the woman is cured. Hooray! Sort of. Do you really care about the nameless, faceless female, though?

Now imagine a Customer Success Story: Gigi Habachi crumples to the ground with a heart attack while walking her dog. As she is wheeled into surgery, all kinds of questions go through her mind. *What if I can't go back to work? Who will take feed my parakeets if I die? Can I ever play beach volleyball again? Will I be okay?* Gigi's doctor explains to her loving and terrified family that because of a new device developed by Medi-Wow, Gigi will be up and at 'em in a matter of weeks, allowing her to resume her normal life, including participating in the Venice volleyball tournament next year.

Which story made you care? Which one helped you understand the problem in a way that lets you identify with Gigi because you can imagine yourself in the same situation?

"We need to understand what's at stake in an emotional way, and we need to be able to visualize in an equally emotional way how good it will be when the problem is solved," writes Gail. "Charts, graphs, and jargon don't do that." If you don't convey a clear picture of how terrible and scary the villain is, your audience won't care about what happens. Make sure your audience can feel the fear, she adds.

The problem you choose will depend on your target audience and what action you are trying to motivate them to take. For example, the same case study would be focused slightly differently, depending on whether the audience consists of people who would use your products or services (in the case discussed here, people like Gigi); gatekeepers looking for good products to recommend (say, a hospital administrator); or check signers who must make sure that neither problem nor solution compromises earnings and productivity (the hospital operations person), Gail says.

3. *The Solution: Be the superhero*.

A case study becomes compelling when you think about it as an adventure, writes Gail. So you have your main character, on which the story centers. The looming problem is the villain, problem, or nemesis.

Of course *(ta-da!)*, your company, product, or service is the superhero, bursting onto the scene. "Your expertise and adaptability are shown in their best light when you share some plot twists; in other words, you tell us about some of the things that didn't work when you tried to solve the problem. Anyone can solve an easy problem. It takes resourcefulness to solve one without an obvious solution. Show us your blind alleys and your flashes of inspiration," Gail writes.

4. *The Results: Live happily ever after*.

Give your audience an emotional feel for just how good life is without the stupid nemesis lurking around, the looming problem having been dusted. If you do it right, Gail says, at that point your reader is saying, "I've got to get me some of that."

You might also mention any takeaways for your audience: Emphasize key points, lessons learned, or (as we do in this book), "ideas you can steal."

5. *Imagine your story in other media—instead of or in addition to text*.

Video is a compelling way to convey the drama and emotion of a customer success story. For example, consider the video case study that Boston agency Captains of Industry created for a company called Vitality (www.vitality.net/glowcaps.html). Its product, the GlowCap, is a drug prescription bottle cap that's connected wirelessly to the Internet and is able to send alerts to remind patients when it's time to take their medicines. In the video that Captains of Industry created for Vitality, the main character is a grandfather, and the story is narrated by his granddaughter, Samantha. The video was featured on *The Colbert Report* in March 2010 as part of a segment on men's health—yet another example of how web content that's good can generate greater visibility for your products and services!

CHAPTER 15

From Dumpy to Sexy

An FAQs Makeover

The Frequently Asked Questions, or FAQ, pages are the unsung heroes of your company web site. Often unappreciated and undervalued, they can nevertheless play an essential role. What's more, they can often help easily and succinctly communicate your brand value to would-be buyers, enticing them to take a closer look at what you have to offer. So as part of your program to produce compelling content, don't ignore your FAQ pages.

An FAQ page is a web page (or series of pages) of answers to questions that visitors frequently ask about your products or services. It functions as an online customer service center, cutting down on repetitive inquiries by anticipating the questions your visitors might have.

But here's the thing: If your visitors are already mining the questions looking for answers, chances are they are already thinking of doing business with your company. So, done right, the FAQ page helps build trust, educate your customers, and ultimately further your relationship.

Write answers, not descriptions. This sounds obvious, right? Don't be tempted to slip in unnecessary product or service descriptions; focus instead on giving your visitors direct and simple answers to their questions. Just like you should approach any content on your site, write for your customer: Tell your visitors what's in it for them.

For example, what's more useful: Knowing that the new Uni-cased Sealy Posturepedic mattresses can be bent up to 15 degrees without damaging the innerspring? Or knowing that Sealy sells a mattress designed for manipulation through tight corners to the guest room at the far end of the hall?

And just because you can spend paragraphs answering every question doesn't mean you should; in general, get to the point and skip the extra words. If you really must expand, answer the question in the first paragraph; you can then go into more detail in the following. That way you satisfy both those who want a quick hit and those who want to dive in deeper.

Don't be afraid to answer the tough questions. Some sites seem to go out of their way not to address certain questions for fear that they'll open themselves up to criticism or other negative feedback. But on FAQ pages (as in life), it's better to address the elephant in the room.

For example: The vintage timepieces at Chicago's Father Time Antiques (www.fathertimeantiques.com) are a little more expensive than you might find elsewhere, and the company takes the opportunity, in its FAQs, to address exactly why:

How do you price your watches?

Our prices may be slightly higher than other watches you may find on the Internet, but this is due to our exhaustive restoration process. When one of our master watchmakers finishes with the restoration of an individual piece, it is timed to within factory specs, or better, in all original rated positions. . . . We also warranty our watches for one full year without an extra charge that some other dealers charge. Included in our price is a good quality watchband at no extra charge.

We also like how ActiveConversion (www.activeconversion .com), a Calgary-based marketing automation services company, has the guts to answer a question in its FAQs that most companies shy away from:

Who are your competitors?

We each approach solving this problem differently, but the closest competitor is Eloqua Corporation. However, their pricing is much higher and geared to large marketing departments. We are also a competitor of LeadLander.

Avoid Franken-speak. Don't use sales-y language and marketing hype on your FAQ pages, and avoid Franken-speak—convoluted text that doesn't sound like it was penned by a human. If the U.S. Copyright Office is capable of writing in a human voice (even adding in a little humor!), so are you. This is from its FAQ page:

How do I protect my sighting of Elvis?

Copyright law does not protect sightings. However, copyright law will protect your photo (or other depiction) of your sighting of Elvis. File your claim to copyright online by means of the electronic Copyright Office (eCO). Pay the fee online and attach a copy of your photo. Or, go to the Copyright Office website, fill in Form CO, print it, and mail it together with your photo and fee. For more information on registration [of] a copyright, see SL-35. No one can lawfully use your photo of your sighting, although someone else may file his own photo of his sighting. Copyright law protects the original photograph, not the subject of the photograph.

Solve; don't shill. . . . Use your FAQs first and foremost to answer your visitors' questions with authority. Answer with facts, not fluffy claims or opinions. Facts will make your visitors trust you more, which ultimately furthers the relationship more than flat-out selling does. Solve, don't shill.

Maybe Sealy is correct that a mattress is one of the best furniture investments you can make, but this answer from Sealy's FAQ page would make us feel, if we were in the market for a mattress, that they are more interested in selling a high-end mattress than meeting customers' needs. In other words, this feels more like shilling than solving:

How much should I spend on a new sleep set?

Mattress prices range greatly, from about $299 to over $5,000 for a queen set. A good night's sleep is one of the best investments you can make, so buy the best mattress you can afford. Keep in mind that most of us spend as much as one-third of our time in bed. Your investment will cost just pennies per night over the next 10 years! In fact, a $1,000 Sealy Posturepedic sleep set costs about 27 cents per night (based on a 10-year life).

...Unless you do so with your tongue planted firmly in your cheek. Clearly, some companies can get away with it, but only because of the irreverent tone of their web site and overall brand positioning. For example, this is from the FAQ page of the Barbarian Group (www.barbariangroup.com), a Boston-based advertising agency:

When should I call the Barbarians?
    Right now.

Show some personality. If it works with your brand, use your FAQ page to extend your personality, just like the Barbarian Group does. Bandcamp, a free publishing platform for bands, liberally douses its FAQs with its quirky personality.

Free!? Then how are you going to stay in business? In your answer, please use the nonword monetization at least twice.
    Our monetization strategy boils down to the simple belief that we should only make money if you make money. So, at some point in the not-too-distant future, we'll begin taking a modest cut from download and merchandise revenue.... In the meantime, we've got plenty of cash in the bank, ...a low burn rate, ...and a proud history of succeeding in the midst of a recession. (Past performance is not a guarantee of future

Figure 15.1   A Clean and Organized FAQ
Source: www.psd2html.com/faq.html

returns. Monetization strategy subject to metamorphosis. Teamocil may cause numbness of the extremities.)

Make your FAQs searchable. This is critical if the page contains lots of information or is dense with text. P2H.com, a web site coding company, has one of the cleanest and most easy-to-navigate FAQ pages we've seen. (See Figure 15.1.)

Use graphics. Many sites neglect to include graphics, art, or other social objects (like SlideShare presentations, explanatory videos, or what have you) when designing compelling FAQ pages, but there are very few that do. The FAQ page from Duke's Hartman Center outdoor advertising collection offers a few vintage images of Wrigley's and Bromo-Seltzer billboards. But graphics and, most specifically, relevant presentations, videos, or other content can help your FAQ page come alive.

Enable printing. Allow users to easily print the FAQs to keep them handy for future reference.

Encourage sharing. Consider embedding direct links in your FAQ page to each question so that it is easier for people to share answers outside of your site. Continually think of ways to make it easier for your online fans to help answer potential customers' questions.

Organize your FAQs into sections. If they are very long, this helps to make it easier on the eye and significantly less unwieldy and overwhelming for your visitors. Hershey divvies its FAQs into broad categories, including corporate questions, investor questions, nutrition issues, product queries, recipes, and so on.

Link to customer service. Another obvious one: Make sure you give your visitors another way to have their burning question addressed if the FAQs don't cut it. You could also link to product support or user guides here, if you have them. Don't bury those links; make them unmissable instead. If potential customers can't figure out how to get ahold of you now, what does that say about how hard it will be *if* they become a customer?

Ask, "Do you have a question not answered here?" In other words, offer a way for your visitors to get answers to *infrequently* asked questions! Allow visitors to suggest a question they didn't find the answer to, like the folks at WEbook do: *"This is an awesome FAQ—but what if I have more questions? Feel free to drop us a note at info@WEbook.com."*

Or here's how California's ShangriLa Furniture handles it:

I've got other questions. Where can I get information?
    Simply write info@shangrilafurnish.com or contact us through our contact form.
    Every new question will help us build a better FAQ section.

Treat your FAQ page as a doorway. Link your answers to other relevant content and information on your web site. The FAQ shouldn't be a final destination; it should be a gateway to areas deeper in your site. So link to other content on your site from within your FAQ page. Also, provide buttons and links to free trials and product tours, or to request a demo, if appropriate.

Guide Dogs for the Blind does a great job linking from its FAQ page to other content on its site to further engage its visitors. Embedded links offer up more information about training guide dogs, donating to the cause, or fostering puppies.

Similarly, be sure your FAQ page isn't a dead end. Offer visitors resources to further their engagement. Hannaford Supermarkets'

FAQ page for its Guiding Stars nutrition program includes relevant links to healthy recipes and budgeting tips, for example.

Practice FAQ prospecting. Continually monitor your FAQs for clues on content that will resonate. Questions offer clues to what your visitors want to know about your products or services, which can inform the process of other creating content they'll care about. Frequently asked questions can be an indicator of information that visitors may need to know more about, such as a prevalent concern that could be better addressed elsewhere on your site.

Keep your eyes and ears open. See which FAQ is most clicked on, talk to customer service or your sales staff, monitor what keywords your visitors consistently use to search, and listen to feedback through e-mail and social channels. You'll gain incredible insight into whether you need to build out content on your site that might more adequately and completely address frequently asked questions.

For example, maybe you could augment a popular frequently asked question with a more detailed article or ebook to share with your customers (and make it available for download on your FAQ page and elsewhere), or perhaps you dig into the issue on your blog with a blog post or series of posts. Or perhaps you produce a slide presentation or a short video on the topic and embed it in your FAQ page as well.

Keeping tabs on what questions your visitors have about your company is also a great way to build content that attracts them to your site in other ways, through other channels.

Set your FAQ page free. Blog, video, or PowerPoint content that you develop (based on visitor FAQs and active monitoring of search and social channels) can also be posted elsewhere. Post it on your Facebook page, blog, LinkedIn, or video channels, for example.

Social media consultant Jay Baer calls this approach creating a "Social FAQ," and he advocates creating meaningful content that can live throughout the social web in addition to your site. "The ideal scenario is that the content performs well enough in search results that potential customers can answer their questions before they ever get to your site," Jay says.

Once your content is posted to your various social outposts, Jay adds, "Invite your current customers to make it better. Talk it up on Facebook and the blog. Send it out to existing customers via e-mail, so they can refer fence-sitters to it. Invite current customers to comment on your answers."

Draft your FAQs to do double duty, informing your content development efforts generally. "Each quarter, commit to answering a few more questions," Jay says. "Involve your customers, and ask them to create their own content that answers other questions (maybe a contest for the best ones)."

He adds, "Now use social listening tools to find blog posts, tweets, forum threads, and other discussions about your brand and your products, and as appropriate, direct fence-sitters to your new social media answers."

Ask the unasked questions. This final one is from friend and colleague John Jantsch of Duct Tape Marketing, who calls such questions FUQs, or Frequently Unasked Questions. (Caution: Do not pronounce phonetically in delicate company.) FUQs are questions "people should be asking but don't know enough to ask," John says.

CHAPTER 16

Video: Show Me a Story

Search engines such as Google and Bing have recently adopted an approach called *blended search,* which means that in their search results they display not only standard web pages but also videos, images, news stories, maps, and tweets from Twitter. Your video content, in particular, is 50 times more likely to appear on the first page of search results than your standard text-based content, according to a recent Forrester Research report. Can you see why it's important to include video as part of your content mix?

Of course, an enormous amount of video is uploaded to YouTube and the like regularly—every minute, 24 hours' worth of video is uploaded to YouTube alone. So how in the world are you going to stand out from the crowd? Clearly, your intent isn't to reach as many people as possible; rather, it's to reach people you want as customers and advocates.

So stop thinking that you need to make a viral video to be successful. Videos that go viral are great for generating buzz and getting people to watch and share them, but they don't necessarily do a lot for getting people to visit your web site or purchase your product. Plus, as we said earlier, you can't guarantee that a video will go viral; instead, focus on the story you are going to tell.

As with any of your content, when creating videos ask yourself, "Why would the people I want to reach want to watch this?" Most of the time, the answer is that they want to be either entertained or educated (about your industry, their area of interest or need, a specific business topic, and so on). The videos you create will, ideally, fall into one of those two categories. If you can make a video that combines the two, better still!

Equipment: What You'll Need

Most of the content we've discussed in this book can be created with the tools and equipment you already have. Video can be accomplished with something as simple as a webcam or a cell phone, though you can also spend thousands of dollars to upgrade your equipment. It is better to start small and build up your equipment and video program gradually.

Be practical. If you're not certain that video is going to play a big part in your content strategy, don't allocate huge chunks of your budget to it. If, for example, you are planning to release your video only on the Web (as opposed to using it on TV), you can get by with a fairly simple video setup.

High-definition video cameras now cost less than $300 and can fit in your shirt pocket. Kodak, Cisco's Flip, and Sony, among others, offer practical options, and the great thing about them is that the video quality is reasonable and you can carry the camera around with you whenever you'd like. Portability is a good thing!

Although going mobile with your camera is a great thing, sometimes you need a tripod so that the camera doesn't move or shake. A tripod is especially helpful if you want to film yourself interviewing someone. You can set up the tripod, hit record, and conduct the interview. You could spend tons of money on a carbon-shaft, ultra-light tripod, but unless you're going to go mountain biking with it, you can get by with any relatively inexpensive, sturdy tripod.

Finally, invest in additional storage in the form of an external hard drive to attach to your computer. Video files are storage hogs, but storage is so cheap these days that you can walk into your local electronics store and walk out with a 500GB drive for a couple of hundred dollars. (You should be regularly backing up your entire computer anyway, so an external drive is a must.)

Creating Your Story

Now that you have your video equipment, what's next?

Video has the potential to tell a more powerful story than text or audio, so you have a tremendous opportunity to create something truly memorable. The difference between a ho-hum video and something that truly engages, according to new-media maven Thomas Clifford, is a true story. So he suggests you create a minidocumentary of sorts that has the following three characteristics:

1. *It features a real story* about your company.

2. *It stars real people* and so shows off your personality and team—as Tom puts it, "Real words from real people." Your video should feature people even if your product or service is technical.

3. *It includes outside sources* (perhaps vendors, customers, stakeholders) to add credibility.

One advantage of minidocumentaries, Tom says, is that they are affordable. Generally, they are filmed with a small crew and don't rely on fancy graphics or effects.

The key to great interviews in a minidocumentary, he explains, is to have a *story sherpa* who lays out a framework or loose script that will help shape the direction of the final product. Each person you interview should speak in his or her own voice, using his or her own words, but you need to guide your interviewees toward your goal for the video. Sometimes, your story sherpa might be an advisor or a director, giving cohesion and continuity, vision, and an outsider's perspective. But more often than not, you will likely play that role.

The best stories, Tom points out, include a *dragon*: a problem or challenge that you or your company faced and overcame. That's much like the way you would craft a customer success story (see Chapter 14), which is why customer success stories are great candidates for being reimagined as videos!

Shooting and Scripting

Although we are about to discuss a few basics of shooting an engaging video, we encourage you to pick up a copy of *Get Seen* by our friend and video expert Steve Garfield (John Wiley & Sons, 2010). If you are going to get serious about video creation, his book will walk you through everything you need to know to do it right.

Every video you shoot will be different, but here are 10 points to keep in mind when filming:

1. *Know your equipment by experimenting with it.* The only way you'll know what your camera can do and what all the options are is to actually get out there and use it. Don't wait until you need the camera for a shoot to use it for the first time.

2. *Get away from as much noise as possible.* You don't have to lock yourself in your office or a studio, but you also don't want to stand on a busy street corner amid noisy traffic. Natural surroundings will add to the human feel of the video, but if viewers can't hear what you are saying, what's the point? (By the way, we essentially ignored this rule when we shot our *Content Rules* announcement video for our blog. Oops.)

3. *Be aware of lighting.* Make sure that you are in a bright room if you're shooting indoors, or there's plenty of daylight if you are filming outside. Lighting is often overlooked, but it is crucial if you want people to be able to see you or what is going on around you. When in doubt, make sure the light source is in front of your subject.

4. *Beware of shadows.* If you film outside, try not to stand with the sun at your back: You'll end up as just a dark shadow in the video. The result will be the same if you are filming in front of a window with light streaming in. Always look at what the shot looks like on the camera. Do a quick test run and play it back. No one enjoys watching a talking shadow onscreen.

5. *Be careful about music playing in the background,* because any music used in your video has to be licensed to legally appear in the video. Plenty of independent musicians would gladly license their music to you. You can also buy royalty-free music online. Keep in mind that it is better to add music in when you are editing the video, not while you are shooting it.

6. *If you are using the camera's built-in microphone*, your subject needs to be fairly close to the camera. The more you shoot, the better you'll understand how sensitive your particular setup is. Most cameras have a headphone jack that a helper can use to listen in during the recording to make sure voices can be heard. Audio is obviously critical to video.

7. *Make sure that the camera is as stable as possible.* Tripods guarantee that the camera will not move. If you need to shoot with a handheld camera, however, try to minimize a shaky hand.

8. *Consider perspective and framing.* If you want the viewer to focus on what you are saying, frame the shot closely around the speaker. But if you want to highlight your surroundings, warehouse, event venue, the commotion in the background, or what have you, zoom out a bit to show more. Composition is important.

9. *After you film each clip,* immediately watch it to gauge its quality. Better to film again on the spot than to have to reschedule a shoot. The worst thing you can do is to spend time filming a lot of footage that, once you get back to your computer, turns out to be unusable.

10. *Smile, relax, and have fun!*

That final rule might be the most important one. Remember the video we mentioned earlier, the one we shot to announce this book? We did it in a single take. As we played it back, we realized that because we'd shot it near a busy street, the sound wasn't great. We decided to use the video anyway, because it conveyed spontaneous energy. In other words, we had fun, and it captured exactly what we wanted.

Was it perfect? Far from it, but we were okay with it because we thought it illustrated our point nicely: You want the quality of your video to be good or great, but it's more important that what is said and shown in the video is what your audience wants or needs.

Show the World

After you've created your video content, the next steps are to post it, share it, and entice people to watch it.

There are many video-sharing sites, and you should put the video up on as many of them as are appropriate for you. You'll need to create accounts on each site, but once you've done that, a tool called TubeMogul (and there are others) will make sharing a snap. You upload a video just once, and TubeMogul will then syndicate it to your accounts on the video-sharing sites.

No matter which site your video will appear on, you need to keep in mind four elements of video sharing. Each service handles these a bit differently, but the basics are the same.

1. *Title*

    The title is the name of the video and is usually the most critical element; it's what people will see and what the search engines will first look at when people do a search. Keep the title short, informative, and on point.

2. *Description*

    Most services allow you to add a content-rich description for the video. The description can consist of several paragraphs and URLs—good to keep in mind as yet another way to drive traffic to your web site.

3. *Tags*

    Tag your videos with every word and phrase that applies to the video. (Less than 20 percent of marketers tag and title their video, according to Forrester. Such a shame.) As with any keyword tagging, consider what search keyword you'd want your video to come up as a result for, and then add those keywords as tags. You should also use the names of the people and companies that appear in the video. Some services on which you can share videos, such as Facebook, will link to the profiles of people tagged in the video if those people are connected to you (as friends, say) via that host site or service.

4. *Thumbnail*

The thumbnail is the image that people see before they hit "Play" on the video. Most video-sharing web sites select several screen shots of the video and allow you to choose from among them; you don't have the ability to pick another image. Some web sites, such as Vimeo, allow you to upload a photo to serve as the thumbnail, but that is not the norm.

Different sites also have different settings for comments, sharing, geo-location tagging, and other options. Check out each service so that you understand how it handles settings, and set them as appropriate for you. In all cases, however, allow others to embed and share your video on their own sites. Too many companies think that they can turn off that setting and drive everyone to the company site to watch the videos. That's a bad business decision. If people are excited enough about your video to want to put it on their site and share with their community, you need to let them spread your message for you.

Even though you are sharing your video across multiple video sites, the most important home you can give your video is your own web site. It's your video, after all.

As with all content, cross-promote your video on all your outlets. Link to it from Facebook, talk about it and link to it from your newsletter, and if it is a regular show, consider putting a link to it in your e-mail signature. Maximize the number of entry points to your content.

But What Am I Going to Shoot?

To answer that question, consider your audience, business, and comfort level. If you are scared to talk on camera and you are a one-person shop, video may not be the best choice for you, and that is okay. (Content Rule Number 11: *Play to your strengths.*) But then again, you could just as easily film around your shop and talk about what people are seeing rather than being on camera yourself.

No matter what your business is, here are some ideas for videos you could shoot:

- *Diary-style videos* of people or groups talking to the camera. These are usually short and insightful. They might offer tips or tricks for using your product, answer a common support question, or simply give an update on how your business is helping its customers.

- *Interviews with staff, customers, or those who might be considered rock stars* in your industry. Putting a camera on a tripod and then having a conversation with someone makes for great content. Think beforehand about the questions that your audience might be interested in hearing answers to. In fact, you could ask your audience via Twitter, Facebook, or your newsletter what questions they might like to hear answered.

- *Product tours highlighting the features of your products.* Think how great it would be for a restaurant to show the specials of the day in a video on its site instead of just listing them on a menu. Or instead of seeing only photographs of your inn, you could watch a video tour of the rooms.

- *Behind-the-scenes videos* are always popular. Musicians have used these for years to give fans a peek into their lives. Businesses can show what goes on in their day-to-day world that people don't see but might be interested in. What about showing, for example, how a popular product goes from concept to rolling off the assembly line? Something that seems completely everyday to you could be exciting and fresh to your fans.

- *Event videos* that share your experiences at a conference or other event are almost always interesting, especially to

B2B customers. Sharing your thoughts and giving people a peek into an industry event they couldn't attend could certainly help gain new customers for you.

The biggest fear most people admit to about appearing on video is that they will look silly. Realize, however, that nearly everyone has this fear . . . and just move beyond it. Cameras are everywhere nowadays and people are sharing their most embarrassing moments online, so any video you create for your business is not going to be as remotely embarrassing as what a quick YouTube search would turn up.

Just get shooting and have fun doing it. Trust us, it will work out.

iContent: Your Own Web Show?

Yes, you can! Are you thinking you could never produce a web show for your brand because of the cost, the technology, and a million other excuses? With a webcam, some free software, and an Internet connection, anyone can do a streaming web show, also called a video podcast. It's easier than ever.

Steve Garfield's *Get Seen* offers some specific advice. So does Rebecca Corliss in a post on the HubSpot blog (for more on HubSpot, see Chapter 23). Rebecca produces HubSpot TV, a weekly video podcast, from the company's headquarters in Cambridge, Massachusetts. What follows is their nine steps to creating your own web show.

1. *Rely on your computer's built-in webcam*, or purchase a webcam from your local electronics store and hook it up to your computer. If you can, use a camera that has a firewire output and also records to tape. "By recording to tape, you also have the recording for post-production later," Rebecca says.

2. *Create a free account with a web-streaming service such as Ustream or Livestream.* Embed the player on your own web site and direct your viewers to watch there. Doing so

allows you to control the content around the player as well as get the benefit of incoming traffic, Rebecca says.

3. *Create show notes as an outline for your episode.* Show notes will help you organize the episode (but keep it free-flowing and not stiffly scripted). They will also allow you to publish the notes later, annotating the published video. As we've discussed elsewhere, this is critical because it adds searchable content to your blog post; Google can't see flash video.

4. *Create an iTunes feed.* HubSpot uses Blip.tv to manage its podcast and iTunes feed. Create a blip.tv account where your episodes will live. Then you can walk through the steps to make your iTunes feed. "Think of a good, descriptive name for your podcast so people searching for similar content in iTunes will find yours," Rebecca writes.

5. *Use an external mic for optimal audio.* What works best are Lavalier mics, especially if you have a live studio audience, she suggests.

6. *Record your show (live or not), and then import the recorded video into something like iMovie for post-production.* Here are the niggly details from Rebecca: "With the firewire and a Mac computer, you can connect the camera to the computer. Open iMovie and it will automatically prompt to import the footage. After you import, create a 'new project' and drag in the footage you want to edit. Then normalize audio volume, clip the beginning and end to remove dead footage, and add fade-in and fade outs! Bam!" (It's not clear whether Rebecca actually utters "Bam!" following post-production work. But we like to think she does.)

7. *Add intro and exit credits, and perhaps add a theme song.* Use PowerPoint to create your credits and save them as a JPG. "Drag that into your project file, and some transitions between the images and the footages, and you're done," Rebecca says. "Export by going to: Share >>Export using QuickTime. This will give you a .mov file."

8. *Upload your footage into blip.tv.* Then, Rebecca says: "After uploading, it will automatically create a flash file (.flv) that you can use for embedding. For the iTunes feed, the paid version can automatically convert your uploaded file into an .mp4 format too and send it to the feed. If you don't want to use the paid account, you can convert your .mov file into a .mp4 file yourself using iTunes. Then upload the .mov as the 'Master' and the .mp4 as 'Portable (iPod).'"

9. *Embed the flash video into a blog post* or onto your site and add the episode show notes, for the reasons noted earlier, in number 3.

10. If you give it a shot (no pun intended), please let us know how it goes!

CHAPTER 17
Podcasting: Is This Thing On?

Podcast (n.): An audio program in a compressed digital format, delivered over the Internet to a subscriber and designed for playback on computers or portable digital audio players such as the iPod.

As you can see by the definition, the term *podcast* is more about the delivery mechanism than anything else. But as the medium has evolved over the past several years, you'll often hear people refer to audio downloads as podcasts. There are also video podcasts (see Chapter 16). Here, we are focusing on audio.

Podcasts are a great way for your organization to share audio content with your audience. Although online video is considered sexier than audio, you can't easily consume videos while driving, walking on a treadmill, or working on a spreadsheet in the office. Think about all the places that your audience might enjoy accessing your content and where audio would work better than video. Quite a few, right?

Podcaster, blogger, and speaker Mitch Joel, who is the author of *Six Pixels of Separation* (Business Plus, 2009), agrees that podcasting appears to have lost some of its appeal in recent years, particularly as video has boomed. But podcasting remains one of the best ways to produce content, because it allows you to essentially be the program manager of your own radio station. What's more, unlike traditional radio, podcasting allows you to target as narrow an audience as you wish, so your show can draw a very specific audience of qualified listeners.

As Mitch suggests, think about a podcast as your company's own radio show, during which you discuss topics that would interest your customers. There are podcasts about every topic imaginable. Mitch's *Six Pixels of Separation* focuses on the changing world of marketing. *Manic Mommies* looks at the life of working mothers, and *The Chillcast with Anji Bee* highlights some of the most mellow music on the Internet. There also networks of podcasts that curate regular shows around specific topics. *SQPN* was started by Father Roderick Vonhögen to showcase podcasts that are faithful to the teachings of the Roman Catholic Church, for example.

Here are nine points to think about as you consider producing a podcast. Chapter 20 also offers some great tips for creating a successful podcast.

1. *You likely already have the equipment you need.* You can spend tons of money on fancy equipment, but you probably already have what you need to start. If you've got a headset and microphone (perhaps one you use for VoIP calls) or a laptop with a built-in microphone, you have what you need to get started. Audacity (audacity .sourceforge.net) is great recording software that's free. If you have a Mac, you probably have GarageBand (pre-installed on most Macs), which is another great tool for recording and editing audio.

2. *Export your audio from videos.* Video-editing software has the ability to export just the audio of any video, so if you've already begun recording videos, then why not also reimagine them for release in audio? (Content Rule Number 5.) This won't work for every type of video, of course, but audio from a presentation, speech, or interview might stand well on its own.

3. *Listen before you record.* What are some of your favorite audio shows, and why? Spend some time on iTunes exploring podcasts to get a sense of varying approaches. Do you like a casual and conversational roundtable approach? Are you more interested in a buttoned-up talk show approach?

Spend some time listening to the kind of podcasts that engage *you*.

4. *Keep length in mind.* How long should your podcast be? Keeping it under an average commute time is a good rule of thumb. (In other words, under 30 minutes.) Of course, that's not an actual rule: Bloggers Shel Holtz and Neville Hobson have for years produced, twice a week, one-hour episodes of their popular business podcast, *For Immediate Release.*

5. *Publishing is easy-ish.* You can use your blog to publish your podcast files. Most blog CMSes (content management systems) can easily accommodate audio files; you need merely upload the file to the blog publishing platform. It's *easy-ish,* because the ease of the experience depends on what publishing platform you use. Pick up a copy of *Podcasting For Dummies* (John Wiley & Sons, 2008) to walk you through the particulars.

6. *Submit to iTunes.* There are other podcast directories, but Apple's iTunes is the premier place to be listed. You can do so directly from the iTunes storefront (click on Podcasts >Submit a Podcast). There is generally a two-week lag time before you are listed.

7. *Plan before hitting "Record."* Some people can record podcasts off the cuff, as C.C. does when he records *Managing the Gray*. But we advise that before you hit the "record" button, you write out some basic notes about the topics you want to discuss, links you may reference, and items that you want to make sure not to forget. When the red light is on and the tape is rolling (so to speak), you'll be comfortable with what you are talking about. In addition, it's good practice to also display show notes that include links to whatever you're discussing on the podcast. By creating notes ahead of time, you'll simplify the task and won't have to transcribe after you are done recording.

8. *Use music wisely.* Music is a great way to open and close a show, but use only music that you have full permission to use. You can find many clips of royalty-free music online, but another option is to license a track from an independent musician. Plenty of musicians would likely love to work with you for the exposure it would bring them. Don't use commercial music or something from your CD collection. Unless you license the tracks (which is not cheap), you'll be in violation of copyright laws.

9. *Editing is your friend.* As Ann says, everyone needs an editor. And that includes podcasters. Take the time to listen to what you've recorded and tweak anything that might need tweaking. This applies especially to interviews, when you'll need to get rid of any periods of silence as the guest ponders a response. (Some podcasters also clean up the "ums" and "ahs" that many are prone to include in their speech.)

Before we end this chapter, we want to remind you that very few people think that they have a good voice for radio, so if that thought is in your head, you are not alone. But the truth is that you shouldn't be the one to judge. Leave it up to your listeners.

Also, a little secret that most successful podcasters don't talk about is that everyone's first few episodes are lacking. Just as with anything, finding your stride takes time. After recording a few episodes, you will feel more comfortable with the process. And you'll have more fun with it, we promise. Plus, remember that you are the one controlling the "publish" button. If it is really bad, no one else has to ever hear it.

CHAPTER 18

Photographs

The Power of Pictures

Most people likely have at least two cameras: a traditional digital camera of some sort and a cell phone that can take photos.

Adding photography into your content mix is not something that needs to be expensive, scary, or daunting. As world-renowned Seattle photographer Chase Jarvis says, "The best camera is the one that you have with you." Keep that in mind as we talk about how photography can add visual interest to your content mix.

What Should I Take Pictures of?

Photography allows you to put a face on your business. Is your company run by machines or does a robot greet people at the front door? Unless you've got something really cool going on, the answer is no. So allow photos to show the human side of your business—not necessarily headshots of all your staff on your web site, but that wouldn't be a bad start.

Capture moments in and around the company. Take photos at the next company meeting, summer picnic, or holiday party, even if you don't have a solid use for them yet. Encourage your staff to bring cameras and take photos, or consider purchasing an official camera for the office to use at business events.

Those photos can be shared online or used in print brochures or other marketing materials for your company. Zappos has gone so far as to publish a yearly Culture Book that, in addition to words of inspiration and other goodies, includes a healthy dose of photos from all around the company.

In addition to taking pictures of the people who work for you, take photos of your products as well. We've all seen the standard glamour shots of the product against a white background from all sorts of angles. But start thinking beyond that. Think about showing the product in real-world situations—so-called lifestyle shots that will give people a better idea of the size and uses of the product.

Threadless.com encourages fans to upload photos of themselves or their friends wearing the T-shirts that the company sells. A quick glance at the Threadless site will reveal a variety of faces from around the world wearing each of the shirts. Those passionate, product-loving shots add a sense of community around the product that a typical product shot could never hope to achieve. Using such images instead of staid, boring stock photos would humanize your company.

Sharing and Tagging

Tagging may not sound sexy, but it is how photography, when added to your content mix, can become really powerful.

Major photo sharing sites, such as Flickr and Facebook, have some sort of person-tagging feature built in. If your photo contains images of Julien and Amber or DJ and Leigh, you are able to click on their faces and add their names to the photo. In most systems, the people in the photo are notified when this happens, and in some cases the photograph will actually show up to others who are connected to the people tagged in the photos.

Did you notice what happened there? That photo you took at the new product launch is suddenly showing up not just to all the employees in the picture you tagged, but also to their friends. Those friends might look at the photo and think, "Wow, what a cool company!" or "I didn't know they had that new design. I should check out their web site."

These are the types of reactions that a simple casual photograph can create, but you need to make sure that you share and tag photos appropriately.

Besides tagging the people in the pictures, add as many descriptive tags to the photo as makes sense. Imagine that you are going to put copies of the photo in a massive file cabinet with unlimited folders, and you want to make sure the photo is in all the folders that you might look in later when searching for it. Those files are the equivalent of the words that you should tag your photo with.

Another way to think about tagging is to consider what search words you would like your photograph to come up as a search result for. All of those words and phrases need to be added as tags.

Each photo-sharing system's tagging is done a little bit differently. Flickr gives you separate fields for entering tags and people's names. Facebook asks you to click on people's faces and then to type in their names, but it doesn't allow tagging (at the time this chapter was written), so you need to put in a really descriptive caption instead.

Getting the Good Shot

The simple truth is that almost anyone can buy a new digital camera and take some pretty amazing photos. Taking a great photo has more to do with the person behind the camera than it does with what camera they are taking the photo with.

Having at least one high quality digital camera on hand will encourage you to take more photos. For under $1,000, your options are massive (and there are plenty of great options under $500 as well), and a quick trip to the nearest electronics store will allow you to play with different models and get hands-on with different models.

Many models today take video as well as stills, so if video is going to be in your content mix (and why wouldn't it?), then look at those specifications as well when you are shopping. It is never a bad thing when a single piece of equipment can be used for multiple tasks.

Ask any photographer and she will tell you that the secret of getting the great shot is to take lots of photos. With storage being a cheap commodity these days, just keep taking photos! At every event, take lots of shots and then afterward keep the best ones and put them in a folder for the event. Save these in the appropriate place and upload the ones you want to share with the world.

Don't have the budget for a new camera? Then use what you've got and make the most of it. Use your cell phone to take casual photos and upload them straight to the Internet using the tool that is integrated with your web site. Don't have anything integrated yet? Then sign up for a free Flickr account and upload them straight to there.

There is nothing worse than being at an event and thinking, "Man, I wish I had a camera right now to capture this." When in doubt, shoot the pictures. You'll have plenty of time afterward to decide if you want to use them in some way or not. But if you never got the photo in the first place, you don't have the option.

Bring In the Big Guns

Just because you have a digital camera or know someone who has a digital SLR (single-lens reflex) camera and seems to take great photos is no reason to not consider hiring a professional. Some people in your very neighborhood likely make a living as photographers.

Although the casual around-the-office shots are great for anyone to shoot, you should consider bringing in a professional for some situations:

- *Trade Shows and Large Events.* If you really want to document a party or other large event, then you want someone who is not going to be distracted by the goings-on and is focused solely on documenting the event. Even though at a wedding everyone is going to be taking photos, you still want someone with a professional eye to really capture the occasion.

- *Head Shots.* These certainly don't have to be the type of static, posed shots that we see in banks around the world. Still, if you want to document your staff with head shots, then bring in a specialist.

- *Product Glamour Shots.* It doesn't matter whether you sell messenger bags or run a boutique hotel, you must have professional photographs of what you are selling if you want people to buy your product. Literally, you want to show your stuff in the best possible light!

Professional photographers range in price and skill, so shop around. Ask friends for recommendations. Keep in mind that many specialize in a certain type of photography, so the great event photographer you hired last year may not be the best person to bring in to shoot head shots of the new executive board.

PART THREE

Content That Converts: Success Stories (with Ideas You Can Steal!)

CHAPTER 19

Reynolds Golf Academy

Greensboro, Georgia

When golf professional Charlie King became director of instruction at the Reynolds Golf Academy, a new golf school located at Reynolds Plantation in Greensboro, Georgia, he wanted to bring in hordes of students—but he had to think of a smart, affordable approach. "I did not have the budget to do direct mail . . . and that was a good thing," as it turns out, Charlie says. A puny marketing budget forced him to consider more creative ways to spread the word about the school.

Inspired by David Meerman Scott's *New Rules of Marketing & PR* Charlie—a 21-year PGA member who is seriously intense about golf but nonetheless light-hearted and quick-witted—decided to pair his teaching philosophy with free instruction and an element of humor to create content that he hoped would spark some word-of-mouth referrals.

Content That Ignites

Charlie set about creating content that would appeal to golfers looking to improve their game engaging them with his friendly, open approach as expressed on his blog, through video, and an engaging e-book. The idea was to both share golf tips to entice golfers to know more as well as position golf as far more approachable and less intimidating a game than the prevailing wisdom suggests. The ultimate goal, of course, is to get golfers to attend the Reynolds Golf Academy: golfers nationwide attend academy instruction each year, through its one-hour, half-day, full-day, or three-day programs.

Blog

Charlie launched his New Rules of Golf Instruction blog.[1] in February 2008, with the idea that he'd share free instruction through blog posts and videos with weekly putting tips, ideas on setting up the perfect shot, or explaining the difference between a true golf swing and a mere maneuver.

Ebook

In March of 2009, Charlie pulled together nine of his favorite golf tactics into a *New Rules of Golf Instruction* ebook, which he makes freely available for download from the Reynolds site and his blog.

The ebook specifically takes to task the old rules, or old-style golf instruction, and suggests a new, less rigid approach. "The old rules preached that golfers were supposed to look a certain way when they swing, without the information they need to understand why the golf ball behaves the way it does," he told the *Wall Street Journal* that year. Charlie's new rules describe seven essential skills in a good swing but place just as much emphasis on the short game, mental toughness, fitness, and smart practice.

"It's too difficult to figure out how to get better at golf," Charlie says. "*New Rules* is the manifesto that explains how to do this," making the game far less frustrating and impenetrable.

As an extension of his approachability and openness, Charlie makes the ebook freely available—in other words, he doesn't require golfers to register with their contact information to download a copy—because he wanted it to reach as wide an audience as possible. Offering content like ebooks with no strings attached means many more people will download and spread your content via email, Twitter, blogs, and the like. Since its release in March of 2009, the *New Rules of Golf* ebook has been downloaded more than 10,000 times.

---

[1] www.reynoldsgolfacademy.com/charlies-golf-blog

VIDEO

Charlie stumbled into video content by accident, but it's become a cornerstone of the school's marketing. During a video shoot in St. Kitts for *Golf* magazine in early 2009, the crew filmed Charlie in an off-the-cuff tutorial, ad-libbing the proper way to angrily throw your club into the water, or "release a club into the watery grave," as the video says.

"Make sure that you get a running start as you head for your throw; you'll be able to throw it a lot farther," he explains earnestly in the video, "The Proper Way to Throw a Club."

Posted on *Golf* magazine's web site (Golf.com), the video went viral; it's now been viewed more than 1.8 million times. That was an *a-ha* moment, Charlie says: He now creates at least two videos a week, posting them on his New Rules blog and the "New Rules of Golf Instruction" YouTube channel, too. Now, his videos run the gamut from the humorous ("Anger Management" and "How to Break Your Club") to the more instructional ("How to Swing a Golf Club Like Tiger Woods" and "How to Hit Long and Straight.") His videographer, Max, and his partner sound man, George, shoot most of his videos with a Kodak Zi8; he relies on a Casio Exilim fh-20 for videos shot at higher speed (for example, when he's demonstrating a golf swing.)

Ka-Ching!

All of the content Charlie produces is focused on attracting and engaging golf students, helping them improve their golf games through video and tutorials, and entertaining them, too. Each page of the site features lots of opportunities to further engage with Charlie and the Reynolds school via Facebook, a LinkedIn golf group, and on Twitter. Each page also offers ample opportunities to sign up for the Reynolds e-mail newsletter, download content geared to specific groups (women golfers, casual business golfers, or junior golfers), or to sign up to attend a one-hour introductory clinic. The content creates momentum for visitors to engage more deeply with Charlie and the school.

This strategy has paid off. Since Charlie began putting his effort into producing video, blogging, and ebooks (he's produced two other ebooks since the original *New Rules of Golf* ebook), the Reynolds Golf Academy has thrived. Despite a lagging economy for much of 2009, "We had a bigger spring [that year] than we'd ever had," Charlie says. "Our business has remained steady in a difficult economy."

Ideas You Can Steal

Have a point of view. The Reynolds Golf Academy has a clear perspective: Learning golf doesn't have to be hard or mysterious. By using its content to debunk the so-called old rules of golf instruction, Reynolds positions itself as a friendly and intelligible alternative—a huge differentiator for its brand.

Have fun. Golf is just a game, right? (Oops! We're ducking while the more serious golfers reading our words launch a driver at our heads.) Charlie's dry sense of humor shines through in his videos ("Anger Management" for golfers) and blog post headlines ("I Just Want a Good Golf Lesson That Doesn't Make Me Worse"). You can tell he's having fun creating content, and his passion is contagious.

Play to your strengths. You don't have to produce every kind of content under the sun; focus on the formats you enjoy and have fun with. "Figure out if you're a good writer, a good radio guy, or a good video guy," Charlie suggests. "I've decided I'm a video guy."

Don't force "viral ....." "The harder you try, [the more] it looks contrived," Charlie says. Keep putting out great content that reflects your brand and your point of view, and you'll occasionally hit on the happy accident of a viral hit, he says.

"... Because you don't necessarily need 'viral.'" Not all of Charlie's videos generate a million views, but they don't need to. Charlie is more interested in whether his video views climb predictably: Are golfers watching the tips consistently? Are the number of views steadily climbing, indicating that the instruction resonates? In his view, it's more important to reach the right *quality* of customer, than a huge *quantity.*

Create momentum. Charlie isn't producing content simply for the fun of it (although he's having plenty of fun doing it). His videos and blog posts are created to inspire his readers to engage more deeply with the school, and reminders on how to do that (sign up for an enewsletter, watch a tutorial video, subscribe to the blog, and so on) dwell in an obvious spot on each page of his site and are sometimes embedded in individual pieces of content.

Measure what works—and then do more of that. Blogs and videos are easily measurable. "When I do a blog post, I measure whether my headline got people's attention, how many people are forwarding it, which ones resonated with people," Charlie says. Then, adjust your content as necessary based on what you learn.

CHAPTER 20

The Cool Beans Group

Greensboro, North Carolina

When Bob Knorpp launched his own marketing consultancy, The Cool Beans Group, in October 2007, he needed to quickly establish credibility. He had plenty of experience, but he didn't want to simply post samples on his site of work he had done for previous clients, because the digital world evolves rapidly and samples age fast. Posting past accomplishments is like "reading a history book and calling it cutting-edge thinking," Bob says.[1]

Rather, he sought to position himself as an expert in the field, consistently feeding his own knowledge and understanding of current trends in the advertising and marketing space, and ensuring he would stay top-of-mind with potential clients.

"I needed to establish that I knew what I was talking about," Bob says. "I needed to somehow distinguish the name, without having completed any projects."

Content That Ignites

So Bob created a living site that focuses on the users' needs. It offers a constant stream of fresh content that includes The

---

[1] Portions of this case study appeared on MarketingProfs in "How Do I Keep My Website Interesting, and Keep Visitors Coming Back?" www.marketingprofs.com/articles/2010/3367/problem-solved-how-do-i-keep-my-website-interesting-and-keep-visitors-coming-back.

BeanCast (www.beancast.us)—a weekly marketing podcast, an accompanying best-practices blog, short audio clips in which Bob addresses current marketing issues, a "best-of-show" feature that offers samples of the site's deeper content, and video clips that augment content on the blog.

How does Bob keep all of this content cutting-edge? "I go where the marketers are hanging out: I post on their blogs and on the professional magazine web sites," he reports. "I tweet on Twitter and I have a Facebook page for The BeanCast. I participate in online forums, and there's even a Wikipedia page for The BeanCast."

How does he keep attracting followers? All of the content is "optimized for relevant marketing keywords," he points out.

The BeanCast, launched in spring 2008, is the centerpiece of Bob's efforts. It's a lively roundtable discussion of top news stories and issues with Bob and three or four guests. Each week, Bob spends four to five hours reading industry publications and identifying five connected trends. Then he gathers an expert panel of marketing and advertising executives to discuss the trends with a freeform, unscripted approach.

To create the podcasts, Bob uses a MacBook Pro, an Alesis 8-channel USB sound board, MXL 920 and 990 XLR Condenser mikes ("very cheap, but excellent quality," Bob says), and Garage-Band and SoundSoap software for editing. The calls are conducted through Skype with guests around the globe calling in to be part of the show.

Ka-Ching!

While Bob's subscriber base is relatively small at 800 individuals, his podcasts reach a broader number of listeners. During the first week after a new podcast is published, shows are typically downloaded 1,500 times or more (some episodes are downloaded over 5,000 times). Bob estimates that, overall, he has reached 10,000 people within the advertising industry with his podcasts and blog.

"I was [initially] surprised at the reach," he says. The podcast was meant to be a credibility tool, but its popularity has become a definite bonus.

According to Bob, the point of creating and maintaining content this way is threefold:

1. *It establishes you among the experts.* "By being seen with the experts in online debate, I make them look good and they make me look good in return," he explains. "Thus, I share in their credibility."

2. *It provides context for clients.* The more content you create, the more archives you have to reference, adding depth to the site, he notes. These days, "there is rarely a discussion or new business-pitch conversation that doesn't involve me referencing a particular show or posting" already at the site, he reports. This referencing of past content is "an amazing tool that over time continues to add value to a business," he says.

3. *It makes you better at your job.* By constantly engaging in debate on marketing subjects in all of these different venues, you avoid stagnation, he notes. "I am always engaged with the latest best practices, which in turn offers obvious benefits to my clients. The value of this cannot be overstated," he says.

"Having your customers engage with a growing body of content is one of the surest ways to raise the perception that you are an expert in your given field, and create a path toward ongoing loyalty and advocacy with your brand," Bob concludes.

Ideas You Can Steal

Play to your strengths. Because Bob is comfortable both speaking and writing, he played to his strengths with the podcast and blog. "If you're running a restaurant and you're great at photography, create a photo blog," he suggests. "Don't try to force the creation of a whole bunch of content you don't feel suited to."

Know the rules, but break them occasionally. Bob admits that he broke a few rules with The BeanCast. Among those he broke:

- *Name the show something that tells clearly what the show is about.* The title of a podcast generally communicates its scope and thrust in the blink of an eye—consider, for example, Boston's PJA Agency's "This Week in Social" podcast, for example, or the "Senior Moments" podcast on coping with Alzheimer's, produced by Day Break Life Center, an adult day services agency serving Kinston, North Carolina. "The BeanCast," doesn't really communicate much, Bob admits: Is it a cooking show? A show for gardeners?

- *Shorter trumps longer.* Many podcasts are shorter, briefer affairs—often less than 30 minutes, and sometimes only 5 or 10 minutes. Bob's show requires an hour-plus commitment from listeners for each episode, but no one is complaining. In fact, they are asking for more.

- *Use a photo of yourself as the show's avatar on iTunes and other outposts*, rather than a logo. Generally, podcasts with a name and face attached attract more listeners on iTunes than a logo avatar, as they appear more human and less corporate. Bob uses his company logo of a trio of what appear to be kidney beans with human faces. It's cute and not so corporate . . . but it's not Bob.

"I broke every rule," Bob admits. "But you can break the rules as long as it's playing into your strategy that you've outlined at the beginning."

Test, test, test. The learning curve for creating podcasts is huge, Bob says—even for people like him with loads of audio recording experience. "From getting the wiring right to recording at the best levels to editing to getting listed on iTunes to getting the logo to display on all devices correctly—none of it was easy and all of it took longer than expected," says Bob. He suggests doing some live, practice dry runs before launch: Once you have a system set up, run a show or two, feed them to iTunes, download them, and listen to them on various devices. All good? Then—and only then—launch.

Let your content be a conversation starter. Bob gives texture and depth to his client conversations by referencing his podcast frequently in conversation and on his blog. He uses it to reach out to potential new clients he thinks might relate to the issues discussed.

Always be learning. Producing any regular stream of content keeps you almost by necessity on the cutting edge of best practices and developments in your particular industry. Perhaps this isn't exactly an idea you can steal, but it is definitely a great argument for the consistent creation of content.

CHAPTER 21

U.S. Army

Fort Knox, Kentucky; Fort Monroe, Virginia

The U.S. Army has long used traditional media to reach potential recruits—young men and women ages 17 to 24. That target demographic, however, is no longer glued to the television set or radio.

"The TV's on, they are IMing, they're texting, they're downloading with the iPod in one ear while listening to TV with the other, the laptop's in their lap," says Bruce Jasurda, chief marketing officer of the U.S. Army Accessions Command, which handles marketing and recruitment.

Because its target market is so adept at media and multitasking, the Army was finding it difficult to grab the attention of prospects through traditional advertising—that is, through TV, print, and radio. Bruce believed that if he could persuade young men and women to join in conversations about the Army, in a way that encouraged them to reach out and ask questions, they would become engaged and so be more likely to visit an Army recruiter.

Content That Ignites

The Army had a web site, GoArmy.com, which offered updated content. "But that isn't a dialogue," says Bruce. "When you're in a dialogue, you're more engaged. You're asking specific and individual questions. We wanted to create a dialogue totally dedicated to conversations about the Army."

So in 2008, Bruce and his team decided to create a web site called Army Strong Stories (www.armystrongstories.com), with the purpose of inviting such dialogue.

Army Strong Stories allows anyone—whether affiliated with the Army or not—to post comments, ask questions, create an account, and blog. It also has a Twitter feed to help disseminate content and a YouTube channel for bloggers who want to post videos.

The user-generated content is almost entirely uncensored. With the exception of profanity and pornography, anything is acceptable, including first-hand stories and other content from soldiers and civilians on the frontlines around the globe.

"We have bloggers from Iraq, from Afghanistan," acknowledges Bruce. "We've been a nation at war for 10 years. If you avoid [the subject], you lose a lot of credibility."

And credibility, he says, is one of the key reasons to be engaging prospects in conversation: "Social media is an honest dialogue. We want people to have a transparent experience. We want them to learn about the Army."

The site is filled with blog posts from soldiers and others involved with the Army, telling their stories, good and bad. One Army reservist talks about the difficulties of leaving jobs, schools, families, and friends when being deployed overseas. A soldier honors fallen comrades. A cadet talks about his excitement at heading off to West Point.

And visitors to the site can get honest answers to questions like these: How hot is it over there? What will happen to my family if I get deployed? Is there medical care? "That's the benefit of Army Strong Stories. The information is individually tailored," Bruce says.

The web site explains itself this way: "On ArmyStrongStories.com you can connect with U.S. Army soldiers to get an inside look at what it's like to be in the Army. Explore these stories to hear soldiers discuss why they serve, get perspectives on Army life, or learn about career opportunities in the Army." It adds:

"Inspired? Share your own Army experience or tell us about the soldiers you support."

Ka-Ching!

Army Strong Stories measures its success mainly by the level of participation. Though slow to grow at first, the site had 170 bloggers by the end of its second year, and in the first six months of 2010, the site doubled the number of monthly unique visits to about 10,000.

While the Army is all about return on investment when it comes to other forms of marketing, they realize that social media is still in some ways "the Wild West," says Bruce. "I could prove any point of view that I wanted; there really isn't a uniform metric across social [media]."

Still, there's no doubt that Army Strong Stories is doing something right: It won a 2010 Gold Quill Award (of Merit)—one of the highest honors in business communications—in the Social Media category, and a 2010 Bronze SABRE Award—presented by a PR industry leader—for Best Blog.

The Army's foray into social media also helps counter the image of the Army as big, amorphous, bureaucratic, and slow moving, Bruce says. "It seems odd on the surface that something perceived to be [as] stilted and almost regimented as the Army would be so into social media."

"There are perceptions out there about what the Army is all about. Many are wrong," he says. By helping to change that perception, Army Strong Stories is making the Army more attractive to its young audience.

And it's doing so even as the Army is spending less money on the social media effort than on the TV, radio, and print media it has traditionally used.

Ideas You Can Steal

Tell true stories. Bruce felt strongly that Army Strong Stories needed to be open to anyone, and that anyone could blog, uncensored, about any topic. But his boss, a three-star general, wasn't so sure. Here's how Bruce explains how the conversation went: "We're having a meeting at the Pentagon, and talking about the release of Army Strong Stories, and this general says, 'You're going to allow folks to say whatever they want on this web site and give unfettered access to the site? Did I understand you right? I'm a little nervous about this.' And I said, 'General, we advertise and market to young men and women around the country, we tell them about the Army and ask them to sign on the dotted line, we give them haircuts, and three days later give them a rifle and live ammunition. I think we'll be okay to give them unfettered access to ask the questions they want, or to answer them, on Army Strong Stories.'" The general agreed.

Invite everyone to participate. Army Strong Stories works because anyone interested in the Army can take part. "We have doctors, journalists, family members, community members, officers, and soldiers," says Bruce.

He adds that recruitment for contributing bloggers happens naturally through the site. "There is no mechanism to say, 'We need a nurse; we need a lieutenant.'"

Offer clean and clear access to decision-makers. Social media works really well when the person with the idea has free access to the person who makes the decisions, Bruce believes. "As you go through committees, things get cloudy. We don't have committees," he says. "The Army is about leadership and making decisions, and we practice what we preach."

To launch Army Strong Stories, he says, "It was two conversations with two different people, and away we went."

CHAPTER 22
AskPatty.com, Inc.
Thousand Oaks, California

AskPatty.com takes a two-pronged approach to the women's automotive retail market: For consumers, the AskPatty.com web site aims to be a reliable source of friendly automotive advice and research. For auto dealers, parts dealers, and other service and repair centers, the AskPatty.com Certified Female Friendly program trains and certifies them on how to attract and serve women customers.

CEO Jody DeVere says her company fills a void in the car-buying market. Purchasing a car is a big and expensive decision, yet good automotive buying and maintenance advice geared toward women is impossible to find; most sites write for a male buyer or enthusiast.[1] "Many sites don't cover the topic, yet it's the second largest purchase you'll make," Jody says.

Content became the cornerstone of her efforts to build her business, Jody says. By creating content about cars with a tone and approach women could relate to, Jody—a successful entrepreneur with more than 25 years of sales and marketing experience—has built brand recognition for her company without costly advertising.

---

[1] Butcher shops often have that same male-centric vibe. Of course, investing $40 in pork chops isn't quite the same as investing tens of thousands in a vehicle. But still.

Content That Ignites

Prior to the launch of AskPatty.com, Jody launched the blog (http://askpatty.typepad.com) as a means of generating early buzz for her new business. She tapped a variety of women as contributors—like auto mechanics, auto retailers, and then-NASCAR driver Deborah Renshaw—to pen posts on their areas of expertise.

"One of my strategies to build my brand is to give away my content for free" to other sites, to build awareness about the AskPatty.com brand, Jody says. "It's not all about driving traffic back your site. It's about meeting your consumers where they are. Marketing is no longer about driving your consumer to a single point of contact."

She broadened the AskPatty.com reach through the following.

PARTNERSHIPS

Jody made a list of all the popular women's web sites and social networks and offered to allow them to run her content on their pages for free, in exchange for a link back to AskPatty.com. She also gave them a listing on her Partners page, and promoted her partners in other ways. For example, AutoTrader.com uses her content on its site with a link back to AskPatty.com; in exchange, AskPatty.com features the AutoTrader car-buying widget. Other partners include Parenthood.com and the *Chicago Tribune.*

SYNDICATION

Jody also syndicated the AskPatty.com content to larger sites and media portals with broad reach, including:

- BlogHer: A publisher network that reaches more than 20 million women each month across 2,500 blogs.

- TwitterMoms: A network of active, connected moms who maintain personal or professional blogs. Many Twitter-Moms have been early adopters of social media—specifically . . . well, *Twitter!*—where they typically have more than 1,000 followers.

- BloggerMomsClub: One of the largest social networks for mom bloggers, with over 9,000 members.

- BlogBurst: A syndication service that places blog content on top-tier, category-specific web sites.

Jody attributes a large part of her success to her syndication efforts. "Say you spend x amount of dollars [on] a traditional campaign . . .. You get a spike in traffic, and then it goes away," Jody says. Syndicating content, on the other hand, is "like a piggy bank. The online articles don't go away," but instead act as a kind of grant that continues to fund traffic and awareness. (Or, as we discussed in Chapter 1, an "information annuity"—a gift that keeps on giving.)

SOCIAL MEDIA

Like a lot of companies, Jody created a Facebook page and a Twitter account to engage and connect with customers. In turn, she syndicates her Facebook and Twitter feeds on other social sites—like groups within the Ning Networks—to cross-pollinate her content, thus extending her reach. (Ning is a service that allows people to create custom-branded social networks; it has some 300,000 active networks.)

"When people visit my profile on Ning, they [also] see my RSS feed, so that's another content syndication point," Jody says.

INDUSTRY PUBLICATIONS

A few times per month, AskPatty.com contributors also contribute advice and commentary to other automotive magazines and web sites. Those contributions "drive a tremendous amount of leads and interest in our program," she says.

Ka-Ching!

Though the broad reach of her content is difficult to measure, Jody estimates that it generates 20 million views a quarter. Most of those are consumers looking for information, but a tiny, profitable portion are dealerships and other service providers who find her through search: Her content generates a steady 10 to 12 solid business leads a day, she says, which she calls "remarkable."

Her content also gives her plenty of visibility, and has earned her media coverage in the *New York Times, Forbes,* the *Wall Street Journal, Woman's Day* magazine, and *O: The Oprah Magazine,* to name a few. She has been an expert guest on radio and TV shows, including Motor Trend Radio, Car Concerns, Oprah and Friends Radio, Disney Radio, National Public Radio's "Talk of the Nation," CNN, Fox, ABC, and NBC.

Ideas You Can Steal

Focus, focus, focus. (Also, *focus.*) Jody's site is interesting because it isn't just another car site: It's a source of information that deciphers car talk for women, empowering them in a personal and relevant way. That might sound obvious, Jody says, but it's tempting to broaden your focus to accommodate more topics with the notion that it'll bring you more fans. It won't: "You need to be an expert at something. Stick with that, and do it long enough that you build a following."

Create great content in your visitors' language. "The strategy around content has to be more than just whipping out five good articles," says Jody. "It's how you tag them, how you title them." What words does your target audience use to describe issues they need help with? Incorporate those words into your content so that you will show up in natural search results, Patty says.

Set your content free. Jody gives away her content to "absolutely anyone" who asks, she says, as long as they link back to her and keep intact any internal link in the post or article itself. Seeding her content to countless sites across the Web raises her visibility exponentially.

Don't be afraid to call yourself an expert. By providing valuable content that helps people, Jody is now seen as an expert, which increases earned media opportunities.

Favor quality over quantity. Initially, Jody published seven blog posts a day in an attempt to generate as much content and as many links as possible. Eventually, though, she realized that one really good article paid higher dividends than a cluster of so-so stuff. Now, AskPatty.com publishes one post per day.

Have patience. A content strategy does not work overnight. "It's like a piggy bank. You put a little bit of money in every day." Be consistent.

CHAPTER 23

Kadient

Lowell, Massachusetts

Kadient sells software to help organizations improve their sales performance. Because Kadient's business relies, in part, on arming salespeople with the right kind of content to move a sale further down the funnel and close it, Kadient understands the value of ebooks and video.

Kadient recognized that much of the content created by business-to-business firms falls short of attracting and engaging buyers. "Marketing often creates content and throws it over the wall to sales, but they're not creating what sales needs" to help close a deal, says Amy Black, then-senior marketing communications manager at Kadient, who now runs the marketing department at TimeTrade.

Like many B2B companies, Kadient contends with a long sales cycle—moving potential customers from the top of the sales funnel (or first contact with a potential customer) to the point of purchase: from recognition to lead-generation to nurturing and closing the sale. In many companies that sell complex goods or services to other companies, the sales process occurs over 6 to 36 months. So Kadient creates content to help buyers at every stage of the cycle, mapping content to engage prospects at specific points in the sales process.

Content That Ignites

Amy began creating a content library mapped to the B2B sales cycle, producing ebooks, white papers, and video targeted toward prospects—those who are just learning about Kadient as well as those further along in the buying process.

Amy created a matrix identifying the various points of the sales process and the types of content needed; now, each piece of content that's created plays a role in furthering a sale. "Every piece of content we create with a goal in mind," explains Amy, "to give a business and marketing objective to why we're creating it."

Generating leads for sales is usually the primary objective. But content is also assigned a secondary priority. Kadient created the ebook *How to Create Killer Sales Playbooks: Four Steps for Designing Sales Playbooks that Win Deals* as a lead-generation piece, but it is also used for lead nurturing, which occurs after the initial introduction but before the closing of any sale.

The lead nurturing stage is when content can come in really handy, to help prospects stay engaged with whatever solution you're selling.

Kadient creates three main types of content to serve various needs.

EBOOKS

At the start of a relationship with a prospect, Kadient avoids white papers, opting instead to create more visually and editorially compelling ebooks, which do "a much better job of breaking through the clutter than a white paper," Amy says.

What's the difference between an e-book and a white paper? Mostly, the differences are in style and tone. A white paper (sometimes called a *research report, summary,* or *technical brief*) plays it straight. It tends to be a topical report focused on a single issue central to your buyers. Ebooks—like Kadient's *Dive Deeper into Your Sales Metrics: 4 Ways to Discover Hidden Sales Treasure*—are looser and more playful. An ebook might be just as long as a white paper—or longer—but with an engaging theme, appealing design, and layout dominated by bold text treatments. (For more on white papers and ebooks, see Chapter 13.)

WHITE PAPERS

This is not to say that white papers don't have a place in the content mix. They do. Kadient's white papers—like those produced by many B2B companies—tend to be bigger-picture, thought pieces that nonetheless appeal to the individual reader—in its case, the sales executive. One recent Kadient white paper, the provocatively titled, *Is Sales Broken?* appealed to busy sales vice presidents by addressing the fundamental question, "Is there something inherently wrong with the sales process, or is it just changing? And if it's changing, are you on board?" Amy says.

VIDEO

Video has a tremendous capacity to nurture leads that are already aware of the company's services, Amy says, as well as give Kadient personality and humor. In *Confessions of a Sales VP,* a sales exec is riddled with guilt about all the bad things he does in his job, and confesses as much to his priest. The last confession he makes: "Father, the worst thing of all is that, when the CEO says to tell him what's in the pipeline, I make it up!" The video pinpoints—in a humorous way—the precise problems that many sales guys have. Inherent, of course, is that Kadient can solve those problems.

"We know our audience likes to laugh at themselves—they're a little edgy," explains Amy.

Most videos are scripted, and Amy sometimes hires actors. She has also hired professional camera crews. She points out, however, that a video "can be shot in your office and still be quality" if the message is strong. For example, Amy used a simple Flip camera at a recent conference to capture a customer testimonial. "The quality wasn't amazing, but it was very specific" to Kadient and created a powerful message that the company uses in nurturing campaigns.

Ka-Ching!

Content is one of the top sources of generating new leads. In 2009, for example, 70 percent of prospects had downloaded the ebook *How to Create Killer Sales Playbooks*. In total, 12,000 people downloaded *Killer Sales.*

The *Confessions of a Sales VP* video earned a healthy click-through rate of 10 percent, a healthy enough response to encourage Kadient to experiment with more video.

Ideas You Can Steal

Create with intent. Especially when you're small, you can't afford to create content that doesn't have a purpose or clear value. Planning is a huge part of the content-creation process. "Before we get to the point where we're creating something, we have to decide how it's going to be used and what point it's going to serve," says Amy.

Create content that makes your buyers run faster and jump higher (so to speak). For B2B companies, there's no better content than helping someone be better at her job, Amy says. Think: coaching tips, concrete steps, hints or how-to guidance to be a better tug boat hauler, or software salesman, or whatever.

Solicit feedback from sales. Constantly ask sales, "Is this useful to you?" You need to create content that will help sales push somebody over the edge or get them over a hurdle, says Amy. She adds, "If you're just doing it on your own without input from sales, you'll miss the mark."

Stay nimble. Be prepared to grab a camera or a microphone or a notebook as opportunities to create on-the-spot content occur, Amy says. Events or trade shows are an obvious place to create on-the-fly content, but look for other opportunities, too: customer visits to the home office, for example.

There's no business like show business. Content that entertains (like *Confessions of a Sales VP*) surprises and engages your buyers, even in a B2B context. When creating your content, try something that's out of the ordinary and has an element of fun.

CHAPTER 24

HubSpot

Cambridge, Massachusetts

HubSpot is the poster child for producing compelling content in the business-to-business world, for two reasons: One, it generates a ton of it, of a broad variety. And second, it manages its well-read blog less like a corporate marketing mouthpiece, and more like a trade publication, or a business magazine.

Based in Cambridge, Massachusetts, HubSpot sells marketing software to small and medium-size businesses. Its Inbound Internet Marketing blog (http://blog.hubspot.com) is the cornerstone of its marketing strategy, says Vice President of Marketing Mike Volpe, because blogs, with their keyword-rich content, are vital in driving traffic from search engines. They are also great vehicles through which to establish thought leadership and build trust and credibility with potential customers. What's more, they are the lifeblood of a social media strategy.

Inbound marketing—an approach to marketing that focuses on getting found by customers through blogs, search, and social media—is critical, Mike says, adding that a blog is "one of the most important things any company can do." Companies that blog generate 55 percent more web site traffic than companies that don't, and they get 97 percent more links coming in to their sites, Mike says, citing HubSpot's own research.

"We've built a brand around having really good content," Mike says, which has "almost nothing to do with our software, but positions us as leaders in our space."

Content That Ignites

At the beginning of this chapter, we called HubSpot the poster child of B2B content. Here's what we meant.

BLOG

HubSpot's Inbound Internet Marketing Blog publishes three or more posts every business day. The content is less about its products and services and more about things that will educate and offer value to its customers, like: "Three Ways to Use Google Webmaster Tools to Increase Search Engine Traffic," or "Five Best Practices for Lead-Nurturing E-Mails," or "How to Successfully Manage a LinkedIn Group." Content on its blog also often has an element of fun—for example, cartoons like the one in Figure 24.1.

Figure 24.1 HubSpot Cartoon

Source: http://blog.hubspot.com/blog/tabid/6307/bid/5932/Facebook-Plugins-in-Real-Life-Cartoon.aspx

VIDEO

In addition to blogging like crazy, HubSpot produces videos, interviews with marketing experts and bloggers, and video tutorials. It's also produced a handful of music videos (like its "You Oughta Know Inbound Marketing" rif, sung to the tune of Alanis Morissette's "Oughta Know") and other "HubSpot Originals" comedy skits, web series, and parodies (http://youtube.com/Hubspot).

WEBINARS

HubSpot produces weekly live webinars on a variety of topics—from blogging to search engine marketing to marketing analytics to press releases, and so on.

RESEARCH AND REPORTS

The company regularly produces larger studies and reports. Its 2010 State of Inbound Marketing Report, for example, looks at how inbound-dominated organizations average 60 percent lower cost per lead than those organizations that market through more traditional tactics like direct mail and advertising. Its State of the Twittersphere report analyzed data from Twitter accounts to show the state of Twitter usage worldwide. All reports are downloadable freely as PDFs (meaning visitors don't need to register with an e-mail address or other information to access them). Most of the content HubSpot publishes is freely accessible, although a handful (like the webinars) do require registration.

FREE TOOLS

HubSpot has released a number of free, informative, valuable tools (called *Graders*) for analyzing the effectiveness of business's social media efforts: "Website Grader" (Website.grader.com) tells you how well your web site is doing (Is it getting traffic? Does it have SEO problems? How popular is it in social media?); Twitter Grader (twitter.grader.com) allows you to measure the power and reach of your Twitter stream.

Video Podcast

Every Friday afternoon, Mike Volpe and Product Manager Karen Rubin host a live-streaming video podcast they call HubSpot TV. Part news channel, part talk show, HubSpot TV covers small business news and topics of the week. They often have a guest join them who is an expert on that week's topic. Episodes are archived with iTunes and are posted, with show notes, to the blog.

Ka-Ching!

The blog is the third-biggest source of new business leads for HubSpot. HubSpot currently has about 30,000 subscribers across e-mail and RSS, Mike says; the more successful blog posts generate 5,000 to 10,000 clicks within the first three days. Roughly 7 to 10 percent of blog visitors ultimately visit the web site; of them, 10 to 20 percent become customers.

HubSpot TV's weekly episodes generally attract about 100 viewers to the live show; another thousand people generally watch the archived version. HubSpot's how-to webinars attract a big crowd, Mike says, of up to 5,000 to 12,000 attendees, depending on the topic.

Some of the company's popular YouTube videos generate tens of thousands of views. "You Oughta Know Inbound Marketing," for example, got 40,000 views within the first week, and was the number one result on YouTube for the search term *marketing*. Other, more serious videos can generate 20,000 views or more. "For a B2B audience, that's very good," Mike says. Not only is an optimized YouTube video 50 times more likely to get on to Page One of Google than an optimized web page, according to a recent Forrester study[1], but a cool, fun video tends to engage in ways other text-based content doesn't, including attracting inbound links, Mike says.

---

[1] http://blogs.forrester.com/interactive_marketing/2009/01/the-easiest-way.html

Ideas You Can Steal

Create key personas. Consistently across all of its content platforms, HubSpot talks less about its products and services and more about things that will educate and offer value to its customers. How does it know what its customers are interested in? HubSpot creates personas to represent the customers they want to attract, and creates content it thinks those customers will find valuable. "Ask, 'What do my customers or prospects care about?'" Mike says. "What information can we provide that helps them do their jobs better?"

Don't forget to talk to actual customers, too. Of course, creating content that attracts your key personas is no substitute for actually talking to your real-life, flesh-and-bones customers. Periodically, create a quick survey on your business blog as a way to get some specific feedback from your readers: What do they like reading about? What kind of content format do they prefer (like audio, video, or text)? Don't forget to offer a comment box for free-form comments. (Online survey tools like SurveyMonkey .com or SurveyGizmo.com have free options to allow you to create and publish custom surveys.)

Spark conversation. HubSpot generates blog posts and other content that sparks conversation, and doesn't simply add to it. It has a point of view with a sometimes controversial tone ("A Message for the Post Office: Direct Mail Is Dying") as well as a distinct how-to approach. The lens through which HubSpot develops content is, "What is the content that they'll want to share with friends? What will get people talking?" Mike says.

Uncover the content creators in your organization. With three or more blog posts a day, videos, webinars, and so on, HubSpot creates a boatload of content. To meet that publishing schedule, it involves employees at all levels of its organization. Its marketing department manages the bulk of the content, including the blog—editing posts, writing descriptive and compelling headlines, and so on—but more than 40 employees throughout the organization contribute. HubSpot does not require employees to post, but "highly encourages" everyone in the company to contribute, Mike says, adding, "Probably half the company has written an article for the blog at one time or another."

What's more, HubSpot looks within its ranks for people with a passion for creating content (and it often hires people based on those passions). Marketing Manager Rebecca Corliss sings after hours in an a cappella group and loves creating video and audio. She's been a driver behind HubSpot's music videos.

Connect your blog to your web site. Make sure your blog and other content is clearly connected to your main web pages. Business blogs can be a key source of new traffic from search engines and social media, Mike says; a blog post—and not your home page—may be the first thing a potential customer sees about your company. Set up your blog as part of your corporate site either as a subdomain (blog.yourdomain.com) or as a page (yourdomain.com/blog). Also, be sure the navigation and the overall look and feel of your blog links it visually to the rest of your site as well as makes it easy for users to find information about your products and services.

Create momentum. Each piece of content you publish should have a call to action: a request or a suggestion to "do something else," or a next step that a consumer could take toward the purchase of a product or service. (The classic example, of course, is "Click here to find out more.") "You want to create a path to [entice] your visitors to consume more," says Mike. On the blog, for example, HubSpot ends each blog post with a related piece of content: perhaps a video, an On Demand webinar, and so on. In most cases, a visitor has to register to access that associated content. Adding that single call to action, Mike says, tripled the number of leads HubSpot generates from its blog. You might also consider adding similar calls to action directly under the navigation bar at the top of the page as well as along the right or left side of the content (depending on your blog's design) to increase its visibility.

Feed your blog. HubSpot's blog thrives on a great mix of various *kinds* of content, not just volume of content. Think of your blog like your local newspaper or favorite magazine: Do you have a similar mix of content? Different kinds of stories and articles, of various lengths?

Rick Burnes, a former journalist, breaks down the HubSpot blog's content into five categories with a memorable foodie metaphor:

1. Raisin Bran—*Useful, everyday posts. "Most of your posts should be [like] Raisin Bran. They're very practical, and usually framed as how-to advice."*

2. Spinach—*Healthy, thoughtful post. "These are the posts that establish your business and your blog as a thought leader. They're posts that probe new developments in technology and changes in your industry. They're generally a little longer than typical posts, and they take longer to write. . . . Do these from time to time (and take the time to do them well), but don't do them too often. Too much spinach, and your readers will get tired of it."*

3. Roasts—*Big, hearty projects. "These are posts that take a lot of time, but that get a lot of attention and inbound links." A research report is one example, Rick says: "It took a lot of time to pull the data together and do the analysis, but it got great traction." Roasts "will introduce your blog to new audiences. . . . This, in turn, will help expand your blog's reach.*

   "The challenge with a roast is to make sure you pick the right project. It's a lot of time to invest in a single article, so you need to make sure you're producing interesting, unique information."

4. Tabasco—*Articles that start fires. "Every so often you need to write an article that asks tough questions. These posts might upset a few of your readers, but they also launch important, valuable conversations. For example, last week I did*

a post called "A Message for the Post Office: Direct Mail Is Dying." This upset a lot of our readers who rely on direct mail. They spoke up—sometimes in sharp tones—in the comments, and we had a lively discussion. Lots of people linked to the article with posts of their own, and the result was that a lot of the nuance about direct mail and its status was uncovered."

5. Chocolate cake—*The sweet stuff. In this category is fun stuff like cartoons, music videos, and the like. "Every blog needs fun stuff that goes down easily and shows that you don't take yourself too seriously." I also think of this category as "show-biz" content: Content that's entertaining and fun tends to get passed around Twitter and Facebook like kisses at a middle school game of Spin the Bottle."*[2]

---

[2] The HubSpot Inbound Marketing Blog, http://blog.hubspot.com/blog/tabid/6307/bid/4524/5-Types-of-Posts-to-Feed-Your-Business-Blog.aspx

CHAPTER 25

Kodak

Rochester, New York

Since the early days of the Internet, Kodak has always tried to engage its visitors with content on its web site. "We want to help people make the most of Kodak products, so we offered articles like the top 10 tips for taking Halloween pictures, or how to photograph babies," says Jenny Cisney, Kodak's chief blogger and senior social media manager.

So when blogs and other platforms became prevalent a few years ago, Kodak readily embraced social media as a way to further expand its reach, as well as to engage in new and evolving technologies.

Content That Ignites

Kodak created a content strategy that was based on the creation of useful content that could then be distributed via social networks. With that in mind, they launched the following.

BLOGS

A Thousand Words (http://1000words.kodak.com). The *Thousand Words* blog has been updated every day since it launched in 2006. "I run it like a newspaper," explains Jenny. "My job as editor is to maintain a schedule. I look at what's going on in the company, if we're going to an event, if we're going to be on a TV show, and plan who should write it." She also includes important holidays like Mother's Day, as well as less obvious dates like April Fools' Day in her coverage, as well as special events like the 2010 FIFA Soccer World Cup from June 2010. Because every contributing blogger also has another job within the company, Jenny makes contributing as easy as possible by giving bloggers a template for posts (see sidebar in Chapter 11). All the author has to do is write the post and forward it to her with photos. Jenny uploads the posts herself.

A Thousand Words topics focus on photography in general, human interest stories, and photo tips, and run the gamut from a pet show in New York City to a concert by the Taiwanese Choral Society of Rochester to honoring mothers through photos to remembering fallen servicemen on Memorial Day. All posts include plenty of rich, gorgeous photos.

Plugged In (http://pluggedin.kodak.com). The *Plugged In* blog is the place for information on Kodak products and services, including news, tips, and reviews. It shares stories about cool new technologies, employee experiences, and other innovations and customer successes, with an eye toward sharing things particularly helpful, insightful, and inspirational.

Grow Your Biz (http://growyourbiz.kodak.com). The *Grow Your Biz* blog covers how Kodak products, services, and technologies can enrich business—typically, the graphics communications industry. The blog is run by an employee in the company's computer graphics business who plans the entries and acts as the administrator for the blog.

Kodak employees throughout the company write all blog posts across all three blogs, largely because they are inspired by their own passion. "You can't force people to do social media," Jenny says. "They have to have a passion for what they do. They're the people who stand out in the company; they're always leaving comments on your Facebook page," and they're usually the people you'd find at a party talking about these topics, anyway. What Kodak does, she says, is encourage them to use their voices online.

FACEBOOK

The company maintains Facebook pages in the United Kingdom, France, Germany, Italy, and Spain, as well as in the United States.

Jenny manually uploads updates to the Facebook pages rather than having them automatically updated every time a new blog post is published. The personal approach is intentional, she says, because Kodak wants to keep an individual behind every Facebook comment, Twitter feed, and blog post.

As with the blogs, Jenny and other employees post on Facebook about news in the photography world at Kodak. They also stay in the Kodak conversation by responding to others, thanking them for kind words, addressing concerns, or answering questions.

TWITTER

Kodak maintains 17 separate Twitter accounts, seven of which are outside the United States. The Kodak employees who maintain those accounts discuss Kodak corporate news, Kodak's community and events, consumer news and deals, or trends in graphic communications.

One of the key points in Kodak's social media strategy is to provide valuable content, not to promote the company—so many of their Twitter posts do not mention Kodak at all, focusing instead on interesting things going on in the world of photography. For example, Jenny has posted on Twitter about a woman who is traveling the world taking pictures of the oldest living things, and about a photographer who takes pictures of people hanging upside down.

When they do talk about Kodak, it's to mention useful things—like firmware upgrades or a reminder that you can take panoramic pictures with Kodak digital cameras. They also retweet when others on Twitter compliment them. "If someone says how much they love using the external microphone jack, I'll say, 'Hey, thanks, glad that's working for you,'" Jenny says. "I make the most of our ambassadors."

USER-GENERATED CONTENT

Kodak created a community, Tips and Projects Exchange (http://exchange.kodak.com), in which "photo passionates" interact and offer advice, tips, and techniques. By offering photo enthusiasts a forum, Kodak stimulates interactivity with its brand while at the same time adding a depth and breadth that's hard for staff writers to replicate.

Ka-Ching!

Kodak's content clearly drives business, Jenny says. Kodak makes a point of tracking online conversation about the company: installing a "chief listener," who uses conversation-tracking tools like Radian6 (www.radian6.com) to measure online chatter. "At the beginning of a campaign, we may only have 20 percent of the conversation," says Jenny. But after blogging and tweeting about a product, and engaging with users as they chat on Facebook and Twitter, "We may have three-quarters of the conversation," she says.

The company also makes use of the brand ambassadors they uncover on their blogs or in social media to give input to improve its products. For example, Kodak recently crowdsourced the name of a new camera by inviting those who follow the company on Twitter to submit ideas. The prize was a ticket to the Consumer Electronics Show in Las Vegas for the product announcement. "We had to pick two people, because one said 'Play' and one said 'Sport,' and we liked the name PlaySport," Jenny says.

Ideas You Can Steal

Hire well. Kodak employees are nuts about photography, so the idea of sharing that passion through sharing photos and ideas on its blogs and other social channels isn't exactly a hard sell. "We're nutty about photography. We kind of geek out on it," Jenny says.

Let your employees tell their stories. Keeping it personal engages readers. That's why Jenny encourages employees to tell their own stories rather than to blog about more generic things. For example, one of the company's IT guys always comes back from vacation with great photos, says Jenny. "So he did a blog post about the best places to take pictures of your kids when you go to Disney World."

Jenny also prospects on social sites to find fans of Kodak. One man attached his pocket video camera to a pole and used it to check his gutters for leaves before climbing up a ladder. "I saw the video on YouTube, contacted him, said that's a really clever idea, and [asked if we could] feature that on our blog," Jenny says.

Just say no to ghostwriters. Kodak doesn't rely on ghostwriters or agencies to write its blog posts, because it sees its tone and voice as personal and approachable, and the results its bloggers get with their photos as easily obtainable. "We're not professionally trained photographers," Jenny says. "We aren't polished and slick. But I'll write a post and post pictures of my dog, and that says to customers, 'She's a person just like me.' If we used professional pictures, people would be saying, 'I could never attain that.' We're giving people the idea that they can do it, too."

CHAPTER 26
Boeing Company
Chicago, Illinois

The defense and aerospace industries aren't typically known for their candor. But five years ago, the Boeing Company made news by being among the first of a handful of major companies to embrace a kind of "management glasnost" when it launched two public blogs, including "Randy's Journal," a blog of thoughts and observations now hosted by Vice President of Marketing Randy Tinseth[1] (http://boeingblogs.com/randy). For industries characterized by security clearances and classified projects, Boeing was an early prototype: a huge company ceding some control and directly exposing itself to potentially harsh public criticism in exchange for what it hoped would be more open and constructive dialogue with its customers and employees.

Fast forward to 2009. "Randy's Journal" and Boeing's second blog (geared toward the business of building airplanes) weren't enough to base a social media strategy on, says Todd Blecher, Boeing's communications director. "Our content was not appropriate for social media," he says. "It was too long, too technical." Boeing didn't want to rush onto various social media platforms without having something interesting to talk about, Todd says, because, "Setting up accounts on Twitter or on Facebook is not a strategy."

---

[1] www.businessweek.com/magazine/content/06_21/b3985098.htm.

Boeing felt that with a million unique visitors per month, Boeing.com needed to be the central hub for its dramatically new approach. Central to its strategy was the premise that Boeing.com would not be a dull, corporate site: "We spent a lot of time thinking how we could transform our content in a way that would resonate with audiences on social media," Todd says.

Boeing "wanted to create an enhancement strategy," to better Boeing's reputation among future employees and the general public, as well as traditional government and aerospace sectors. It wanted to focus not on lifeless technology or utilitarian products but rather on its customers and employees, and the interesting ways in which Boeing intersects their lives. It wanted to embed writers in its midst who would tell the stories of these people, a discipline David Meerman Scott calls brand journalism; others call it corporate journalism or business journalism. (Borrowing a phrase from the Dutch, Matthew Stibbe calls the function *bedrijfsjournalist,* which is both fun to say and, on a business card, is a conversation starter!)

Unlike product-centric marketing-speak meant for brochures and other collateral, brand journalism is about the creation of videos, blog posts, photos, webinars, charts, graphs, ebooks, and other information that delivers value to your marketplace. A brand journalist works inside the company, writing articles or blog posts or producing videos or podcasts to attract a specific audience. "Brand journalism is not a product pitch. It is not an advertorial. It is not an egotistical spewing of gobbledygook-laden, stock-photo-enhanced corporate drivel," David writes on his blog in his characteristically brusque style.[2]

---

[2] The phrase brand journalism was coined in 2004 by Larry Light, then McDonald Corp.'s chief marketing officer, who said in a speech at an industry event that McDonald's has adopted it as a new marketing technique. The term has evolved since then, although the basic idea of customer-driven versus corporate-driven marketing remains fundamental.

Content That Ignites

Boeing morphed its web site into a digital hub, with the goal of enhancing the company's reputation with good, shareable, human stories—or, as Todd describes it, "People-oriented feature stories that were on interesting topics and that told Boeing stories from that person's perspective."

Todd heads up an editorial board of about a dozen people that Boeing.com created to oversee the new content. It also created three new Twitter accounts to amplify and engage—one each for its military, corporate, and commercial businesses (@BoeingCorporate, @BoeingAirplanes, and @BoeingDefense). Boeing also creates a steady stream of content through the following.

BYLINED ARTICLES

Extending its brand journalism approach, the Boeing site includes bylined feature weekly stories penned by employees who write the stories of the company's products, people, or competencies, packaged with "an interesting, personal angle," says Todd. "We're open to a lot of different topics, as long as it helps bolster the reputation of the company." Articles are either original to the site or sometimes repurposed from its internal magazine or from its internal employee news service, but in any case they are more like a feature you'd find in a magazine than a corporate site.

- Aboard the USS *Dwight D. Eisenhower* aircraft carrier, a Boeing writer gets a firsthand look at how the U.S. Navy is conducting missions in the Persian Gulf with support from Boeing, and reports on the Boeing site in *Dispatches from the Gulf.*

- In *When the Volcano Blows,* a writer talks about ways the airlines are looking to predict the path of volcanic ash and procedures to avoid it.

- In another, Rocky, a Belgian Malinois, retires after serving for 56 dog years as one of Boeing's 18 explosive-detection dogs.

Video

Many articles include embedded video to enhance the narrative and bring the story to life. Boeing employees with video skills—a few employees are former television journalists—take the lead on video. Unlike other companies, Boeing does not seed its videos on YouTube or other platforms. Boeing worries about the videos it produces showing up on YouTube along with less desirable results, like crash videos or the like. "I understand [YouTube's] usefulness as a tool, but my concerns are the possibility that a good video we post could be compromised by a bad video that gets posted right next to it," Todd says. "We'd rather have people come to our site."

Twitter

Boeing is active on Twitter, amplifying its own published content, retweeting third-party links, and responding to followers reasonably well. They could be doing more to engage and interact with their audience there (for example, the accounts follow a paltry number of people, and they lack any sense of a human behind the accounts). But, that said, Boeing gets points for its active monitoring: When Harry Winsor, an eight-year-old boy from Boulder, Colorado, sent an original airplane design to Boeing with the suggestion that they manufacture his plane, he received a terse, canned response: "Like many large companies," Boeing wrote Harry in a form letter, "we do not accept unsolicited ideas. Experience showed that most ideas had already been considered by our engineers and that there can be unintended consequences to simply accepting these ideas. The time, cost, and risk involved in processing them, therefore, were not justified by the benefits gained."

Harry's father, John, an ad agency exec, shared Boeing's response on his blog and with his Twitter followers. Boeing responded, owning its mistake (see Figure 26.1).

"That took off, and [the responses ranged] from some number of people being critical of us for sending a form letter to an eight-year-old to a much larger number of people saying, 'Isn't it great that Boeing responded to that?'" Todd says.

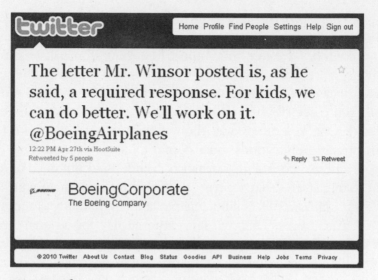

Figure 26.1   Boeing Apologizes on Twitter

Source: http://twitter.com/BoeingCorporate/statuses/12953083392

Ka-Ching!

The site was less than two months old when this chapter was written, but Boeing's word-of-mouth has been increasing gradually but consistently since it began its new content initiative in April 2010. The best-performing feature story thus far—a piece about new airplane testing—generated more than 50,000 views in a month.

Better yet is the shift in public perception of Boeing, from a dull, turgid corporation to something far more interesting, approachable, and human. "The perception of our willingness to engage with the public is slowly changing," Todd says. " I don't think people expect a company that is known to be rather stodgy and engineering-based to be engaged in the way we are."

Ideas You Can Steal

Find the human angle. Content that's engaging is about people. Find the ways your company intersects the lives of living, breathing humans, and tell their stories.

Tell the truth. Hiring writers or former journalists to function as embedded brand journalists with your organizations can give your content a fresher, more appealing shine. Journalists know how to write, and they can give your content a patina of objectivity because they understand innately how to create a more balanced piece (versus, for example, a PR-heavy bit of Frankenspeak). One key difference, though: Journalists who write for mainstream publications must depict all sides of a story or an issue, whereas corporate journalists do not. But both need to tell interesting stories that are true, and they must tell them well.

Have patience. When Boeing first launched "Randy's Journal," in the early weeks of 2005, it weathered flak for its unauthentic tone, lack of feedback functionality ("Randy's Journal" didn't originally allow comments), and apparent heavy reliance on marketing spin. Instead of quitting, then-author Randy Baseler took the criticism constructively. He eventually found his voice, and in June 2010, the blog marked its fifth anniversary. (During those five years, 2.9 million unique visitors stopped by the site.) "It's very easy to get wrapped up in minute-by-minute, day-by-day tracking of hits, and you can end up being pretty frustrated pretty quickly," Todd says. "You have to track your audience over time, but you need to give yourself time to build an audience before you start saying it's working or it's not." At the same time, be clear on your purpose, he adds: "If it's reputation-building you're after, try to get everyone involved to agree at the start that you're going to do it for many, many months before you decide if it's working or not."

CHAPTER 27

Indium Corporation

Clinton, New York

"The mantra of my marcom program is simple: content to contact to cash," says Rick Short, director of marketing communications at Indium Corporation, a manufacturer and supplier of specialty alloys and solders.

Indium sells electronic assembly materials globally to the electronics, semiconductor, solar, and other markets. As part of its marketing, it publishes white papers, a Facebook page, and a YouTube channel. But what's most impressive is its blogging program, which has been a key driver of business leads.

We know what you're thinking: a blog about solder paste? Seriously? The Indium blog (actually, *blogs*) are so hyper-specific that, "most people in the world chuckle when they look at it," Rick admits. "They can't believe people really care about this stuff. But my customers do . . . They love this stuff! [So often] we hear, 'You're so into solder paste that you have a blog about it? You must be the dude for me!'"

Content That Ignites

Rick realized several years ago that social media could be a powerful marketing force, and he set about experimenting with it. He jumped in and began blogging on his own, about topics of personal interest but unconnected to Indium. "I wanted to be a leader, and I didn't want people to say I led us astray," he says.

"My first phase was to learn a lot myself, so I could establish respectability and integrity," and speak from a point of knowledge.

Once Short had learned everything he could about blogging, he approached a handful of his more gregarious engineers who worked in the field. Most of them were already producing content of sorts—delivering tech papers and giving workshops, he says.

"And one of them in particular really aligned with the concept" of blogging, and pretty soon started blogging about the technology the company's customers use to manufacture electronics. He added personal asides and insight into his own life to give the blog some personality, which Short encouraged: "Don't be a machine, I told him." One by one, Short added other engineers to the mix. Now, he has between 12 and 15 bloggers who author their own blogs. In addition, the company actually publishes 73 additional blogs with subject-specific, aggregated content produced by those dozen-plus bloggers.

Why? Through keyword research, Short identified several dozen keywords that were hyper-specific to his company's niche industry, so he made a glossary of the 73 most important keywords potential customers search on, and then set up separate blogs to aggregate any content produced for that keyword. "We don't want to be the engineering blog; that's too big," says Short. "So I asked, what do we really do, and what do the customers that we care about *call* what we really do?"

Short worked with Compendium Blogware, a company that offers blogging software for businesses. With Compendium, every time an Indium blogger writes a blog post that includes any of the keywords on the list, the content is automatically posted to that keyword's blog. If the post contains 2 of the 73 keywords, it is posted to those two blogs, and so on. So for example, if Product Manager Carol Gowans pens a post about the specific properties of fusible alloys, the post is auto-posted in at least two places: on Carol's blog (http://blogs.indium.com/blog/carol-gowans) and on the Fusible Alloy blog (http://blogs.indium.com/blog/fusible-alloy). If you were the sort of person searching for a source of "fusible alloy" on a major search engine, guess which company shows up first or second? (Answer: Indium.)

Social networks were also important to Short's content strategy, but there are too many networks to connect to them all. He surveyed customers to discern which networks they were using the most, and based on the results, ultimately decided on Facebook, Twitter, YouTube, and LinkedIn. Now, when people at the company post to their blogs, that content is also auto-posted to those networks.

Ka-Ching!

"The results were astounding," Short says. Once Indium began using a keyword-rich strategy to populate the 73 blogs, customer contacts increased 600 percent in a single quarter. Furthermore, every time someone raises a hand—in other words, every time someone contacts the author of a post to ask a question or make a comment, or downloads a white paper—they opt in to the Indium database. That means those contacts have willingly opted in to receive more information about a specific topic, making it that much easier for salespeople to close a deal.

Additionally, Short's bloggers have nearly become celebrities in their fields, raising the profile of the company as a whole. At conferences, they are stopped in the exhibit halls. "People say, 'I know you,' and it's because of the blog, because of social media," Short says.

Ideas You Can Steal

Look for good listeners (not just good writers). Like HubSpot (see Chapter 24), Indium seeks out those employees who have a passion for creating content and who enjoy sharing. But Rick says the best bloggers are good listeners as well as good writers, because they enjoy the give and take of online conversations with customers or prospects. In other words, it's not all about them.

Trust your employees. It's still scary for some executives to give their employees the freedom to write whatever they'll write about. Indium bosses worried that bloggers would reveal trade secrets, or just merely mention something the company would prefer to keep quiet. But Rick sees social platforms like blogs and Twitter and Facebook as offering companies a direct opportunity to address issues their customers have, and perhaps are already talking about. "Our bloggers are already in contact with customers every day," he says. "Should we also disconnect the phone and e-mail?" The bottom line, he says, is to "trust your people."

Be human. Indium's blogs have a definite personal vibe, which goes a long way to humanizing an otherwise soulless product. That's intentional, Rick says. The Indium bloggers aren't "slick spokesmen"; they're "real people," who write what they think and believe, and don't just spew corporate spin. The approach pays off with customers, Rick says, adding, "The minute there's the whiff of spin in the air, [my customers'] antennae go up. My philosophy is to sweep the entire Mad. Ave. spin out of the picture and put my engineers up front, talking the way they want, [with] the words they want to use."

Embrace your niche. There is no topic that is too niche-y to be embraced by social media. If you are passionate, then there certainly are people out there who will also be passionate about it. Create the content, share it, and those people will find you.

CHAPTER 28
PinkStinks
London, England

PinkStinks is an advocacy group and social movement designed to create positive female role models for girls, so as to inspire them to achieve great things.

Twin sisters Abi and Emma Moore launched the group in 2008 to challenge the "culture of pink," or the pervasive gender stereotyping of products meant for girls. Some of that stereotyping they saw expressed in persistently pink and princessy stuff intended for girls, while toys that promoted adventure and exploration were typically marketed to boys. But there are other, more disturbing examples, too: toys and clothing that sexualize little girls—such as a U.K. clothing chain selling padded bikini tops to girls as young as seven; or a pole-dancing toy marketed by U.K. retailer Tesco.

"We believe that the media's obsession with stick-thin models, footballers' wives, and overtly sexualised pop stars is denying girls their right to aspire to and learn from real role models," Abi and Emma write on the PinkStinks site (www.pinkstinks.co.uk). "PinkStinks aims to redress the balance by providing girls with positive female role models—chosen because of their achievements, skills, accomplishments, and successes."

The sisters had a passion to effect change, but—with zero funding—had few resources to devote to the cause.

Content That Ignites

Abi and Emma set about creating content on the cheap to educate their audience and draw attention to their cause.

Blog

Emma, Abi, or Lucy Lawrence—a third member of PinkStinks—create posts on the PinkStinks blog (http://pinkstinks.wordpress .com) on issues of gender. Topics vary from gender stereotyping in popular advertising campaigns to positive news stories, such as one that appeared in the spring of 2010 about four intrepid women who orbited into world record books as the greatest number of female astronauts ever to fly in space at the same time. The goal is to highlight positive and nontraditional role models for girls, Abi says, adding, "We don't want to be a bunch of moaners."

Newsletter

The PinkStinks monthly newsletter includes

- A "Pinkstinks Approved" section, which features books with great girl characters, stores with gender-neutral clothing, and other products or vehicles that match the PinkStinks philosophy.

- "Name & Shame," a section that highlights the worst examples of negative gender roles.

- "Role Model of the Month," which showcases positive role models, often from current news stories.

- "Blogs of Interest," which are links to other blogs that support similar causes.

Twitter

"We use Twitter to recruit people," explains Abi. Every time the women publish a newsletter, they tweet about it, inviting people to sign up.

The sisters also use Twitter to highlight current events about the issues of interest to Pinkstinks, or to highlight their own appearances in the press.

FACEBOOK

Facebook has become the backbone of the PinkStinks effort, as it's been instrumental as a forum for parents (and sometimes grandparents) united around issues of gender equality. What's evolved is a global forum of close to 13,000 people, many of whom actively share links and their own PinkStinks stories. The active Facebook group "has helped us be broad in our reach and sustain momentum," Abi says, which is remarkable for "three women who don't have a proper organization, as such," she jokes.

Ka-Ching!

What's impressive is the degree to which PinkStinks has effected real change: In 2008, the group persuaded the Early Learning Centre, a U.K. toy chain, to reconsider the way it color-coded products for children (pink aisles for girls filled with vanities and makeup kits, every other color for boys). That campaign generated press in 43 countries, including top media venues such as Sky News and the BBC.

More recently, Pinkstinks persuaded British supermarket chain Sainsbury's to repackage children's dress-up costumes so that the doctor costume did not specify for boys and the nurse's costume did not specify for girls. It also persuaded the Prince's Trust (a U.K. charity founded by Prince Charles) to withdraw its sponsorship of a campaign by St. Tropez, a company that makes fake tanning products.

Ideas You Can Steal

Simplify your core message. After the Early Learning Centre success and the huge amount of press it generated, the group learned it needed to refine its message. By trying to convey too much, the message was clouded. "The tabloid media said we wanted to ban the color pink. Quite frankly, we weren't ready to deal with it. We decided to be much more specific with what we were targeting," Abi says.

Take a stand. You can't be all things to all people, and that's okay. While a huge number of people agree with PinkStinks, there's an equally large number who disagree with the group's philosophy. But Abi says that tempering the group's message would lessen its impact. "It's much easier to be wishy-washy about it, but we didn't want that. We had to learn to pick over the responses and ignore the vitriol that came in," says Abi. "We are really passionate about what we're doing and why we're doing it. There's no point in being Mrs. Nice Guy all the time. You have to stick your neck out."

Stoke the campfire. The PinkStinks Facebook group functions just like a virtual campfire, with like-minded members swapping stories and comments and posting photos. The group's founders participate but intentionally don't police, Abi says, so as to give the group's participants a sense of freedom and ownership of the cause.

PART FOUR

This Isn't Goodbye

CHAPTER 29

This Isn't Goodbye, and a Gift for You

Often, when we are nearing the end of a particularly good book, we linger over the final chapters because we don't want it to end. We hope you don't have that feeling now, and that rather than feeling morose you are feeling motivated. We also hope you are looking forward to applying the principles and Content Rules in this book to create content that engages your own customers.

Also, unlike most books, this book doesn't end with the final chapter. This isn't goodbye; it's an invitation to connect further. The conversation continues online at our web site (www .contentrulesbook.com), on Twitter (@thecontentrules), and on Facebook (www.facebook.com/ContentRules).

Drop by for some drinks! Or better yet, tell us how the ideas in this book have inspired or helped you.

Tell us how your own content has ignited your business. If you're game, we'd love to profile your success as part of an ongoing series of how the Content Rules have helped organizations. So share with us your fun video series, captivating blog, winsome webinar, or ebook that spread like wildfire! (Tag any content you create with #ContentRules so we'll see it.) We'd love to hear how you did it, and would love to add your story to our growing library of Success Stories!

In parting, for now, here's a gift: a handy 12-point content checklist to help set you on the right path. (You can also download this checklist as a PDF at www.contentrulesbook.com/extras.)

A 12-Point Content Checklist

- ☐ Have you embraced the notion that publishing is a fundamental shift in how to market your business—but nonetheless an exciting opportunity?
  - ☐ Are you patient? Have you recognized that a content strategy is a commitment—not just a one-and-done?

- ☐ Do you know what keeps your customers up at night?
  - ☐ Do you know their concerns? Objectives?

  - ☐ Does your content answer the question "What's in it for me?" from the perspective of your customer?

- ☐ Are you creating with a distinct voice and an unmistakable point of view?
  - ☐ Are you communicating like a human, not in Frankenspeak?

- ☐ Are you showing how your product lives in the world, and how people actually use it?

- ☐ Do you occasionally surprise or awe?

- ☐ Are you sparking interaction and a community campfire?

- ☐ Are you giving your content roots and wings?
  - ☐ Do you need to require registration? If so, which information do you really need to collect up front, and which can you seek down the road, after you've established a relationship?

- ☐ Does your content have at least one trigger to action?
  - ☐ Have you created a unique landing page for each content asset?

- ☐ Are you reimagining what you create?
  - ☐ Have you inventoried your content to discover and organize the content you already have and how you might reimagine it?

  - ☐ Have you developed an editorial calendar to help you deliver consistently great content?

☐ Can you measure the effectiveness of your content?

☐ Can prospects easily find, access, and share your content?
    ☐ Are you accessorizing your content with social bling (like Twitter, Facebook, or LinkedIn sharing options) to help it spread like crazy?

☐ Are you prepared for doing something—or at least one thing—really, really well?

Index